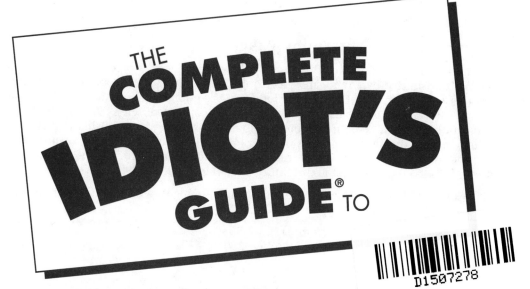

THE COMPLETE IDIOT'S GUIDE® TO

Business Statistics

by Sunny Baker, Ph.D.

ALPHA

A Pearson Education Company

To Kim Baker, my other half and a great resource on completing the graphics!

Copyright © 2002 by Sunny Baker

THE COMPLETE IDIOT'S GUIDE TO and Design are registered trademarks of Pearson Education, Inc.

International Standard Book Number: 0-02-863987-1
Library of Congress Catalog Card Number: 2001094732

04   03   02   8   7   6   5   4   3   2   1

Interpretation of the printing code: The rightmost number of the first series of numbers is the year of the book's printing; the rightmost number of the second series of numbers is the number of the book's printing. For example, a printing code of 02-1 shows that the first printing occurred in 2002.

Printed in the United States of America

Publisher
Marie Butler-Knight

Product Manager
Phil Kitchel

Managing Editor
Jennifer Chisholm

Senior Acquisitions Editor
Renee Wilmeth

Development Editor
Michael Koch

Production Editor
Billy Fields

Copy Editor
Rachel Lopez

Illustrator
Jody Schaeffer

Cover Designers
Mike Freeland
Kevin Spear

Book Designers
Scott Cook and Amy Adams of DesignLab

Indexer
Amy Lawrance

Layout/Proofreading
Mary Hunt
Mark Walchle
Juli Cook

Contents at a Glance

Part 1: Charting Your Future   **1**

  1 Statistics and Business Go Hand in Hand   3
Understand why knowing statistics is important for your business success.

  2 Understanding and Organizing Business Data   11
Discover the types of data used in business and statistics.

  3 Visualizing Profit and Performance   21
Learn about the charts, graphs, and tables used in descriptive statistics.

  4 Predicting Profits with Measures of Central Tendency   39
Know how to recognize a mean from a mode from a median.

  5 Improving Quality with Measures of Dispersion   47
Go from central measures to variance and the standard deviation.

  6 Solving Problems with Curves and z-Scores   57
Know when curves are normal and how associated z-scores help answer business questions.

Part 2: Facing Probability and Forecasting   **71**

  7 Playing the Probability Game   73
Discover the importance of probability in business and statistics.

  8 Forecasting Your Business Results   91
Learn statistical ways to look at your future results.

  9 Making Decisions That Count   103
Develop decision techniques that can handle big problems.

Part 3 Using Business Research and Inference   **115**

  10 Using Research in Your Business   117
Describe the basic reasons for quality research in your company.

  11 Eliminating the Bias in Your Research   129
Understand the importance of random samples in business research.

12 Being Confident About Your Sample   137
   *Make sure your sample represents the population in
   question.*

13 Testing Your Hypothesis   149
   Know when your test results are significant.

14 Learning from Contingency Tables   163
   *Discover how to use tables and the chi-square statistic to
   answer questions of relationship.*

Part 4: Seeing the Industry Relationships   175

15 Recognizing the Relationships of Business Variables   177
   *Know when variables are correlated and how they can
   be predicted with linear regression.*

16 Estimating the Probability of Success with the *t*-Test   193
   Learn how to use the t-test to study small samples.

17 Are These Customers the Same or Different?   205
   *Compare means to ascertain the similarity and difference
   between two groups.*

18 Getting Results from ANOVA   215
   Compare the means of several populations.

Part 5: Going On from Here   225

19 Interpreting Business Data Correctly   227
   *Avoid statistical pitfalls and understand the correct use of
   statistical tests.*

20 Using Statistics Programs for Your Company   239
   *Discover how computer software programs can make sta-
   tistics fast and easy.*

21 Advancing Your Business with Statistics   253
   Review all you've learned and find out how to learn more.

Appendixes

A Answer Key   261

B Statistics Formulas   267

C Sample Statistical Tables   273

D Glossary   285

  Index   303

Contents

Part 1: Charting Your Future   **1**

1 Statistics and Business Go Hand in Hand   **3**

The Origin of Statistics 5
Some Real-World Business Examples of Statistics...............6
Determining Advertising Effectiveness.............................6
Understanding Demand for Your Products..........................6
Improving Quality 7
Introducing the Branches of Statistics 7
The Relationship Between Probability and Statistics 9

2 Understanding and Organizing Business Data   **11**

Understanding Observations...12
Organizing Observations into a Datafile...........................13
Exploring the Four Basic Data Types................................14
Nominal Data 14
Ordinal Data 14
Interval and Ratio Data 15
Understanding the Limitations of Your Data Choices 16
Try It On Your Own 17
Start Making Decisions by Creating Datafiles....................17

3 Visualizing Profit and Performance   **21**

Turning Raw Data into Information 22
Using Tables 22
Using Pie Charts 24
Using Histograms..26
Using the Bar Graph 31
Examining Relationships with Scatterplots 31
Stem and Leaf Plots 33
Understanding the Types of Variables 34
Common Questions About Research Data 36

4 Predicting Profits with Measures of Central Tendency   **39**

The Meaning of the Mean...39
The Mode—Not an Operation, but a Count....................41
The Median—In the Middle of Everything......................42
When to Use a Measure of Central Tendency 44

5 Improving Quality with Measures of Dispersion   **47**

Getting Started with Dispersion Measures 48
A Simple Way to Measure Dispersion 48
The More Meaningful Interquartile Range 48
Calculating the Interquartile Range....................................49
Getting Even More Meaningful Information
   on Dispersion 50
Recognizing the Variance 51
Introducing the All-Important Standard Deviation 51
How to Interpret the Standard Deviation..............................52
The Real Standard Deviation 52
Some Important Notes on the Standard Deviation.................53
Choosing Among Dispersion Measures 53
Some Simple Practice—No Computer Required 54

6 Solving Problems with Curves and z-Scores   **57**

Introducing the Bell-Shaped Curve....................................58
Measuring the Standard Normal Distribution 59
Estimating the Number of Units That Are Substandard....62
Two-tailed and One-tailed Analysis 62
Translating Standard Deviations into Values 63
Predicting Percentages with z-Scores................................63
Calculating the z-Score...65
Answering Questions with the z-Scores 66
Skewed Curves and the Relation to a Standard
Distribution 67
Kurtosis—or How Long Is Your Tail? 68
Providing Your Own Answers 68

Part 2: Facing Probability and Forecasting   71

7 Playing the Probability Game   73

Introducing the Classic Theory of Probability 75
The Classic Formula 76
When the Stakes (or Numbers) Are Bigger..........................77
Figuring the Odds of 46 Heads in a Row...........................77
Figuring Out the Possible Outcomes 79
Calculating Factorials 79
Sampling with Replacement 81
The Addition Rule 82
Dependent Events and Probability 83
Understanding the Probability of Joint Occurrences 84
*Using Conditional Probability for More Informed
  Judgments* 85
Exploring Normal Curves and the Binomial Scale 85
Determining the Success or Failure of an Outcome 86
Using the Poisson Limit 87
Getting to the Heart of the Probability Theory 87
Try Some of Your Own 89

8 Forecasting Your Business Results   91

Introducing the Components of Time Series Data............92
Now for Something Trendy 93
The Cyclic World—What Comes Around Goes Around........95
What About Adjusting for the Season? 96
Working with Precalculated Business Data 100
Price Indices and the Role of Inflation............................101

9 Making Decisions That Count   103

Understanding the Key Decisions 104
Charting a Decision Tree..105
Learning by Example..106
List Your Options 106
Evaluate Your Options 108
Calculate the Benefits of Your Decisions 108
Incorporate the Cost of the Decision 109
Always Use Objective Variables 110
Select the Right Path with the Payoff Table....................111
Devising Strategies for Decision Making........................113
Try It On Your Own 114

Part 3 Using Business Research and Inference 115

10 Using Research in Your Business 117

Deciding When to Use Research 118
Developing a Basic Research Methodology.....................119
Identifying Appropriate Research Projects 120
Understanding the Levels of Research 120
Comparing Research with Evaluation *122*
Developing Your Research Literacy *123*
Understanding Validity and Reliability in Research *124*
Developing a Model for Your Research..............................*125*
Three Steps to Prepare for Statistical Analysis *126*

11 Eliminating the Bias in Your Research 129

The Infinite Population in Applied Statistics 130
The Importance of Random Sampling 131
Choosing the Appropriate Sampling Methods 131
Random Sampling *132*
Systematic Sampling...*133*
Cluster Sampling *133*
Stratified Sampling...*134*
How Big Should the Sample Be? 134

12 Being Confident About Your Sample 137

Conducting Bernoulli Trials 138
Back to the Sample *139*
The Confidence Interval *139*
Larger Sample Means Smaller Spread *140*
What About Interval and Ratio Samples?.....................141
Determining a Confidence Interval 143
It Won't Work with Small Samples 144

13 Testing Your Hypothesis 149

Using the Normal Distribution to Answer Questions 149
Stating Hypotheses to Test Assumptions 152
Using a Five-Step Procedure for Testing a Hypothesis 152
Step 1: State the Null and Alternative Hypothesis *153*
Step 2: Select a Level of Significance *154*
Step 3: Compute the Test Statistic...................................*155*

Step 4: Formulate the Decision Rule 156
Step 5: Make Your Decision 157
Understanding the p-Value in Hypothesis Testing 157
Testing a Hypothesis 158
Try One on your Own..160

14 Learning from Contingency Tables   163

How to Create a Contingency Table 164
A Positive Relationship Example..165
A Negative Value Contingency Table 165
Contingency Examples with No Relationship 166
How Confident Are You in These Conclusions?.................167
A Real Example of How It Works 169
Using Chi Square for Other Expected Frequencies..........171
When Expected Frequencies Are Equal 171
Unequal Expected Frequencies and Chi Square 173
Try Using a Contingency Table On Your Own 174

Part 4: Seeing the Industry Relationships   175

15 Recognizing the Relationships of
Business Variables   177

Starting with Correlation of Business Variables 178
Other Relationships to Consider 179
Revealing Hidden Relationships with the
Correlation Coefficient 181
An Example and What It Means 182
The Coefficient of Determination 183
Calculating the Significance of r..184
Going Beyond Correlation to Prediction 184
How Linear Regression Works..184
The Goals of Regression Analysis 185
Try Some Regression Calculations on Your Own 186
The General Form Equation 187
Predicting Business Values...187
The Standard Error of the Estimate.....................................189
The Confidence and Prediction Intervals 189
What Happens When You Have More Variables?............190

16 Estimating the Probability of Success with the *t*-Test   193

Understanding the Student's *t* Distribution 194
Using *t* to Test a Mean.....................................195
Comparing Two Population Means Using *t* 196
Are the Processes the Same? 197
The t Distribution Calculations 198
A Paired t-Test Example..................................200
Understanding Dependent and Independent Samples..........201
Try Using a t-Test on Your Own 202

17 Are These Customers the Same or Different?   205

Testing the Mean, Standard Deviation Known...............206
Using z-Tests When the Standard Deviation Is
Unknown 206
What's the Investment Turnover? 207
Working with Proportions and the z Distribution 208
Electing the New Chairman of the Board 209
Testing Two Population Proportions........................211
Do Customers Prefer the Same Packaging? 211
Try Solving a Problem on Your Own 213

18 Getting Results from ANOVA   215

Introducing the *F* distribution 216
Comparing Training Results 216
Do Customers Who Like Our Advertising Buy More? 219
Inferences About Treatments.............................221
Considering Two-Way Analysis of Variance 221

Part 5: Going On from Here   225

19 Interpreting Business Data Correctly   227

Beware of Nonrandom Nonsamples 229
Beware the Ploys of Advertisers..........................229
Use the Correct Scale....................................230
Correlation Needs Matched Pairs 231
Beware of Significant but Unimportant Findings...........232
Beware of Data Mining Without Hypotheses.................233

Avoid Extrapolation That Goes Beyond
  Observed Ranges 234
Avoid Basic Mistakes That Affect Business Results 234
From Inferences to Your Future.....................................237

20 Using Statistics Programs for Your Company   239

Using Software That Simplifies the Details......................240
What Can Statistics Programs Do? 240
  So What's in It for Me? 242
  Simple vs. Complex Software Tools 242
The Types of Statistical Programs 242
  Basic Spreadsheet Programs 243
  Robust Data Analysis Programs 243
  Excel Functions You Might Want to Know 244
  Corporate-Level Statistics Programs 246
  Choices and More Choices 246
How Do You Choose? 247
  Cost/Feature Analysis...247
  Ease of Use and Consistency of the Interface..................248
  Flexibility to Adapt to Various Analyses 248
  Compatibility with Other Programs 249
  Documentation and Support for the Program 249
  Reputation of the Product Manufacturer 250
  Word-of-Mouth Experiences 250
  Technical Support..250
Things Statistics Software Can't Do 250
Go Get Yourself Some!..252

21 Advancing Your Business with Statistics   253

More Statistical Functions to Learn................................254
Where Can You Learn More? 256
You're Ready to Compute!...258

Appendixes

A Answer Key   **261**

B Statistics Formulas   **267**

C Sample Statistical Tables   **273**

D A Glossary of Statistical Terms **285**

Index   **303**

Foreword

In the cartoon, a rather stuffy looking executive is sitting at the head of the conference table, pontificating to two subservient staffers. "Of course I realize that statistics are misleading," he says. "That's why we generate so many of them!"

I ran that cartoon a year or so ago in the *Journal of Business Strategy* because I knew it would strike a chord with the executives who read the magazine. My readers know a lot about numbers, and they're learning more and more every day. Over the last decade or so, business metrics have swarmed out of the finance department to infest every function in the company. Yes, the finance people are still preparing balance sheets and computing earnings per share, return on assets, and myriad other ratios. But now every other department has its own spreadsheets in which managers and their staff compute such things as customer retention rates, productivity, return on training investments, product/service defect rates, market share, cross-sell ratios, and on and on and on.

In fact, there can't be many jobs today in which workers have no contact with statistics. Assembly-line workers know how much product they must generate daily; part-time telemarketers know their sales per hour numbers; and wait staff knows the average number of table turns per shift. Even retirees or stay-at-home parents can't escape statistics—all they have to do is pick up the daily paper.

The problem is that, although we're confronted with statistics every day, most of us are innumerate. We have difficulty understanding the calculations that produced a statistic we are told to accept as fact. So we're at the mercy of the cartoon executive—and anyone else—who deliberately generates misleading numbers. And, worse, we may be guilty of inadvertently lying with numbers ourselves. It's all too easy to generalize too broadly, based on unexamined statistics, or to combine numbers that *seem* to go together to produce a new statistic that looks wonderful but is just plain wrong.

So what's an innumerate to do? Going back to school to enroll in a stats course is just not on. Spending night after night memorizing endless formulas and conquering complex math just to set up a spreadsheet would be an inefficient use of time.

A really good alternative, of course, is to read this book. In it, Sunny Baker provides solid grounding in the most important statistics terms you need to know, and even defines those cryptic symbols the digiterati love to confuse you with. She's made it all the more palatable by limiting the amount of math you'll have to use in order to grasp the concepts. And, best of all, she offers numerous tips on how to tell the difference between damn lies and solid statistics.

By the time you finish reading this book, you'll be able to pick up a business report and understand what the research results really mean. Even better, you'll have the tools you need to design your own research and use the results to make informed decisions. In short, you'll be able to drill down into that massive database your company has collected and draw out information that can help you hone your company's—and your own—competitive edge.

In an era in which "You can't manage what you can't measure" is a mantra heard in every company, large and small, no one can afford to remain ignorant of business statistics. The joy of this book is that it enables you to gain enlightenment painlessly.

Pamela Goett

Editor & Publisher
Journal of Business Strategy

Introduction

Mention the word "statistics" to businesspeople or students in business school and loud groans are the inevitable response. Students in business programs and the social sciences alike agree that statistics is a course to avoid or put off as long as possible. Math phobia and boring teachers give statistics a negative image—but it doesn't have to be that way.

Because statistical textbooks typically focus on calculations and symbols at the cost of understanding the underlying concepts, businesspeople and students who finish their mandatory stats course may master the equations but may still not know how to choose and apply the correct statistical test to analyze a given problem. Even worse, they may not know how to interpret the statistical results in important business reports.

This is a book for people who hate math but who need to know how to choose, use, and interpret a statistical analysis. (And that's most of today's managers and professionals in business.) This book provides tons of real, illustrated examples and offers fanciful but informative diagrams to illuminate the concepts. The statistical examples in this book are all taken from real business scenarios. If you ever dreaded the statistics requirement in your program of study, or need to understand a complex report but don't know the difference between a standard deviation and a standard deduction, this book is for you.

A New Focus for a Computerized Age

Statistics is all about numbers—however in today's age of computerized statistics, the primary focus on mastering the equations is entirely unnecessary. Statistics is more about concepts than it is about doing the math. Businesspeople need to understand what the equations do and how to use and interpret the results—but the complicated math can be handled by computer programs.

Businesspeople and students, even those who received A's in their statistics courses, frequently choose the wrong test, apply it ineptly, or misinterpret the results. Almost every business person, even those with statistical training, asks questions like these, "But what statistical test should I use?" Or, "What does this data mean to the business?" These will be the questions you learn to answer in this book.

Getting the Most from This Book

Obtaining or purchasing a statistical calculator is useful but not necessary to complete the exercises in this book. A number of calculators that will perform the necessary functions are available and many cost less than $20. As the reader, you are responsible for learning how the calculator functions, so a manual is absolutely necessary. The calculator must be able to do bivariate statistical analysis. If the index of the manual has an entry for linear regression, regression, or correlation, then the calculator will do the functions necessary to complete the exercises. Even better get a copy of Microsoft Excel and read Chapter 20 to learn how to use this software program to complete the exercises.

In addition, an attempt has been made to tie together the various aspects of statistics into a theoretical whole by closely examining the scientific method and its relationship to statistics. In particular, this is achieved by introducing the concept of models early in the book. Throughout the book I show how the various topics are all aspects of the same approach (using models) to knowing about the world.

What This Book Is All About

This stress-free book presents statistics and quantitative analysis in language the average business reader and student new to statistics can understand. The book is not only informative, but also fun to read and work through. The book supports (traditional) statistics concepts so it can also be employed in colleges and universities as an adjunct teaching aid and as a tool for basic research design in business.

Unlike other introductory statistics books, this book focuses almost entirely on statistical evaluations as concepts, not on arithmetic, symbols, and calculations alone. It assumes that you are using any one of the multitudes of inexpensive statistical programs or spreadsheet programs to do the math. (The book even offers suggestions on where to find such programs and which ones to buy.) That doesn't mean you won't see some math in the book—it can't be entirely avoided—but I do promise to concentrate on the meanings of statistics and how to use them, not on the memorization of the calculations.

How to Use This Book

The book has five parts, which I recommend you read from beginning to end. Together, the parts demystify the steps and tools behind basic business statistics and offer practical advice that can be used in a variety of business situations that involve making decisions, analyzing risk, and understanding relationships among people, things, and data.

Part 1, "Charting Your Future," explains what statistics are used for in business and how statistics can help you reduce risk and make better decisions about your business operations. You'll also learn how to describe the important data in your business world using graphs, charts, and measures of central tendency, including averages and standard deviations.

Part 2, "Facing Probability and Forecasting," presents the basic laws of probability and the connections between probability and statistical hypothesis testing (important in researching ideas, processes, and operational results in business). This section is important because you must grasp several concepts about probability in order to understand the predictive nature of inferential statistics.

Part 3, "Using Business Research and Inference," presents information on making generalizations from samples of people and applying them to larger groups. This information assumes you've already read Part 2 of this book. You'll also learn about designing your research and choosing the right statistical reports or tests for your purposes.

Part 4, "Seeing the Industry Relationships," covers concepts of relating the impact of one variable on the outcomes or causes of another. You'll learn about the purposes of correlation and regression analysis in business and why these big words are really not that difficult to understand (given the practical examples you'll find in this section).

Part 5, "Going On from Here," talks about ways to further your statistical knowledge and even venture into traditional statistics textbooks to learn about more advanced statistical analyses.

Finally, the appendixes are provided for those who really want more details on the subject of statistics; you'll also discover the answers to the exercises that I've sprinkled throughout the chapters. I've included an appendix of math formulas as a reference for future work in statistics. And all the terms defined in the text of the book are repeated in the glossary in Appendix D so you can look up anything you might forget on a moment's notice.

Extras

A series of sidebars throughout the book highlight specific items that can help you understand and implement the material in each chapter:

Statistical Lingo

This box defines the most important concepts in statistics, research, and analysis. These are the words you should use in meetings to impress your boss and your co-workers.

Reduce the Risk

Use the suggestions in this box to reduce the risk in using statistical techniques. Hopefully the advice will spare you the embarrassment of choosing the wrong statistical technique or coming to the wrong conclusion about your data. You'll also pick up on a variety of tips used by veteran statisticians to make better decisions using statistical tests.

Watch Out!

Sometimes things just go wrong, no matter how well you plan your statistical analysis. Luckily, there are usually things you can do to avoid common mistakes before you make the wrong decision. This sidebar provides tips to help you do just that.

Statistical Wisdom

This sidebar provides quotes and tips from my experience and that of other experts that may help inspire you to greater achievements, or simply help keep you motivated to do your best, even when the statistical concepts seem impossible to master.

Acknowledgments

Over the years and through countless research efforts and business analyses of all sizes, people too numerous to mention have offered advice, shared techniques, and provided examples (good and bad) that have helped me hone my skills as a user of statistics. All of these people deserve my appreciation, as they've provided me with research models to copy (and avoid) as I bring my own statistical analyses to bear on real-world issues.

Regarding this book, all of the people at Alpha Books—editorial mentors, production professionals, and marketing authorities—deserve my special thanks for their hard work, skill, and good ideas. Renee Wilmeth and Michael Koch deserve special kudos for their patience and support of this project. I appreciate the opportunity to again work with such a special group of people. I also want to express gratitude to my agent, Mike Snell, who is always smart enough to see an opportunity with low risk and high probability of success.

Most important, I want to thank you, the reader, for considering the thoughts, tools, and techniques I lay out in these pages. I understand the importance of your business analyses, and appreciate that you are taking time to consider my ideas for using statistics to make better decisions on the potential, quality, and performance of your enterprise and your career. I hope this book, with its practical examples, will revolutionize your understanding of statistical analysis, without burdening you with the details that keep you from getting the business information you really need to know.

Trademarks

All terms mentioned in this book that are known to be or are suspected of being trademarks or service marks have been appropriately capitalized. Alpha Books and Pearson Education, Inc. cannot attest to the accuracy of this information. Use of a term in this book should not be regarded as affecting the validity of any trademark or service mark.

Part 1

Charting Your Future

Modern business requires a focus on priorities, better management techniques, and effective structures for communication. Believe it or not, statistics can help you with all of these things. Statistics can help you extract meaningful information from piles of raw data, see trends in your marketplace, and help you communicate important concepts using charts and graphs. The processes and methods of statistics provide the structure, focus, insight, and control to help guide your decision making. With statistics you'll get a clearer view of your enterprise—yes, even with the math involved. As you read on, you'll see that it's not really that hard to master the concepts.

In this first section, you'll be introduced to the ways to use statistics in business and how statistics can help you make better, more informed decisions. You'll also learn about the core concepts in statistics, the descriptive statistics (including charts and graphs) that form the basis for more advanced statistical analysis. So if you don't know a mode from a mean or a median, you will when you finish this section—and that will give you the power to master the rest of the book.

Chapter 1

Statistics and Business Go Hand in Hand

> ## In This Chapter
>
> ➤ Why statistics is a vital subject in today's business world
>
> ➤ What statistics can help you do in business
>
> ➤ The common statistical questions
>
> ➤ The basic concepts in understanding statistics

The world of business is filled with uncertainty. We continually make decisions without knowing how they might affect future events. When we are careful we try to think logically, assessing situations and determining our priorities. Using the mathematical theory of probability, statisticians, also called statistical scientists, formalize this decision-making process to improve it.

The steps involve collecting observations, coding it as data, evaluating the data, and drawing conclusions. The information might be a test group's favorite amount of sweetness in a blend of fruit juices, the number of men and women hired by a city government, or the velocity of a burning gas on the sun's surface. Statisticians can provide crucial guidance in determining what information is reliable and which predictions can be trusted. They often help search for clues to the solution of a scientific mystery, and sometimes keep criminal investigators from being misled by false impressions.

Statistical Wisdom

Florence Nightingale (1820–1910) is most commonly known as the "Lady of the Lamp," an English hospital administrator, and a reformer who organized and operated hospital units during the Crimean War. However, you probably don't know that she was also a skilled statistician and a pioneer in using data to demonstrate the need for change in medical care. Here's what she had to say about statistics: "[Statistics is] ... the most important science in the whole world; for upon it depends the practical application of every other science and of every art: the one science essential to all political and social administration, all education, all organization based on experience, for it only gives results of our experience."

How is *statistics* useful in business? Some people might say statistics has no place in the real world of inventories, sales, and bottom lines. But what if numbers derived from data you already have on hand could help you get more return on your investment dollars? What if statistics could help you see a downward trend in the sales of your main product so you could adjust your product mix before you lose your market share?

Statistical Lingo

The word **statistics** has two meanings. In common usage it means a collection of numerical data; formally, the word refers to a branch of mathematics that encompasses descriptive statistics, statistical inference, and the analysis of statistical data.

Well, statistics can do all that and a lot more. No matter what your type of business, it's important to know who your customers are and what they are thinking. Research and statistical analysis of the research data enables you to do that. For example, by surveying a sample of potential or actual customers you can better determine whether your new product line will be a major success or a megaflop.

However, before you can use any of the advice in this book, you need to understand what statistical analysis is, and what it can and can't do. In this chapter you'll learn to recognize the importance of statistics and explore the reasons statistical concepts are vital to success in business in almost every department. This is the first step toward speaking the language of statistics—and because most professionals know that a working knowledge of statistics will improve their odds of career success, it's a pretty important language to speak.

The Origin of Statistics

The original idea of statistics was the collection of information about and for the "State." The birth of statistics often is attributed to a mid-seventeenth-century commoner named John Graunt. A native of London, Graunt began reviewing a weekly church publication issued by the local parish clerk that listed the number of births, christenings, and deaths in each parish. These so-called Bills of Mortality also listed the causes of death.

Graunt, who was a shopkeeper, organized this data in the forms we call descriptive statistics, which was published as *Natural and Political Observation Made upon the Bills of Mortality,* and shortly thereafter was elected as a member of Royal Society. Thus, statistics borrowed—and continues to borrow—some concepts from sociology such as the concept of population. It has been argued that because statistics usually involves the study of human behavior, it cannot claim the precision of the physical sciences.

Probability, the mathematics that much of statistics uses, has much longer history. Probability theory was a branch of mathematics studied by Blaise Pascal and Pierre de Fermat in the seventeenth century. It originated from earlier studies of games of chance and gambling during the sixteenth century. Today, *probabilistic modeling,* an advanced application of probability theory, is used to control the flow of traffic through a highway system, a telephone interchange, or a computer processor; find the genetic makeup of individuals or populations; quality control; insurance; investment; and other sectors of business and industry.

Even though ever-growing and diverse fields of human activities are using statistics, it seems this field remains obscure to the public. Professor Bradley Efron of Stanford University expressed this nicely:

> "During the twentieth century statistical thinking and methodology have become the scientific framework for literally dozens of fields including education, agriculture, economics, biology, and medicine, and with increasing influence recently on the hard sciences such as astronomy, geology, and physics. In other words, we have grown from a small obscure field into a big obscure field."

> **Statistical Wisdom**
>
> "Today, in most organizations, if you can't speak statistically, no one listens."
>
> —*Terry Dickey,* Using Business Statistics, *1994*

Some Real-World Business Examples of Statistics

Statistical methods usually are developed for a particular purpose, but then find use in a range of endeavors. For example, experimental techniques that help farmers choose appropriate varieties of wheat also assist manufacturers in improving their products, and are a key part of the testing of therapeutic drugs before they are approved for the general public. Similarly, methods used to study radio waves from distant galaxies also help businesspeople to understand fluctuations in financial markets. In each of these cases, statistical principles designed to solve one problem now solve problems in very different disciplines.

Business owners, managers, and professionals use statistics to analyze trends and make decisions. They use statistics to measure profitability, quality, performance, and customer attitudes. Every business and every department can benefit from statistical analysis of relevant data.

Determining Advertising Effectiveness

If you are an air-conditioning service company you might want to know the geographic area in which your customers fall (called the *catchment*). To figure your catchment, you can draw a scatter diagram based on customer ZIP codes showing your market penetration in various geographical areas. By pulling this information from your accounting database and importing it into a statistical package, you can determine whether advertising in more local periodicals would serve your needs better than an ad in the city newspaper. Once you've placed your ads, if you've coded them you'll be able to accurately evaluate their effectiveness.

Understanding Demand for Your Products

Statistical techniques also can help you sort out the separate effects of several different factors on the demand for your products. For example, if you're selling ice cream, you can expect that the price of the ice cream, the flavors you have available, the income of the community, the number of children in the area, and the temperature all will have an impact. If you have data on all these different factors, you can use *regression analysis* (a technique I'll introduce in Chapter 15, "Recognizing the Relationships of Business Variables") to determine which factors are most important in affecting demand for your ice cream (thus determine how to modify your marketing strategies to maximize your sales).

Statistical Wisdom

"... statistics, like broccoli, is a very good thing, even though both may have a slightly malodorous aftertaste. Statistics is even more useful than broccoli in helping companies make decisions about types of products they should produce, the ways in which they should market those products, and the production processes that are to be used to make those products. Broccoli, by contrast, is of very little use in formulating a marketing plan or operating a factory, even though it is a good source of iron."

—*Jefferson Hane Weaver,* Conquering Statistics, *1997*

Improving Quality

Statistics also can help manufacturers with quality control. Say you develop software in your company. If you want to keep track of how well your staff is packing the materials in the boxes, you can regularly take a sample of your product, enter the data such as the day of the week, hour of the day, number of workers, and rate of production, and then enter the number of mistakes made. If you run a statistical analysis you'll be able to determine whether the day, the hour, the workers, or the production rate most affect shipment quality.

Wouldn't it be interesting to know that when a certain manager or worker is on vacation or sick, productivity and quality improve? Or that certain workers always take sick leave on Monday? A statistical analysis could help you determine where the dead wood is—and where the rotten apples are—in your organization.

Introducing the Branches of Statistics

There are two distinctly different but equally important branches of the formal mathematical branch known as statistics. The first branch is known as *descriptive statistics*—the branch that summarizes and organizes *raw data* into meaningful information. You probably are already familiar with some aspects of descriptive statistics. For example, you know how to calculate the average cost for your monthly utility bills or can summarize the percentages of the response choices on a marketing survey. These both are examples of descriptive statistics. You'll learn about these and many more descriptive statistical techniques in Chapters 2 through 6.

Statistical Lingo

Raw Data *Data* are a statisticians raw material. Raw data are lots of numbers related to an observation, study, or research project. In statistics, data are coded in an explicit way that will make them more meaningful. (You'll learn more about that in Chapter 2, "Understanding and Organizing Business Data.")

Population In statistics, the word refers to the total group of people, things, or characteristics you are interested in studying, understanding, or predicting.

Sample A group of items or data selected from a population.

The other major branch of the mathematical field of statistics is referred to as *inferential statistics*. Statistical inference (or inferential statistics) is the process of obtaining information about a larger group from the study of a smaller group. The total group of people, things, or characteristics you are interested in studying, understanding, or predicting is called the *population*. A *sample* is a group of representative items chosen from the population and used to predict the behavior or characteristics of the total population with the help of inferential statistics.

Examples of populations and samples include:

Example 1

Population: The 31 flavors of ice cream at a 31-flavor Baskins Robbins ice cream parlor.

Sample: The six flavors of ice cream you have tested to determine whether the store sells high quality, tasty ice cream.

Example 2

Population: All registered voters in the United States.

Sample: The 3,000 registered voters who are interviewed as part of a Gallup poll to determine the most likely winner in the next election. (Obviously, if you consider the year 2000 presidential election, the predictive capabilities of inferential statistics and the polls that use it are not perfect!)

Example 3

Population: All products produced on an assembly line.

Sample: Items randomly selected to undergo quality tests to ascertain the predictable quality of the products being produced.

Why use samples, you ask? Wouldn't it be more accurate to use data on the entire population? Well, you're right about your assumption—but samples are used in statistics because it's often too expensive and time consuming to survey entire populations. It wouldn't be prudent to survey an entire population if the predictions made from a sample are almost as accurate. However, there are times when large populations are surveyed to make sure the absolutely most accurate data is obtained. The population census taken by the Census Bureau every ten years in the United States is one such example.

Statistical Wisdom

"How to study statistics: Do well in it—if you do well, you are much more likely to enjoy it. (And in later years you may even make some money tutoring other students!)"

—T. P. Hutchinson, author and professor of statistics

The Relationship Between Probability and Statistics

As you can see in reviewing the previous examples, inferential statistics from sample data often involve the laws of probability (the laws of chance) to make the prediction or draw a conclusion. Probability and statistics are very closely related because they ask the opposite kinds of questions. In general, probability asks what is likely to happen and statistics answers questions about events that have already occurred.

After covering descriptive statistics, you'll learn a bit more about probability. In statistics, you don't know how a process works but are able to observe the outcomes; conversely, in probability you already know how a process works but want to know how to predict what will happen—the outcome of that process. Learning how probability works will help you understand how statistical inference can be used to learn about the nature of unknown processes and behaviors.

Statistical Lingo

Descriptive statistics The process of obtaining meaningful data from raw data, often, but not always, consisting of large sets of numbers too large to deal with directly.

Inferential statistics The science of drawing statistical conclusions about a population from specific data (usually a carefully selected sample from the population) using probability and specific statistical data prediction techniques.

Probability The laws of chance or the likelihood that something will happen based on what you already know about a process. Most inferential statistics depend on the science or laws of probability.

At this point you have a good idea of the importance of statistics to business and why you need to understand the fundamentals of the field; you're ready to move on to descriptive statistics. I think you'll find the information a lot more useful than you expected when you bought this book. Besides, you already use statistics every day and probably don't even know it; you'll discover this as you read on.

The Least You Need to Know

➤ If you are in business, it helps to have a working knowledge of statistical principles and their applications to better understand your business operations and customer behaviors.

➤ Statistics can help you make better decisions about a wide range of business operations.

➤ Data are the raw material of statistical analysis.

➤ Samples are used in statistics because usually it would be too expensive to survey large populations.

➤ Statistical analyses can be applied to many aspects of business.

➤ The two major branches of statistics are descriptive and inferential statistics. Most inferential statistics depend on the laws of probability.

Chapter 2

Understanding and Organizing Business Data

In This Chapter

➤ Distinguishing between observations and data

➤ Categorizing and describing data

➤ Building a datafile for further analysis

Data is the core of statistics. Without data, there would be no statistical analyses. All statistics are derived from data that are based on observations—including observations that are made directly by people (such as counting the number of red cars in a parking lot), to data gathered in formal research (such as a study of a group of customer's preferred color for the packaging of your battery products).

In this chapter you'll learn about a lot of different categories of data and observations such as those used in various types of statistical analyses in the business world. However, before you can even start doing meaningful business statistical research and analyses (or reading statistical business reports, for that matter), it is important to be able to recognize the categories for one reason—the statistical analyses you'll learn about later in the book will only work on specific categories of data and observations—so you need to know which categories of data you're working with. (If this is unclear to you now, you will understand it by the time you've finished the chapter.)

Understanding Observations

To compute or arrive at a statistical understanding of your observations, you must have observations (usually in terms of measures, tests, or counts) of some event, factor, or occurrence. These observations can be the result of a formal study, reviewing numbers on sales history, or simply numbers or facts available to you from various other sources.

Assume for a moment that you are selling an innovative type of battery to the general public. To make your sales, you'd need to prove that your product is more effective than the competitor's. What would you do? Well, the first step would be to gather some observations about your product (and the products of the competition). We can assume we can all agree on what we mean by observations; however, some discussion points about observations definitely are worth mentioning. They are sort of philosophical, so you don't have to agree with them all.

In general, observations you can use in your analyses:

➤ **Need not be scientific.** Indeed, everybody observes; not everybody is engaged in science. For example, you simply know the number of batteries sold by your company—that's a fact; it's not a scientific study.

➤ **Need not be empirical.** In fact, in quite a few disciplines (including anthropology and philosophy, for example) people observe by using introspections, intuition, or empathy. These terms are not easily explained, but they do not seem to involve the senses, and they certainly don't involve numerical measures; thus they are not empirical (meaning related to numbers). But because people use these internal processes, there seems to be no obvious reason for excluding them from the domain of observations—they are simply called *subjective observations,* because they're based on personal feelings that can't be measured scientifically.

➤ **Are not just sense impressions.** Most observations are interpreted and, at least in principle, public for others to observe—except for those subjective feelings I was just talking about. Most observations, even the subjective ones, can be communicated to others, although often they are not. Thus observations usually are coded in our brains and filtered through language and cognition.

➤ **Need not be quantitative.** Some people say observations are never truly quantitative. There always has to be some sort of operation performed on observations to make them quantitative. For example, the sales of batteries for the month have to be totaled based on the submission of sales records from the salespeople. No one actually observes the total sales. The sales total isn't an observation until the number is created based on raw numbers from the submitters.

Despite all these truths about observations, you'll find most statistical observations involve numerical data of some kind, whether it's been derived from other data or directly observed. Empirical analyses (meaning number related) are used in statistical analyses because numbers can be manipulated with mathematical operations (statistics). This helps researchers and observers understand the data in ways that make them more meaningful for decision making and other business assessments.

Organizing Observations into a Datafile

In the example of selling the new type of batteries you might make the following observation:

> The battery power is between two particular marks on your power-measuring device.

You also might observe the qualitative nature of the responses your customer gave in a questionnaire about how she liked the new batteries:

> The customer gave response *a* to multiple choice item 1, response *b* to multiple choice item 2, and response *d* to multiple choice item 3.

Although all these observations are coded, at least implicitly, it is more important to turn them into data that are explicitly coded so they seem more empirical and quantitative. This way we can better understand them with statistical analyses. If you're the person collecting the observations about the batteries you'll need to develop a codebook or data file of the observations. This will help you transform the observations to data, which in part determine the statistical tools you can use to understand which battery really is the better choice for the customers.

A data file can help you record all the possible observations you collect. For instance, you might decide to code income in four categories. If you ask the potential customer for her religion, we need some rules on how to enter the responses into the datafile. You should not have categories for only the major religions; you must take into account that somebody might answer "republican" or "agnostic."

Statistical Wisdom

"A fact is like a sack—it won't stand up if it's empty. To make it stand up, first you have to put in it all the reasons and feelings that caused it in the first place."

—*Luigi Pirandello (1867–1936), Italian author and playwright,* Six Characters in Search of an Author *(1921)*

Exploring the Four Basic Data Types

In coding observations into a codebook or data file, there really are only four basic types of data you can record: *nominal, ordinal, interval,* and *ratio.* Let's take a look at each of these types of data and see how they might be used to help you understand the observations about your batteries.

Nominal Data

Nominal data uses numbers as names for classification purposes only. For example, you might have three groups of people who responded to your questionnaire about the batteries and you identified them as Groups 1, 2, and 3. Nominal variables are useful for identifying groups within the data such as gender, location, experimental versus control group, and so on.

For example, you might want to measure the actual performance of the batteries for those who actually used them compared to those who didn't use them. Thus, you would need to record *used-battery* (a nominal variable) for each person who completed the questionnaire. You might want to record another nominal variable to record opinions about the battery for each participant (for example, 1=Yes, I like it and 2=No, I don't like it).

However, in spite of their usefulness for classifying people into groups, nominal data contain too little information to use with many powerful statistical techniques—even something as simple as an average. For example, if you were to record group numbers for every participant in the questionnaire survey and then average the number of the groups, the result would be meaningless.

Ordinal Data

Ordinal numbers are *rankings*—first, second, third, and so on. For example, to measure the lifespan of your batteries, you might select the length of time each battery lasts in running the toy rabbit with the beating drum. The battery that lasts the longest in the toy rabbit—drumming contest would be first. Such a ranking would be ordinal data. It would tell you more than nominal data (I like it versus I don't like it), but less than if the time actually was measured in the rabbit drumming contest.

Ordinal data are useful in situations where it is difficult to get better measurements. For example, you would have trouble using ordinal data alone, saying that the battery lasted twice as long as the competitor's battery. You could say only that your battery lasted longer when put into the toy drumming rabbit.

Statistical Wisdom

"*Data* originated as the plural of Latin *datum,* 'something given,' and many maintain that it still must be treated as a plural form. The *New York Times,* for example, adheres to the traditional rule in this headline: 'Data Are Elusive on the Homeless.' But the practice of treating *data* as a plural in English often does not correspond to its meaning in modern research. We know, for example, what 'data on the homeless' would consist of—surveys, case histories, statistical analyses, and so forth—but it would be a vain exercise to try to sort all of these out into sets of individual facts, each of them a 'datum' on the homeless. Seventy-seven percent of the Usage Panel on English accepts the sentence *We have very little data on the efficacy of programs for the homeless,* where the singularity of *data* is implicit in the use of the quantifier *very little* (contrast the oddness of *We have very little facts on the efficacy of such programs*)."

—*Adapted from* The American Heritage® Dictionary of the English Language, Third Edition

Ordinal data still contains too little information to use statistics based on the average, but it does allow use of more powerful tools than does nominal data. For example, if you tested ten different batteries, you could pick out the battery that lasted in the exact middle of the rankings and have some basis to claim this as a typical battery.

Interval and Ratio Data

Interval and *ratio* data are similar. Interval data means you can measure the size of the difference between numbers. Not only do you know that your battery is "powerful" and the other battery is "weak" (nominal measurements), or that your

Statistical Wisdom

"Where I am not understood, it shall be concluded that something very useful and profound is couched underneath."

—*Jonathan Swift (1667–1745), Anglo-Irish satirist.* The Tale of a Tub, *Preface (1704).*

Statistical Wisdom

"Darkness is to space what silence is to sound, i.e., the interval."

—Marshall McLuhan (1911–80)

battery finished longer than the other battery (an ordinal measurement), you also know how many minutes longer—and you know the size of the *interval* between the other battery wearing out and yours continuing on. *Ratio data* is the same idea, except it is measured on an absolute scale with a zero in it (so the ratios are meaningful).

For example, let's consider the length of time your battery and the competitor's batteries are able to operate the drumming toy rabbit. If you know that your battery ran for two hours and the other battery ran for only one hour, you could create a meaningful ratio. Your battery lasted twice as long as the other battery.

If you know only that your battery lasted 10 seconds longer than the other battery—you know the interval (10 seconds), but you can't compute the ratio, because both batteries might have been running for days, hours, or minutes.

Interval and ratio data are sometimes called *parametric data*. They allow the use of statistical techniques based on averages (which you will learn about soon in Chapter 4, "Predicting Profits with Measures of Central Tendency"). If you are going to compare averages across groups of batteries by name brand (nominal variables)—such as length of time that the batteries are able to power the toy drumming rabbit—you must use interval or ratio data to measure the overall power life of the competitive batteries.

Understanding the Limitations of Your Data Choices

The type of data you choose limits the type of statistical techniques you can use. You want to choose the type of data that provides the most information: ratio over interval, interval over ordinal, and ordinal over nominal. Why, you ask? Well, the length of the battery life (a ratio measurement) also provides interval information (the difference in battery life between two batteries), the ranking of the battery life for all the batteries you tested (ordinal information), and nominal information ("long" battery life versus "short" battery life). However, if you record only nominal information ("short" and "long") the other information is lost—and you won't be able to justify your claims of having a better battery.

Try It On Your Own

Here are some types of data (ratio, interval, ordinal, and nominal). See if you can determine which is which: (The answers are at the end of the book in Appendix A—but don't peek until you try it yourself.)

1. The lengths of a group of skyscrapers

2. Your personality type (introverted, shy, friendly, or assertive)

3. The amount of the mortgage on your house, in dollars

4. A rating, on a scale of 1–10, on your job performance

5. The manufacturing order of a group of computers

6. The finish order in a race to complete a set of paperwork

7. Time from start to finish on the set of paperwork

8. Time between finishers on a set of paperwork

9. Classification of "slow" or "fast" in completing a specific job task

10. One person is 15 miles ahead of another in a race and 20 miles behind a third person

Reduce the Risk

Know that data are only crude information and not knowledge by themselves. The sequence from data to knowledge is: from data to information, from information to facts, and finally, from facts to knowledge. Data becomes information when it becomes relevant to your decision problem. Information becomes fact when the data can support it. Fact becomes knowledge when it is used in the successful completion of a decision process.

—Professor Hossein Arsham, University of Baltimore (quoted from his home page at http://ubmail.ubalt.edu/~harsham/)

Start Making Decisions by Creating Datafiles

Remember: Business statistics is a set of mathematical tools that can assist you in making business decisions under uncertainties based on some numerical, measurable, and organized data. Decision making (using statistics) must be based on data—not on personal opinion or on belief. However, before you can begin decision making, you need to organize your data.

After you collect appropriate data to help you sell your batteries, the next step is to organize your measurements into a data file. (A data file sometimes is called a *data set* in statistics or in formal business research.) Statistical software (such as SPSS, a

Statistical Wisdom

"At first, many people think statistics is a dull subject that is not very much fun. However, think about how much *more* dull work you would have to do if you didn't know statistics. If you've just been given a large pile of numbers, you have no hope of understanding them unless you can figure out some way to summarize them. And that's what statistics is all about."

—*Douglas Downing and Jeffrey Clark,* Statistics the Easy Way, *3rd Edition*

popular statistics software program from a company of the same name) or a statistical calculator can use a data file or data set similar to the one described here. Even if you are creating statistics by hand, you still will need to code and organize your data in a useful way, such as a codebook that is similar to the data file you'd create on a computer.

In general, there are four important parts to any data file: the variables, the cases (a case also is called a *record* in a computer database), the values, and the table that lists values or variables by each case.

Let's create a data file for your batteries and the competitor's batteries. Start with the cases, which are named (the nominal data). For example, let's use these names: Our Battery, Their Battery, The Other Battery. Each case (or record) will contain all the data elements about the battery named Our Battery, Their Battery, and so on. The variables are the specific measurements recorded for each individual case. The values you are going to record are brand name, voltage, component metal, finish order, and total battery life.

Statistical Lingo

Variable   A variable simply is a measurement recorded for an individual, object, or entity in an experiment or an observation. A variable is a quantity that varies over different instances, which is why it is called a variable. For example, if the volts of 30 batteries were measured, the volts would be a variable. A statistical variable varies in another sense. X might be the weight of a particular person. Repeated weighing of that person might, and probably would, yield slightly different values from weighing to weighing. Maybe this is because of an error in the scale, or maybe the person's weight actually fluctuates because of water retention or sweating; the reason isn't important. What is important is that on any given weighing there is uncertainty about what the exact measurement will be.

If we make a statement such as $y = x + 3$ about statistical variables, we mean that x is subject to chance variation as in the previous paragraph; and whatever value x happens to assume, we add 3 to it to obtain y. Y therefore is subject to the same chance variation, but it is still related to x—which itself might vary on different weighing of the individual. In statistics, we call statistical variables *random variables* and refer to the actual value taken on by a random variable at the time it is measured as its *realization*.

Nominal scale   Nominal measurement, or the nominal scale consists of assigning items to groups or categories. No quantitative information is conveyed and no ordering of the items is implied. Nominal scales are usually qualitative rather than quantitative. Gender, your name, a brand, colors are all examples of nominal scales. Variables measured on a nominal scale are often referred to as *categorical* or *qualitative* variables.

Quantitative and qualitative variables   Variables can be *quantitative* or *qualitative*. (Qualitative variables sometimes are called "categorical variables," just like nominal scales are called categorical.) Qualitative variables are measured on a nominal scale because you can't measure a quality such as good, excellent, or even poor—except on artificially created scales produced by the researcher. Quantitative variables are measured on an ordinal, interval, or ratio scale; these types of variables can be measured using numbers. If you asked someone about his favorite brand of battery, the variable would be qualitative. "Oh, that Bunny brand is a great battery." In this example, "great" would be the qualitative variable. Things such as your name, a brand of equipment, and gender all are nominal variables; but they are not qualitative because there is no judgment or subjective observation associated with these nominal variables.

If you measured the time it took someone to respond to the question about the favorite battery, the variable would be quantitative. For example, it took 30 seconds to reply to the question. Thirty seconds is a quantitative amount because it is numerical data.

Independent and dependent variables   Some variables are manipulated by an experimenter; others are measured from the subjects who respond to the independent variable. For example, you might want to know how the temperature (independent variable) affects people's attitudes in a shopping mall. The attitudes are being manipulated by the temperature change, which you can control. The attitude or sale level or other measure of the subjects' behavior is a dependent variable: It is affected by or dependent on the independent variable of temperature. Sometimes independent variables are called *factors*, and the dependent variables are frequently referred to as *dependent measures*.

Frequency distribution   A *frequency distribution* is an arrangement of a number of observations from zero to infinity. The arrangement and order of a frequency distribution graph helps you analyze the type, range, and frequency of specific occurrences or variables. A frequency distribution can be used to display everything from the smallest to the largest numbers of occurrences in a set of data. There are many ways to display a distribution of frequencies, including plotted or graphed distributions such as tables, histograms, and polygon plots.

The values are defined by a particular case and a particular variable. Our Battery's value for the value "voltage," is 12 (a ratio variable); the component metal is "nickel hydride." Here is a data table of the batteries. Most statistical software accepts data organized like the table shown here. In most ways, it's similar to entering data into a spreadsheet such as Microsoft's Excel product. (In fact, Microsoft Excel can even perform a wide range of statistical analyses on the data.)

Brand Name	Voltage	Component Metal	Finish (Lowest Rank Means Longer Performance)	Total Operation Time (Start to Finish)
Our Battery	12	Lithium Ion	First	3.4 hrs.
Their Battery	11.5	Carbon-Zinc	Third	1.1 hrs.
The Other Battery	12	Nickel Metal Hydride	Second	1.5 hrs.

You can see it's much easier to explain your battery's superior performance when the data is put in a table like the one shown here. But there are many other ways to display statistical data that make the information easier to understand. You're going to learn about more ways to describe data in the next chapters.

The Least You Need to Know

➤ Measurements, or observations, often represent different types of information; the type of information limits the choice of statistical tools.

➤ There are four basic types of data used in statistics: nominal, ordinal, interval, and ratio.

➤ Nominal measurements are names or categories.

➤ Ordinal measurements indicate ranking.

➤ Interval measurements tell the difference between measurements.

➤ Ratio measurements use an absolute scale with a zero in it.

➤ Data files organize information like a spreadsheet; for example, every column represents a different variable and every row represents a different case (or record)

➤ An individual number in a data set or data file represents the values of a particular variable for a specific case (or record).

➤ A variable is a quantity that varies over different instances or measurements.

Chapter 3

Visualizing Profit and Performance

In This Chapter

➤ Making data visually understandable

➤ Representing data in useful ways

➤ Displaying data in various charts, graphs, and plots

➤ Understanding the concept of "skew"

If you've been given a list of daily numbers for all the sales in the country over the last two work weeks for your new battery product, you'd have little hope of understanding the numbers by themselves. You need to summarize the numbers in some way. Suppose you have observations of the following sales numbers over ten days (two work weeks) for boxes of batteries sold by your western regional distributors:

49, 37, 89, 63, 65, 55, 66, 104, 41, 66

This list of numbers is an example of raw data, as you might remember from Chapter 1, "Statistics and Business Go Hand in Hand." Raw data are numbers that haven't been transformed with other statistical (mathematical) operations. How can you see underlying patterns in a row of naked numbers? There must be a more productive way to view the information.

Reduce the Risk

Before any statistical calculation—even the simplest—is performed, your data should be
tabulated, graphed, or plotted.

Turning Raw Data into Information

Raw numbers need to be organized in a way that makes them understandable. You could simply state that on Monday of the first week we sold 49 boxes of batteries, on Tuesday 37, on Wednesday 89, and so on—but there's got to be a better way to represent and understand the data than a simple narrative. There are three main ways to present raw statistical data such as this: in tables, graphs, and charts. I'll start with tables, move on to graphs, and then discuss pie charts (which look exactly like pizza pies without the pepperoni) and other charting options.

Using Tables

Tables provide an easy format to present raw data in an orderly way that (hopefully) also is easy to read. However, if tables contain hundreds or thousands of numbers, they might not be too easy to understand. Things must be summarized (which I'll talk about later in this chapter). You'll be working with simple tables for now. The following table simply displays the number of boxes of sales for each day of the two weeks using the same data from the beginning of this chapter.

Western Region Battery Sales in Boxes for Two Weeks

Days	Week One	Week Two
Monday	49	55
Tuesday	37	66
Wednesday	89	104
Thursday	63	41
Friday	65	66
Totals for the Week	**303**	**332**

Sometimes you might want to use tables to make comparisons. Suppose you want to compare the sales of the Western and Eastern regions. Here's a table that represents and compares two weeks of sales both:

Western and Eastern Region Battery Sales by Boxes for Two Weeks

Days	Week One Western	Week One Eastern	Week Two Western	Week Two Eastern
Monday	49	102	55	97
Tuesday	37	95	66	89
Wednesday	89	37	104	42
Thursday	63	41	41	45
Friday	65	55	66	66
Totals for the Weeks	**303**	**330**	**332**	**339**

You can graph the numbers with dots for each number or actually connect the dots (as shown in later examples in this chapter) with a line that makes a pattern of what is happening with the data. One of the most basic (and important) statistical tables is the *frequency table*. You can construct this type of table by dividing scores or instances into intervals, and counting the number of scores or instances in each interval. An interval or instance can be 1, but in large frequency tables the frequencies likely will be put into groups such as all frequencies ranging from 1–5, 6–10, and so on. The actual number and percentage of scores in each interval typically are displayed.

Cumulative frequencies also are displayed in a frequency table. A frequency table for the range of chess moves for the players in a chess tournament is provided in the following table as an example of a typical frequency table.

Chess Moves by Number of Players: Cumulative Frequencies

Lower Limit	Upper Limit	Players Count	Cumulative Count of Players	Percentage	Cumulative Percentage
25	35	1	1	5	5
35	45	3	4	20	25
55	65	5	10	50	75
75	85	9	19	45	95
85	95	1	20	5	100

Note: Values are > lower limit and < upper limit of moves per game.

Statistical Wisdom

Good graphic display is part art and part science.

—*Larry Gonick and Woollcott Smith,* The Cartoon Guide to Statistics, *1993*

You'll probably agree that, simple or complex, tables generally are boring. However, you can add color and dimension to them with today's software—even Microsoft Word 2000 will enable you to do that. Even better than playing with various designs for the tables, you can turn the same data into more interesting graphs and plots that help you interpret the data quite easily.

Using Pie Charts

Pie charts, also called graphs, are a good way to show the relative percentages of a total amount that has been sold, delivered, or manufactured in a business—among other business uses. The following figure shows a simple pie chart that represents the Western region's first week of sales of boxes of batteries.

Example of a pie chart.

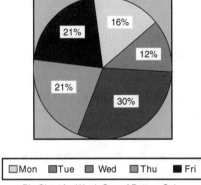

Pie Chart for Week One of Battery Sales

Line graphs (also called *plots*) are another simple way of representing data. The following figure shows a line graph that represents the first week of sales for both the Western and Eastern regions on one graph. You can see that even though the total sales by week is very similar—that days on which the most boxes are sold vary. This is the power of graphing raw data—the ability to see things more easily than you can see them in tables or as raw data.

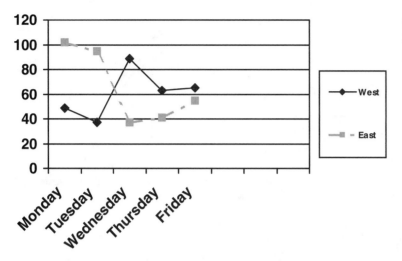

Graph of Western and Eastern regional sales for one week.

A *polygon* plot is *skewed* if one of its *tails* is longer than the one in the other direction. The first graph shown in the first of the following three figures has a positive skew. This means it has a long tail in the positive direction. The distribution graph shown in the second of the following figures has a negative skew because it has a long tail in the negative direction. Finally, the third distribution, shown in the third figure is symmetric and has no skew. The tails are the same length and shape on each side. Distributions with positive skew sometimes are called "skewed to the right;" distributions with negative skew are called "skewed to the left."

This is a little bit confusing. Remember, it's the long tail—not the big area of the plot—that determines the direction of the skew. You'll be learning more about skewed distributions in Chapter 6, "Solving Problems with Curves and *z*-Scores."

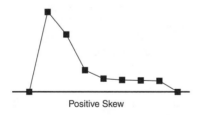

Graph of positive skew.

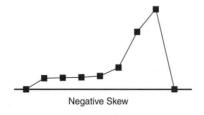

Graph of negative skew.

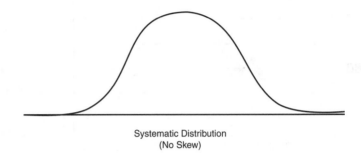

Graph of symmetric distribution (no skew).

Systematic Distribution
(No Skew)

Understanding about skew will become more important and meaningful as you learn more about inferential statistics (including variance) later in the book.

Using Histograms

You can create many different charts and graphs from a frequency table. A *histogram* is one of the basic graphs that can be constructed from a frequency table. The intervals are shown on the *X* axis; the number of scores in each interval is represented by the height of a rectangle located above the interval. The following chart is a histogram for the number of moves by the players in a chess tournament.

Histogram of chess moves by number of players in a tournament with that frequency per game.

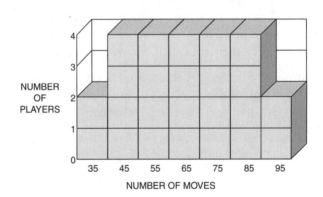

NUMBER OF PLAYERS

NUMBER OF MOVES

Histograms vary based on the class intervals you use. For example, a histogram of the sales of your boxes of batteries by quarter might look much different than those by month. This is because the shapes of histograms will vary depending on the choice of the size of the intervals. In the first quarterly histogram, I've used intervals of 500 boxes on the X axis. In the second histogram on the same data, I've used intervals of 100 boxes on the X axis. For the monthly histogram, I'm using an interval of 10. Look at the following examples to see how the histograms change based on the size of the intervals.

Monthly Battery Cases Sold in 2002

Jan	700
Feb	800
March	700
April	600
May	757
June	550
July	867
August	1067
Sept	883
October	567
November	933
December	683

Sales Boxes Sold by Quarter

Qtr 1	2200
Qtr 2	1907
Qtr 3	2817
Qtr 4	2183

Histograms of quarterly sales of batteries.

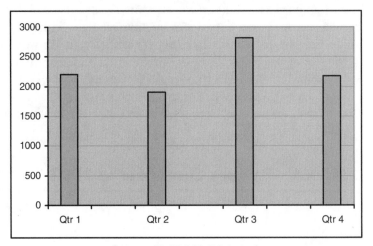

Sales with 500 Unit Intervals

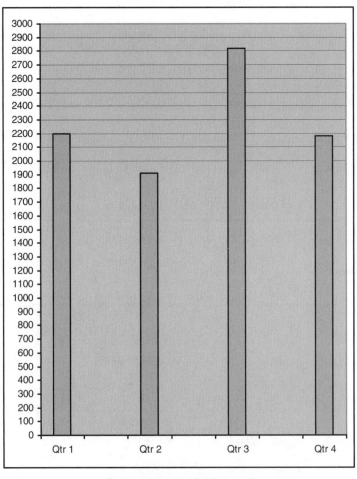

Sales with 100 Unit Intervals

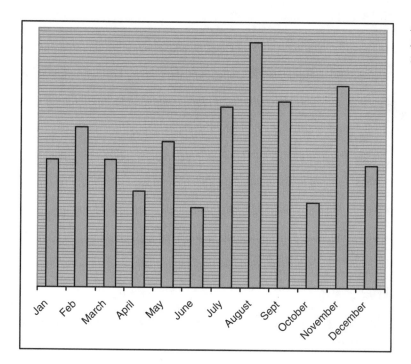

Histogram of monthly sales of batteries with 10 unit intervals.

You can see how the length of observation and interval can affect someone's perception of sales during the various months and quarters in 2002. Thus, choosing the interval is important in developing histograms. Here are some helpful steps for you to follow:

➤ Use intervals of equal length with midpoints at convenient round numbers.

➤ For a small data set, use a small number of intervals.

➤ For a large data set, use more intervals.

Another way to display frequencies is with the *cumulative frequency distribution. This* is a plot or histogram of the number of observations falling on, in, or below an interval. The graph shown in the following figure is a cumulative frequency distribution in the form of a histogram of the scores on a single statistics test. Forty students took the test. The *X* axis shows various intervals of scores (the interval labeled 35 includes any score from 32.5 to 37.5). The *Y* axis shows the number of students scoring in the interval or below the interval.

Any cumulative frequency distribution can be displayed as either the actual frequencies at or below each interval (as shown here) or the percentage of the scores at or below each interval. A cumulative frequency distribution can be a histogram, as shown in the next figure, or a polygon plot as shown in the following figure.

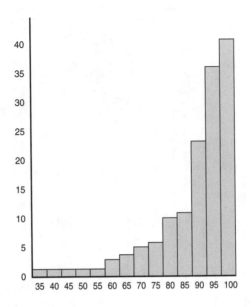

Cumulative scores on a statistics test for forty students.

There are many ways to display frequencies in a series of related observations, such as people attending the doctor's office over a period of a month, numbers of people riding on the train each month over a year, or the number of boxes of batteries sold each month in a year. One way of displaying the cumulative frequencies over a period is using a *frequency polygon* as another graphical display of a frequency table.

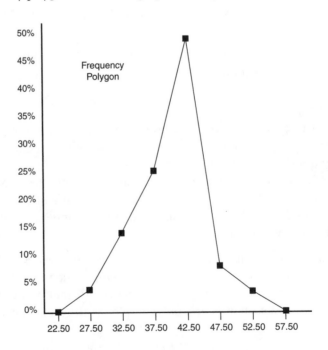

The cumulative frequency of batteries sold over a period of twelve months.

In a frequency polygon the intervals are shown on the X axis; the number of scores, observations, or counts in each interval is represented by the height of a point located above the middle of the interval. The points are connected so that with the X axis they form a polygon, which sometimes looks like a mountain or two mountains; other times it looks like a hill or bell shape, depending on the way the frequencies distribute themselves on the plot. You'll see a lot of frequency diagrams in other chapters.

Using the Bar Graph

A bar graph is much like a histogram, except the columns are separated from each other by a short distance. Bar graphs are commonly used for *qualitative variables* such as colors, brand names of cars, or other such nominal data. The following chart is a bar graph of the colors of toy wagons sold by color.

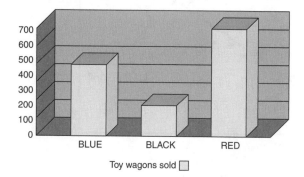

Sample of a simple bar chart.

Examining Relationships with Scatterplots

One of the most important steps in examining the relationship between two variables is to create a *scatterplot.* A scatterplot is simply a graph that plots a score for one variable (for example, attitude toward your product) against a score on a second variable (for example, income level). They are used to examine any general trends in the relationship between two variables.

If scores on one variable tend to increase with correspondingly high scores of the second variable, a positive relationship is said to exist. If high scores on one variable are associated with low scores on the other, a negative relationship is apparent in the scatter plot. (In Chapter 15, "Recognizing the Relationships of Business Data," you'll learn to calculate these type of relationships, called *correlations* between variables.)

The extent to which the dots in a scatterplot cluster together in the form of a clear directional line (up, down, sideways, and so forth) indicates the strength of the relationship. (again, we'll be talking more about these types of correlation relationships in Chapters 15, "Recognizing the Relationships of Business Data," 17, "Are These Customers the Same or Different?" and 18, "Getting Results from ANOVA." Scatterplots with dots that are spread apart almost randomly represent a weak relationship between the variables. The following figure shows a scatterplot for attitudes toward your product compared to the salary levels of the subjects being interviewed.

Scatterplot with generally positive direction: As the variable on the left gets higher the variable on the bottom also gets larger.

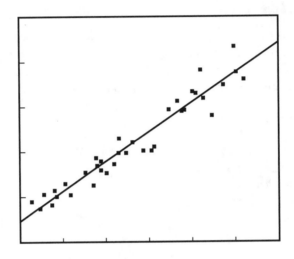

Statistical Wisdom

Factual science may collect statistics and make charts. But its predictions are, as has been well said, but past history reverse.

—John Dewey, American philosopher and educator

Stem and Leaf Plots

The following raw data often is referred to as an *array*, which is a list of numerical data. It would be nice to order this data and know what the range of accuracy is in this particular manufacturing application. One way to display this easily is to use a *stem and leaf plot*, shown in the diagrams that follow for this array of data for fifteen pistons manufactured in a Porsche plant. A stem and leaf plot looks somewhat like a tree; hence the name for the chart.

Data Accuracy in 1/1000 millimeters for fifteen pistons manufactured for Porsche engines:

2.6, 0.6, 1.1, 0.1, 0.4, 2.0, 1.3, 0.8, 1.3, 1.2, 1.9, 3.2, 1.7, 2.2, 1.9

The following diagram is known as a stem and leaf plot *as they come,* which means the data is entered in the order it appears in the array (as shown in the preceding example).

Unordered Stem and Leaf Plot

Stem	Leaf						
0	6	1	4	8			
1	1	3	3	2	9	7	9
2	6	0	2				
3	2						

To create the type of plot shown in the preceding diagram you must abbreviate the observations to two significant digits. In the case of the grinding accuracy data, the digit to the left of the decimal point is the stem; the digit to the right is the leaf. First write the stems in order down the page; then work along the data set, writing the leaves down as they come. Thus, for the first data point, we write a *6* opposite the *0* stem. These are given in the preceding figure. You then order the leaves, as in the following example.

Ordered Stem and Leaf Plot

Stem	Leaf						
0	1	4	6	8			
1	1	2	3	3	7	9	9
2	0	2	6				
3	2						

33

The advantage of first setting the figures out in order of size and not simply feeding them straight from notes into a calculator or computer program (for example, to find their average) is that the relation of each to the next can be looked at. Is there a steady progression, a noteworthy hump, a considerable gap? Simple inspection can disclose irregularities.

Furthermore, a glance at the figures gives information on their range. The smallest value is 0.1; the largest is 3.2 (based on 1/1000 of a millimeter). Of course, if you don't have time to lay out a large dataset into a stem and leaf plot, most statistics computer programs (such as the popular program, SPSS) will do this for you in a snap.

Understanding the Types of Variables

The first step, before any calculations or plotting of data, is to decide what type of data variable and variables you're working with. There are a number of typologies but one that has proven useful is provided in the following table. The basic distinction is between the type of variables: *quantitative* variables (for which you ask "how much?") and *categorical* variables (for which you ask "what type?").

Quantitative variables can be continuous or discrete. In theory, continuous variables such as weight can take any value within a given range. Discrete variables have a limit and can be counted or observed directly. Examples of discrete variables include number of employees in a department within the company, number of boxes of batteries sold, or the number of different models of a product.

Categorical variables are either *nominal* (unordered) or *ordinal* (ordered). You learned about this difference when you read about data types and variables in Chapter 2, "Understanding and Organizing Business Data." Some simple examples of nominal variables are male/female, alive/dead, regional area, and product style.

For nominal variables with more than two categories the order does not matter. For example, one cannot say that people in the Western regional sales group lie between those in the Southern regional sales group. There is no natural ranking among named regions. However, sometimes people can provide ordered responses such as grade of product quality; or they can agree, neither agree nor disagree, or disagree with some statement. In this case the order does matter and usually is important to account for.

Typology of Variables and Data

Quantitative Variables

Continuous Data	Discrete Data
Height, weight, age Salary from $1 to infinity Number of product defects	Number of batteries sold

Categorical Variables

Ordinal (Ordered categories) of Data	Nominal (Unordered categories) of Data
Product quality Better, same, worse Disagree, neutral, agree	Gender (male/female) Styles of Jaguar Cars (XJS, S Type, XJ8) Sales Region (Western, Eastern, Southern, Northern, Midwestern)

Variables shown at the left of the preceding table can be converted to those farther to the right by using *cutoff points*. For example, salary can be turned into a nominal variable by defining "high salary" as an annual salary of more than $200,000, "moderate salary" as less than or equal to $200,000 and more than $75,000, and "low salary" as less than or equal to $75,000. Height (continuous) can be converted into short, average, or tall (ordinal).

In general it is easier to summarize categorical variables; thus quantitative variables often are converted to categorical ones for descriptive purposes. However, categorizing a continuous variable reduces the amount of information available and statistical tests in general will be more sensitive; that is, they will have more power to predict outcomes or results for a continuous variable than the corresponding nominal one, although more assumptions might have to be made about the data.

Therefore, categorizing data often is useful for summarizing results, but not typically useful for statistical analysis. The choice of appropriate cutoff points can be difficult and different choices can lead to different conclusions about a set of data.

The definitions of types of data and variables in this section are not unique, nor are they mutually exclusive; they are provided to help you create or read a report that uses statistics, and to decide how to display and analyze the data. You should never debate too long about the typology of a particular variable in your analysis!

Common Questions About Research Data

This section presents a series of questions and answers about displaying business research data.

How many groups should I have for a histogram?

In general you should choose enough groups to show the shape of a distribution, but not so many that you lose the shape. It is partly aesthetic judgment but in general, between 5 and 15, depending on the sample size, gives a reasonable picture. Try to keep the intervals (known also as "bin widths") equal. With equal intervals the height of the bars and the area of the bars are both proportional to the number of subjects in the group. With unequal intervals this link is lost, and interpretation of the figure can be difficult.

What is the distinction between a histogram and a bar chart?

Alas, with modern graphics programs often the distinction is lost. A histogram shows the distribution of a continuous variable and, because the variable is continuous, there should be no gaps between the bars. A bar chart shows the distribution of a discrete variable or a categorical one so the resulting chart will have spaces between the bars. It is a mistake to use a bar chart to display a summary statistic such as a mean; particularly when it is accompanied by some measure of variation. It is better to use a *box-whisker* plot (which can be produced by most computer statistics programs.). A box-whisker plot is a type of frequency diagram that displays the most common frequencies of data in a box and extends the total range of the data with a line from the box, called the whisker.

What is the best way to display data?

The general principle should be, as far as possible, to show the original data and to try not to obscure the design of your research or business findings in the graph or chart. Within the constraints of legibility show as much information as possible. For example, when displaying the relationship between two quantitative variables, use a scatter plot rather than assigning a category to one or both of the variables.

There are many other ways to graph and chart data. If you have a statistical program such as SPSS (one of the most popular ones), you'll have instructions for creating literally a hundred or more versions or modifications to charts for displaying statistical data. I'll show a few more of these charts and graphs as I continue through the book.

The Least You Need to Know

➤ Raw data should be ordered, summarized, and displayed in appropriate tables, charts, or graphs before applying other statistical techniques.

➤ Some of the most common ways to display raw data are tables, pie charts, line diagrams or plots, stem and leaf plots, histograms, scatter diagrams, and polygons.

➤ One of the most basic (and important) statistical tables is the frequency table. A great number of charts and graphs can be created from a frequency table.

➤ It generally is easier to summarize categorical variables; for this reason, quantitative variables often are converted to categorical ones for descriptive purposes.

➤ The categorization of quantitative variables is useful for summarizing results, but not normally good for statistical analysis.

➤ Charts and graphs help you see trends, anomalies, and other information and relationships in your data without performing more complicated statistical analyses.

Chapter 4

Predicting Profits with Measures of Central Tendency

In This Chapter

➤ Understanding the concept of central tendency in a data set

➤ Determining the important central tendency measures of mean, median, and mode

➤ Learning when to use one measure of central tendency rather than another

---

If you were the vice president of sales for the battery company we've discussed in previous chapters, one thing you probably would want to know about the sales of your batteries is the average number of boxes sold each month for a period of time (say six months). You probably already know how to calculate this simple statistic from your grade school mathematics classes. You've already calculated this type of average, called the *mean* in statistics, many times: Simply add all the numbers and divide by the number of observations.

The Meaning of the Mean

The mean is one measure used to establish the characteristic of most data to *cluster* around a central value, often near the middle of all the other values. For example, if you have a list of all the people who have retired in the United States and their ages on the day they retired, most of the people would have retired around the age of 65.

Thus, 65 is a central value because most of the people retired at about this age. Some might have retired when they were a few years younger or a few years older—but the majority would have been 65. This clustering function of data around a central value is called the *central tendency of data.*

Statistical Wisdom

Defendit numerus: There is safety in numbers.

—*Anonymous*

Here an example of calculating the mean for a number of values. In the following example of monthly sales numbers, the numbers would add up to 1440 and the number of observations is 6; 1440 divided by 6 is 240. This is the average boxes sold per month based on a six-month sales period. This average, which is a measure of central tendency, is called the *mean* in statistics. The formulas for establishing the measures of central tendency are so simple that you will easily understand them; the *mean* formula for the example looks something like this:

$$\frac{249 + 337 + 163 + 289 + 298 + 104}{6} = \frac{1440}{6} = 240$$

The simple mean is 240 of boxes sold for each of the six months. In statistics the symbol used for the simple mean of a variable in a sample is $\overline{X}$ (called x-bar). (The symbol for the mean of a population is μ (the Greek letter mu). The mean is only one way to measure central tendency in a data set; there also are the *mode* and *median.*

Reduce the Risk

"Averageness is a quality we must put up with. Men march toward civilization in column formation, and by the time the van has learned to admire the masters the rear is drawing reluctantly away from the totem pole."

—*Frank Moore Colby (1865–1925), U.S. editor and essayist. The Colby Essays, vol. 1, "The Reading Public."*

The *sample mean* is an example of a statistic, or characteristic of a sample, that you are able to compute based on available data. Hopefully the mean represents the population you are studying (but sometimes it won't). The sample mean also is used in a wide range of statistical calculations. It is one calculation performed on almost every data set of *interval* or *ratio* data (defined in Chapter 2, "Understanding and Organizing Business Data"). Calculating the mean is not usually possible on nominal or ordinal data—unless the data has been altered in some way, and that's not usually a good idea.

Watch Out!

Don't confuse statistics with *parameters*. Parameters are characteristics of the population that you usually cannot know; typically they are designated with Greek symbols. Statistics are characteristics of samples that you usually are able to calculate. Statistics correspond to parameters but are not the same thing. For example, the sample mean $\overline{X}$ is a *statistic* which is the mean of a sample taken from a population. μ is the mean of a population—it's a *parameter* that cannot be known absolutely unless the population is very small. Remember: You compute statistics in order to estimate parameters.

The Mode—Not an Operation, but a Count

The *mode* is another interesting member of the central tendency measures of a data set. The mode is quite simply the most frequent value in a data set. It is appropriate for all types of numbers (nominal, ordinal, interval, and ratio), but is best used when at least one value occurs more frequently than most of the others.

In the sales example used earlier, there is no mode. No number appears more than once. However, in the following example of the years of employment at a company, there is a mode—it tells you that most of the people have been at the company a pretty long time. Here's an organized data set with the list of years each employee has worked at the company:

1 2 2 4 4 4 9 9 9 9 9 9 9 10 11 12

Statistical Wisdom

At first, many people think statistics is a dull subject that is not very much fun. However, think about how much *more* dull work you would have to do if you didn't know statistics. If you've been given a large pile of numbers, you have no hope of understanding them unless you can figure out some way to summarize them. And that's what statistics is all about.

—*Douglas Downing, Ph.D. and Jeffrey Clark, Ph.D., Statistics the Easy Way, 3rd Edition*

To calculate a mode, you need to list all the data values from low to high or from high to low; then count the number of times each value occurs to find the most frequently occurring value. The mode for this data set is 9—it is the most frequently occurring number in the data array.

Statistical Wisdom

"... Certainly statistics can claim to have as great a stake in the modern economy as chemistry and physics because statistics alone makes possible the functioning of the market economy and the management of massive multinational corporations."

—*Jefferson Hane Weaver, Conquering Statistics: Numbers without the Crunch, 1997*

The Median—In the Middle of Everything

The median is another central tendency measure. It is a value such that 50 percent of the data elements or cases are equal to or below it. Using the preceding ordered data from low to high for the 17 employees' years with the company, the median would be in the middle of the list (or an average of the two numbers in the middle if there is an even number of values). Thus, the median for the example also is 9 because 8 values are below the middle 9 and 8 examples are above the middle 9.

Statistical Lingo

Here are the definitions of the measures of central tendency so you won't forget the difference among the "three m's":

Mean The simple average you learned how to calculate in grade school.

Median Using a list arranged in order from low to high, the value such that as many numbers in the list are above it as below it.

Mode The value in a data list that occurs most frequently.

It's interesting to note that the rounded mean for this data is 7.8; thus the central tendency for this data around the 8–9 number is very strong. The closer the three central tendency measures are (mean, mode, and median)—the more perfectly centralized the data is around a single value.

To return to the monthly sales example, the median is the number halfway between 163 and 269—because in this even list of numbers, these are the two numbers closest to the middle. Here's the list of sales numbers ordered from high to low:

104 163 249 289 298 337

Since there isn't a clear median that is exactly in the middle, it must be calculated as the number half-way between the two middle values. In this case that halfway number between the two values is—a number that is half-way between 249 and 289. (If you add 249 and 289 and divide by 2 you get 269, the average of the two numbers.) It (269) is a number that is somewhat close to the mean of 240—but not a complete match. However, it would still be a reasonably accurate estimation of the average sales per month. Even so, the mean is a much better measure of central tendency in this case.

Watch Out!

In general, when a list of numbers contains one extreme value (an *outlier*), the mean (average) will not be representative of the numbers in the list. In that case the median might be a better measure of the central tendency. However, the average often is faster to calculate (by hand that is) so it is used more often.

When to Use a Measure of Central Tendency

The mean usually is the best indicator of central tendency. For nominal data, it's meaningless—the mode is the best choice with nominal data. For ordinal numbers, the median usually is the best choice. Even when the mean can be used with ordinal data (such as selections on a multiple-choice questionnaire), the median is a better estimate as a few extreme values distort the mean. To help you remember how to calculate the various measures of central tendency, you can refer to the diagram that follows.

Step-by-step central tendency calculations.

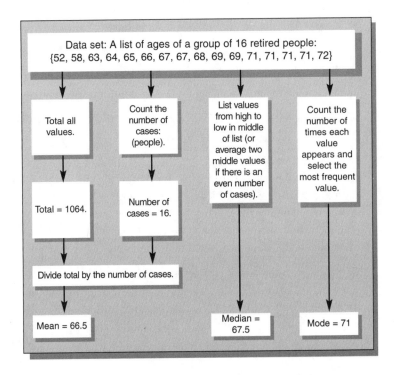

In this chapter, I've discussed the ways you can look at the tendency of data to center around a central number, called a measure of central tendency. We've discussed the mean, the mode, and the median. These types of averages are useful but don't tell you a lot about the distribution of values in a data set (prices, quality, sales, and so forth).

Now that you understand averages, you're ready to look at the ways data move around the measures of central tendency—especially the mean—so you can understand the distribution and variance in data. You're going to learn how to do that in Chapter 5, "Improving Quality with Measures of Dispersion." Get ready! It will be fun—I promise.

The Least You Need to Know

➤ Most of data you use in business tends to move toward a central value, called the central tendency of the data.

➤ The three most common measures of central tendency are the mean, mode, and median.

➤ The mean usually is the best indicator of central tendency, but is a useless measure on nominal data and a questionable one on some ordinal data.

➤ For nominal data, the mode is the best measure of central tendency.

➤ For ordinal data, the median is the best measure of central tendency.

Improving Quality with Measures of Dispersion

In This Chapter

➤ Describing the spread (or dispersion) in data and understanding its use in business

➤ Calculating range, interquartile range, variance, and the all-important standard deviation

➤ Creating your own measures of dispersion with a simple calculator

Wouldn't it be wonderful if you had a way of measuring the unpredictability of the daily, weekly, and monthly sales figures in your business? You'd have some data to help you understand exactly how to plan the payment of your expenses, distribute your advertising efforts, and understand what you need to make the sales averages higher and more predictable.

Variability (also called *dispersion or spread*) also is a good measure of quality in business. For example, a reduction in variability on product manufacturing means an increase in quality, because the production is consistently closer to the design specifications for the product. If variability is reduced the range of values (the spread) in the dataset (from low to high) is also reduced.

Getting Started with Dispersion Measures

In statistics you can start to understand the sales performance and work on improving quality by analyzing the *spread* or *dispersion* of the sales numbers away from their mean. For example, consider the battery business we discussed earlier. If you sold the same number of boxes of batteries—say 200—every day there would be no dispersion. However, if you sold 400 boxes one day and no boxes the next day, the average boxes sold for these two days would be the same, but the degree of dispersion would be much greater.

A Simple Way to Measure Dispersion

One way to measure the dispersion in data is to simply take the difference between the highest number and the lowest number in relevant data. This number is called the *range*. For example, if your highest sales day for the month was 650 boxes and your lowest sales day for the month was 45 boxes of batteries, the range would be 650 – 45 = 605.

The range gives you information on the spread between the highest value and the lowest value. However, it is not a truly accurate measure of the spread of the entire distribution of data. To prove the point, look at the following two lists, both of which have the same range:

List 1	List 2
500	500
300	490
300	420
300	40
300	10
0	0

It is clear when you examine the lists that the overall spread of List 2 is much greater than the spread of List 1.

The More Meaningful Interquartile Range

One problem with the range as a measure of dispersion is that the overall range will be greatly affected by the presence of a few very large or very small values that are far removed from the average (called *outliers*).

One way to make the range more representative of the actual spread in the data is to ignore the bottom and top quarters of the data and calculate the range of the remaining numbers. This calculated value is called the *interquartile range* or *IRQ*.

Watch Out!

It is important to understand the difference between a *percentage* and a *percentile*. A percentage usually is the expression of a number as a fraction of 100. For example, 50 percent is one-half of the total number of occurrences or things. The percentile is the ranking of a score compared to other scores; the percentile range of a score represents the percent of cases in a group that achieved scores lower than the one stated. You probably remember getting your percentile score for your SAT exams in high school. If you received a score of 567 on the verbal SAT test and that score had a percentile of 71, it means you earned a higher score than 71 percent of the people who took the test.

Calculating the Interquartile Range

Here are the steps for calculating the IRQ. (Remember, only simple calculations are presented here.)

1. Put the list of data in order from highest to lowest.

2. Find the data value such that $3/4$ of the other values are at or below it. This value is called the *third quartile* or 75th percentile.

3. Find the value such that $1/4$ of the other values are below it. This value is called the *first quartile* or 25th percentile.

4. Calculate the difference by subtracting the first quartile value from the third quartile value. This calculated value is the IRQ.

If the data sets are small or the sample size is not divisible by four, it might not be possible to divide the data set into exact quarters. However, there are a variety of proposed methods to estimate the quartiles. A simple, consistent method is to find the points midway between each end of the range and the median.

Statistical Lingo

You should know that the median is equal to the *second quartile* value in an array of numerical data.

Getting Even More Meaningful Information on Dispersion

Even with the more useful statistic called the *interquartile range,* a good dispersion analysis still must account for all the numbers being analyzed in a data set. One way to do this is to find out how far away from the mean each value is in the data set. To find the distance from the mean, you can simply subtract the mean from each value in the data list and derive the absolute values (values without negative signs or values). Absolute value calculations are represented by algorithms inside two vertical lines like this:

| |

The following table is an example of calculating the absolute value distances from the mean of a week of battery sales.

Calculating Absolute Values

Boxes of Batteries Sold	Distance from the Mean
235	68 = |235 – 303|
337	34 = |337 – 303|
248	55 = |248 – 303|
317	14 = |317 – 303|
402	99 = |402 – 303|
237	66 = |237 – 303|
345	42 = |345 – 303|
mean = 2121÷7 = 303	

To understand the dispersion, you could simply calculate the average distance from the mean, like this:

$$\frac{68 + 34 + 55 + 14 + 99 + 66 + 42}{7} = 54$$

This particular mean calculation is called the *mean absolute deviation;* it is a good measure of dispersion because it provides the average distance of each number from the mean.

Recognizing the Variance

For many purposes in statistics, the mean absolute deviation is not really useful for further analysis of the data. Often it is more useful to square each deviation and calculate the average of all the squared deviations. This number is called the *variance*. Here's the calculation with the absolute distances from the mean, which we calculated earlier for sales on each day of one week:

$$\frac{68^2 + 34^2 + 55^2 + 14^2 + 99^2 + 66^2 + 42^2}{7} =$$

$$\frac{4624 + 1156 + 3026 + 196 + 9801 + 4356 + 1764}{7} =$$

$$\frac{24981}{7} = 3568.714 = \text{Variance}$$

Variance of a population often is represented by the symbol σ^2 (sigma squared); σ is the lowercase Greek symbol sigma. The symbol for the variance of a sample is S^2. Typically, statisticians use the abbreviation Var(x) to represent the variance of a single value(x) for a sample.

However, it's important to remember the sigma squared symbol may be used erroneously in papers that report statistical results. The report may use the population symbol for variance (sigma squared) when a sample is used instead of data from the entire population. Most times, when calculating the variance of a sample, you should use the symbol S^2 for variance since you'll also likely be using a sample and not data from the entire population (unless the population is very small).

The calculation for the sample variance also is a bit different, as you can see from the diagram provided in this chapter. You divide the average of the squares by number of cases minus 1 (n–1). This provides a more accurate estimate of the population variation.

Introducing the All-Important Standard Deviation

Even though the calculated variance is a good measure of dispersion, it still suffers from a major disadvantage: The variance is difficult to interpret. Does the variance of 3568 in the preceding example really mean there is a lot of variance in general? Or does it mean there is also a little among some of the values? The problem arises because the variance is measured as a square of the unit in which the data values are measured. In the previous example, there is a variance of approximately 3568 boxes of batteries squared ... whatever that means. This number doesn't really tell you too much.

Statistical Wisdom

The idea of variability or variance sounds complex; really it is very simple. If you were planning a trip to a tropical island, it would be easy to pack. Daily temperatures wouldn't vary more than 10 degrees from the annual average. However, if the trip were to the American Midwest, the same mean annual temperature would be the result of blizzards and heat waves. The daily temperatures there are much more widely disperse around the mean; they are much more variable.

—*Terry Dickey,* Using Business Statistics, *1994*

This brings us to the calculation we've really been working toward: the *standard deviation*. This is the most difficult calculation we'll discuss in this book. Nonetheless, the standard deviation is a statistic of considerable magnitude because it is used in so many other analyses of statistical data.

How to Interpret the Standard Deviation

In simple terms, the standard deviation is simply the square root of the variance (which we just learned to calculate); the variance is the standard deviation squared.

$$\text{Standard deviation } = \sqrt{\text{variance}}$$

If you want to know more about calculating the standard deviation and all of these measures of dispersion, check out Appendix B, "Statistics Formulas," which explains and shows the calculations as standard accepted symbolic equations. (These are the ones that make statistics seem so hard initially—it really isn't, as you've been learning in the last few chapters.)

The Real Standard Deviation

In the example for calculating the variance in the sales of batteries over a week, the standard deviation is the square root of 3569 (approximately), which equals almost 60. The standard deviation is measured in the same units as the data: boxes of batteries sold. At first glance this seems like a relatively large deviation from a mean sales of

303 per day. The larger the standard deviation, the larger the dispersion in a sample or population. However, the standard deviation alone doesn't tell the whole story of the dispersion relative to the mean.

If you want to know whether the dispersion is very large relative to the mean, you can calculate (or your computer can) a statistic known as the *coefficient of variation.* You get this percentage by dividing the standard deviation by the mean and then turning the result into a percentage. In the battery sales example, the coefficient of variation = 60/303 = 0.198= 19.8%. This is a moderate to large variation—and certainly one that needs further examination if you're the one responsible for producing batteries.

Some Important Notes on the Standard Deviation

For now there are some interesting properties worth mentioning about the standard deviation. (You'll learn more in later chapters.) First, in any list it will always be true that at least 75 percent of the numbers will be within two standard deviations of the mean. Second, it generally is true that the proportion of numbers in the list within k standard deviations of the mean must be at least

$$1 - 1 \div k^2.$$

This result is known as *Chebyshev's theorem*—and it applies to every single possible list of numbers.

Choosing Among Dispersion Measures

Once you understand the summarizing numbers for dispersion—variance, standard deviation, mean absolute deviation, and range—you'll see that they all do what you originally set out to do when you were trying to understand the unpredictability of sales figures for the battery company. The measures all are related to each other and are relatively simple calculations of the dispersion of scores around the mean.

Statisticians typically use the standard deviation as the most commonly employed summarizing number to represent dispersion (the standard deviation of a population is represented by the Greek symbol sigma shown here with no square: σ). The standard deviation of a sample is represented by S.

The standard deviation is useful and understandable because it is represented in the same units as the original measurement. You'll recall that the variance is not. Still, in some cases statisticians will use the variance in advanced statistical calculations and analysis. You'll see a lot more of the standard deviation in the next chapters and learn how it is used to represent the spread in data.

Some Simple Practice—No Computer Required

If you want to get your hands into actually calculating the dispersion measures we've been talking about, here are some simple practice exercises. You can find the answers for this exercise in Appendix A, "Answer Key." A calculator probably would make this a lot faster—so I recommend you get one if you want to really create some statistics. Use the data sets to calculate the measures shown in the following table.

If you need help you can refer to the calculation steps for populations provided in the earlier step-by-step figure. Note that the calculations for samples are slightly different—and when you start using your computer program to calculate these measures you can specify whether you want measures for a population (*if* you have access to the data for the entire population as you do here) or a sample.

Data Set	Range	Variance	Standard Deviation
50, 52, 48, 52, 48			
50, 0, 100, 25, 75			
50, 25, 75, 25, 75			
50, 45, 55, 40, 60			
50, 52, 48, 54, 46			

If you know more about the standard distribution of the numbers, usually you can make more precise statements or predictions about the numbers. For example, when a list of numbers follows a common pattern called the *normal distribution* (which we'll discuss in more detail in Chapter 6, "Solving Problems with Curves and *z*-Scores"), 68 percent of the numbers will be within one standard deviation of the mean; 95 percent will be within 2 standard deviations of the mean. If this doesn't make sense now, it will when we discuss *normal* and *skewed distributions*—and what they mean when you're analyzing your business data; you'll find this information in the next chapter.

The Least You Need to Know

➤ Measures of spread or dispersion can help you understand how data relates to the mean and other averages.

➤ The range is the easiest way to calculate measure of dispersion but also the least useful.

➤ You need to calculate the mean of the data to determine the more meaningful measures of dispersion.

➤ The variance is calculated from the square of each case's absolute deviation from the mean, then calculate the average of all the squared deviations.

➤ The sample standard deviation, one of the most important statistics used to understand data, is simply the square root of the variance.

➤ To understand the dispersion in your data relative to the mean, you can calculate) a statistic known as the coefficient of variation by dividing the standard deviation by the mean and presenting the result as a percentage.

Chapter 6

Solving Problems with Curves and z-Scores

In This Chapter

➤ Exploring what's normal about the normal curve

➤ Understanding the standard normal distribution

➤ Looking at the interplay between the mean and the standard deviation

➤ A little about skewed curves and kurtosis (not halitosis!)

The manufacturing group in the innovative battery company I've been talking about in the last few chapters has difficulty meeting consistent charge results: Some of the batteries are falling short of their overall charge—and those under or over .2 volts beyond the specification of 12.0 volts need to be tossed. After reading the previous chapter on standard deviation, the manufacturing director knows that the batteries have a standard deviation of .1 volt from perfect spec of 12.0 volts based on 100,000 batteries produced each week.

The vice president suggests that the manufacturing director store all the substandard batteries that are over or under .2 volts beyond specification, and then scrap or rework them all at once each week. However, he wants to know how many batteries that would entail. What if you had to figure this out? What would you do? Well, the first step would be to understand how the *standard normal distribution* can help you; and before you can do that, you'll need to understand a bit more about normal curves and the standard deviation on a curve.

Introducing the Bell-Shaped Curve

Suppose you make a graph of all the batteries you produce each week. This is a graph of a large number of measurements. Because it is a large number of observations, it's likely that the distribution graph (you learned about those in Chapter 3, "Visualizing Profit and Performance") will look at lot like the following curve.

A bell-shaped curve.

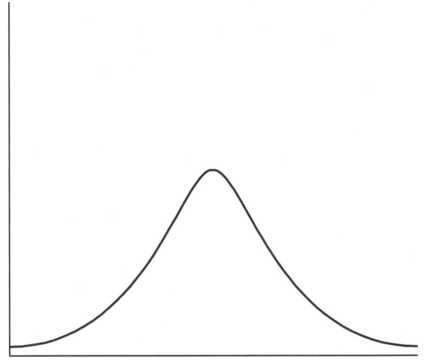

This is known as the *bell-shaped curve.* (The reason is obvious—it looks like a big church bell.) This bell-shaped curve also is known as the *normal curve,* or the *standard normal distribution.* It's one of the most important curves and distributions in statistics.

To be fair, only the middle of the bell-shaped or normal curve is bell-shaped. The curve also has tails extending to the right and left. There are many examples of quantities and values that are distributed according to the normal curve:

➤ The IQ of all people in the United States or the height of a large population

➤ The number of weekly customers at large retail businesses

➤ The production output of large volume manufacturing businesses

Statistical Wisdom

Back in 1995 Richard Hernstein and Charles Murray immortalized the curve with their best seller, *The Bell Curve*. The main thesis of the book is that IQ (intelligence quotient) is the most important factor in determining our earnings. So the smarter you are, the more you are likely to earn. Although this book is highly controversial, few people actually read it—perhaps because it's 872 pages long and somewhat technical.

—Steve Slavin, Chances Are: The Only Statistics Book You'll Ever Need, *1998*

The normal distribution applies only to ratio and interval data. (The normal distribution also is an approximation of the *binominal distribution,* which you'll learn about in the section on probability that follows this chapter.)

Measuring the Standard Normal Distribution

The mean of a data set or group of measurements literally is the central score in a normal distribution (it's right smack in the middle of the curve). And because half the values or scores are below the mean and half the values are above the mean, the mean and the median are identical in a standard normal distribution.

Because the standard normal curve has so many uses in statistics, it doesn't make sense to label it in units that apply to only one situation. Instead, the normal curve is marked off by standard deviations from the mean. Specifically, the normal curve is marked off by 1, 2, 3, and –1, –2, and –3 or more standard deviations from the mean, as shown in the following diagram.

Statistical Lingo

Normal distribution is the most important continuous *random variable distribution.* It is bell-shaped, and many real populations and observations of large sets of values of a continuous variable are distributed according to the normal distribution.

Standard normal distribution divided into sections and bound by standard deviations.

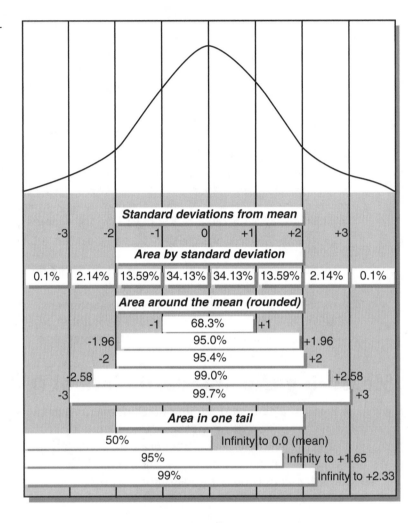

According to the central limit theorem, a large number of observations will always have a normal distribution (a mystery in some ways, but it's true—at least from the theoretical perspective). The normal distribution can be defined with only two numbers: the mean and the standard deviation.

In a standard normal distribution, you already know that 50 percent of the observations or values lie above and below the mean, respectively. Amazingly, if the curve is a standard normal one, you also will know that the percentage of the curve between 0 and 1, and 0 and –1 standard deviations is always 34.13 percent for each section away from 0. And the percentage of values between the 1 and 2 and –1 and –2 standard deviations is always 13.59 percent of all scores or observations for each section away from the last section of the standard distribution. (This makes more sense if you refer to the previous diagram.) Between 2 and 3 standard deviations, and –2 and –3 standard deviations respectively, 2.14 percent of the observations lie at this distance from the mean.

Only a very small percentage of the observations (.13 percent) lie beyond 3 and –3 standard deviations. If you've added it up already, you'll know that approximately 99.9 percent of the observations or values are within 3 standard deviations each way from the mean.

Following is a diagram to make it clearer. I've also added a percentile rank of the scores as they relate to the standard deviations. A value at the mean would be in the 50th percentile. As you can see, a standard deviation of –3 is equal to .13 percentile, meaning that only .13 percent observations have values below this number. A standard deviation of –2.0 would be at the 2.28th percentile (0.13% + 2.15%). This value would be higher than only 2.28 percent of the scores—or lower than 97.72 percent of the values.

Reduce the Risk

The standard or normal curve and the central limit theorem are two related concepts. You'd learn more about the central limit theorem in an advanced statistics course; for now, you should only know that the *central limit theorem* (CLT) is central to statistical practice. For practical purposes, the main idea of the central limit theorem states that the average of a large number of independent, identically distributed random variables will have a normal distribution if certain conditions are met.

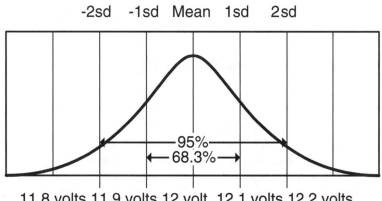

Standard Curve for Mean Volts of 12 and Standard Deviation of .1 Volt

Areas of the standard normal distribution.

Estimating the Number of Units That Are Substandard

Now that you know the percentages at each stage around the bell-shaped normal distribution, you can estimate an answer to the question that led this chapter: How many batteries will be beyond 2 standard deviations, one way or the other, from the mean manufacturing standard for last week's production run? Of the 100,000 batteries produced in a week—and if the rate of error in production remains the same—with .2 volts being the 2 standard deviations in each direction, 95.4 percent of the batteries will be within the .2 volts (or 2 standard deviations in this case) of the desired mean production standard. Additionally, approximately 4.6 percent of the batteries will need to be reworked each week. (Again, refer to the figure earlier in the chapter that shows precisely how the percentages around the mean work on a normal curve.)

This is not quite a total quality-oriented plant at this point—with 4,600 batteries being manufactured out of specification each week. To be a truly high-quality manufacturer, the standard deviation needs to be a smaller number in the future, so less than .1 percent of the batteries are out of spec. However, for this example .1 volt and 1 standard deviation being the same is an easy way to learn how the standard normal curve works in numbers and percentages.

Statistical Wisdom

All science requires mathematics. The knowledge of mathematical things is almost innate in us ... This is the easiest of sciences, a fact which is obvious in that no one's brain rejects it; for laymen and people who are utterly illiterate know how to count and reckon.

—Roger Bacon, British philosopher, 1267

Two-tailed and One-tailed Analysis

In the example of the batteries and the manufacturing specifications, the question requires a *two-tailed analysis,* because you want to look at values in terms of voltages produced above and below the mean in the percentage analysis. If you were interested only in voltages –.2 volts away from the mean (or –2 standard deviations in this example), you'd be looking at a *one-tailed test* with a question such as this to answer: How many of the batteries are manufactured at less than .2 volts from the standard specification (which in this example also is –2 standard deviations from the mean manufacturing voltage)?

Translating Standard Deviations into Values

Can you see in your head how one standard deviation means .1 volt away from the mean, and 2 standard deviations means .2 volts away from the mean? Yes, because in the example the standard deviation conveniently is a full 1 volt. It is easier to calculate—but remember that this is only an example. The standard deviation usually is a less obvious number or something more difficult to play with.

Read the section again until you can switch between standard deviations from the mean and the volts example (or any other value for that matter). Look at the following diagram to see how easy it is; then let's learn about other uses for the standard normal distribution.

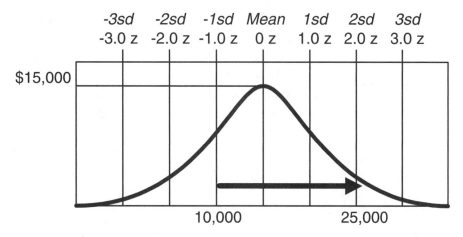

Average Customer Sales on a Standard Normal Curve

Average customers sales between $10,000 and $25,000 on a standard normal curve with z-scores shown.

Predicting Percentages with z-Scores

Your calculation of the number of out-of-spec observations is not always so easy to figure out in terms of percentages of predicated observations or values. There is another distribution that is the same as the standard normal distribution: the *z distribution;* values in it are called *z-scores*. This distribution can predict the percentage of cumulative area under the standard normal curve based on any multiple or fraction of standard deviations. Remember it's the area under the bell-shaped normal curve that determines the percentage of scores that are represented in the space under the curve. Look at the diagrams in this chapter to understand the concept of z-scores and how they relate to standard deviations away from the mean score.

As you look at the diagrams, you'll see that z-scores are equal to standard deviations. The following table shows a simplified example (but still more exact than the averages we've used in earlier diagrams) of a z distribution using a table. Most statistics texts (and z distribution tables available over the Internet and in Appendix C of this book) offer more precise, detailed tables. If you need more precise estimates of the percentage of values under the curve, refer to a detailed statistics text or do a search for "z distribution table" on the Internet.

Proportions of Area Under the Normal Curve Using z- Scores

z-Scores in Absolute Values(+ or –)	Area between Mean and z (read this as percentage away from the mean of one tail of the curve)	Area Beyond z (read this as percentage away from the z-score on one tail of the curve)
0.00	.0000	.5000
0.50	.1915	.3085
1.00	.3413	.1587
1.65	.4505	.0485
1.96	.4750	.0250
2.00	.4772	.0228
2.33	.4901	.0099
2.58	.4951	.0049
3.00	.4987	.0012

Z-scores also translate into percentile ranks (refer to the preceding table). As an example, if you earn a salary of $45,000 a year and the z-score of your salary compared to all the others in your profession was –1.96 or |1.96|, you'd know that you were pretty poorly paid, because only 2.5% of the people in your profession make less than this, and 97.5% make more! That's the power of understanding how to read a z-score table—you can discover the relative performance of all sorts of scores on normally distributed results: personnel performance on standard tasks, questionnaire responses on product and service research, and manufacturing questions about quality and production.

Reduce the Risk

All standard normal tables using z-scores do not use the same format. It is important to know what area of the curve (or probability) the table presents as corresponding to a given z-score. For example, the table might give the area of the curve lying at or below z. In this type of table, the area to the right of the z-score (or the probability of obtaining a value above z) is simply 1 minus the tabled probability.

Calculating the z-Score

Z-scores are composed of a number whose sign (+/–) indicates how many standard deviations lie between the value in question and the mean. Thus, if you know what a standard deviation is, you understand the concept of a z-score. A z-score of 1 is a number equal to 1 standard deviation from the mean. The formula for calculating a z-score for a sample is pretty simple, too—it's the score or value minus the mean, divided by the standard deviation of the representative sample. You can refer to the actual formula in Appendix B, "Statistics Formulas."

You can use this formula and z-scores to solve more complex problems than those you've been looking at so far. For example, you might want to find out the percentage of customers with battery purchases between $10,000 and $25,000 per year. To calculate this you'd have to have the mean sales per customer and the standard deviation of customer sales. Then you'd need to find the area on the standard curve between the sales of $10,000 and then $25,000. To do this you need to use z-scores.

As an example, if the average customer purchase is $15,000 per year and the standard deviation is $5,000, you need to find the area of observations on the curve between a z-score of –1 and a z-score of 2.0. Based on the table of the proportions of

Statistical Wisdom

Nobody before the Pythagoreans had thought that mathematical relations held the secret of the universe. Twenty-five centuries later, Europe is still blessed and cursed with their heritage. To non-European civilizations, the idea that numbers are the key to both wisdom and power seems never to have occurred.

—Arthur Koestler (1905–83), Hungarian-born British author

area under the normal curve this *z*-score would equal –1 minus 2 = |3| (a *z*-score area of 3 as an absolute number). Based on the preceding table of *z*-scores (also available in Appendix C, "Sample Statistical Tables"), this means approximately 99.9 percent (rounded) of the customers have annual purchases within these two amounts.

Here is the visual of a standard normal curve that shows the sales values and *z*-scores in this problem:

A negatively skewed curve.

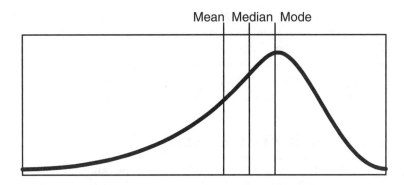

Negatively Skewed Curve - The Mean Is Lower than the Median

Answering Questions with the z-Scores

When a normal distribution is a good representation of the frequency distribution of a variable—such as the battery production voltage in the example we've been using—the distribution (and the related *z*-scores) can answer a variety of useful questions, such as

➤ What percentage of a population of customer prospects would find your product appealing?

➤ How many prospective applicants will qualify for one of your open positions based on company test scores?

➤ What percentage of a manufacturing run will be above or below the specifications?

➤ In a marketing survey where the mean and standard deviation are known, what percentage of the population will prefer the proposed blue product over the current red version?

Basically, there are only two steps to answering all these types of questions:

1. Translate the values into *z*-scores.

2. Look up the critical areas on a *z*-score table and state the conclusion based on the percentage of area below the normal curve that is relevant to the answer. You'll be able to come up with a probability percentage of the total number of people or tests that will equal this value, or the percentage of scores or values that will be above or below this value.

Skewed Curves and the Relation to a Standard Distribution

Unfortunately, not all distributions of variables are perfect standard normal distributions. When a distribution of values is a standard normal distribution, the mean, median, and mode would be the same number. These measures of central tendency would be at the exact center of the symmetrical bell curve.

In Chapter 3 I discussed pictures of skewed curves. Here are some others to remind you how they look—and how the mean and median are positioned compared to a normal curve. A negatively skewed curve, such as the one shown in the following figure, has a tail off to the left. You'll notice that the mean is lower than the median because it is pulled down by a few extreme low scores—say a few bad production days at the battery factory.

Mode Median Mean

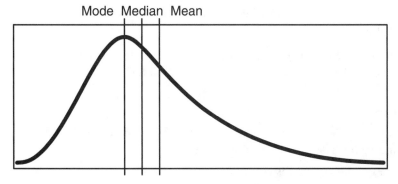

A positively skewed curve.

Positively Skewed Curve - The Mean is Greater than the Median

A positively skewed curve, such as the own shown in the following figure, tails off to the right. In positively skewed curves, the mean is greater than the median because it is pulled up by a few extremely high scores, such as some great sales days that were way beyond expectations.

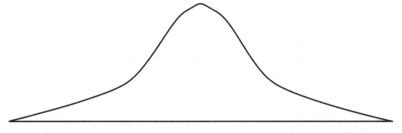

Standard deviation of battery production shown on a normal curve.

Kurtosis—or How Long Is Your Tail?

Kurtosis is a measure of the size of a distribution's tails; the formula for calculating it is in Appendix B, "Statistics Formulas," at the back of the book. The kurtosis of a normal distribution is 0. Distributions with relatively large tails are called *leptokurtic;* those with small tails are called *platykurtic.* A distribution with the same kurtosis as the normal distribution is called *mesokurtic.* You don't need to remember these definitions, but they're nice fodder for conversations with friends (or even better, co-workers you want to impress).

Providing Your Own Answers

Here are some simple questions regarding the standard normal distribution and *z*-scores. See how many you can answer on your own or with the tables and diagrams from this chapter. The answers are given in Appendix A, "Answer Key," but no peeking until you've tried them at least once.

1. What percentage of values is lower than a value equal to a standard deviation of 3 on a normal curve? (Use the diagrams from this chapter if you don't know already!)

2. What is a *z*-score equal to?

3. What two numbers do you need to produce a standard normal curve for a question you're trying to understand about your business?

4. If you have a *z*-score of 1.0, what is the area between the score and the mean in percentage terms?

5. If a curve is negatively skewed, which is the larger value, the mean or the median?

6. What types of data are necessary to make frequency estimates using a standard normal curve?

The Least You Need to Know

➤ One reason the normal distribution is important is that many business and psychological variables are distributed approximately normally.

➤ Theoretically, the percentages of values between the standard deviations on a normal curve are always the same.

➤ Many kinds of statistical tests can be derived for normal distributions.

➤ Although many distributions are only approximately normal, they are usually quite close. Almost all statistical tests discussed in this book assume normal distributions as the tests work well even if the curve isn't exactly normal.

➤ The z-score is equal to the standard deviations a value is from the mean.

➤ The z-score is useful in calculating the percentage of values between z-scores and the percentage of values above or below a value in a distribution.

➤ The standard normal curve and the related z-scores are descriptive statistics that can be used to calculate the answers to a number of common questions in business related to the number of values in a distribution of ratio or interval data.

➤ When a distribution tails off to the right or the left, the distribution curve is not normal; it is skewed.

Part 2

Facing Probability and Forecasting

Probability is the study of chance phenomenon. You probably know something about probability already, especially if you play the Lotto or have visited Las Vegas or Atlantic City. But probability isn't all about gambling—it is a core part of understanding how statistics work to predict information about your business.

I'll start the discussion using coin tossing as an introduction to probability. Of course, most business decisions depend on more than the outcome of a coin toss. But the study of probabilities associated with coin tosses provides valuable practice for the concepts you'll encounter later in this section and the book. After tossing coins, you'll learn about the value of probability distributions, forecasting using time series calculations, and the odds associated with decision theory.

Okay, this seems like it might get complicated, but if you know how to toss a coin, you really can master the principles of forecasting sales and assessing your chances of consistently producing a quality product.

It seems there may be some truth in the notion that business is a gamble. So what's your bet on mastering probability? Heads you win, tails you lose.

Chapter 7

Playing the Probability Game

In This Chapter

➤ Introducing the classic theory of probability

➤ Understanding the probability of simple events

➤ Understanding the difference between dependent and independent events

➤ Determining total probabilities with the addition and multiplication rules

➤ Understanding conditional probabilities

You might think that the most obvious benefit of studying probability is that it will help prepare you for the glittering halls of the casinos. However, often in business you need to understand how probable it is that something will happen that might affect your business productivity, profitability, or position in the marketplace. For example, when you are manufacturing batteries in the hypothetical company we've been talking about, you will want to know how probable it is that a defect in manufacturing will materialize on a production line. Or you might want to know if a major downturn in the economy is more or less probable than it was last year, as this could affect your budget planning or the timing of your release of a new type of battery to the marketplace.

Not all of these types of questions can be answered or predicated 100 percent of the time. However, grounded in the theory of probability, often statistics can help you make better educated predictions. As you learn more, you'll see that the theory of probability, also known as the "law of chance," plays an important role in many statistical analyses in business and elsewhere. In fact, to understand statistical inference—which enables you to infer the conclusions to your questions (the topic of Part 3, "Using Business Research and Inference")—you need to know the basic concepts of probability.

Statistical Lingo

There are a few basic terms you should understand when working with probabilities:

Probability   The study of chance, or random, phenomena.

Probability of an event   The number of outcomes that corresponds to an event in question divided by the total number of possible outcomes, with the proviso that all outcomes are equally likely to occur.

Factorial   When dealing with a whole number, the factorial of that number is the product of all the whole numbers from 1 up to that number. Factorial is designated with an exclamation point. For example, the symbol for four factorial is 4! Thus, the factorial of four (4!) is equal to $4 \times 3 \times 2 \times 1 = 24$.

Hypothesis testing   You'll learn more about this in later chapters on research design and testing; for now you should know *it's a statistical procedure that involves establishing a hypothesis* (the expected outcome of an experiment) *and then collecting evidence* (data) *and making a decision on whether the hypothesis should be accepted or rejected.*

As I discuss more about probability in this chapter, you'll likely find much of probability theory very familiar. Probability usually can be reduced to questions you ask casually in business all the time (especially if you like a nice weekend in Las Vegas or Atlantic City now and then): What are the odds that this event will occur? What is the likelihood that this or that will happen?

Probability and statistics are closely related because they ask the opposite kinds of questions. In probability, you know how a process works and then want to predict what the outcomes of the process will be. In statistics, you don't know how the process works, but you can observe the outcomes of the process. The information about the outcomes is used (with the help of statistics) to learn about the nature of the process.

In practice, there are three kinds of probability:

➤ **Classical probability** is based on gambling ideas. The fundamental assumption is that all elementary outcomes have the same probability and that the game also is fair.

➤ **Probability of relative frequency** is a type of probability that can be repeated. In this type of probability, an event probability is the proportion of times an event occurs over a large number of repeated experiments.

> **Statistical Wisdom**
>
> If you bet on a horse, that's gambling. If you bet you can make three spades, that's entertainment. If you bet cotton will go up three points, that's business. See the difference?
>
> —*Blackie Sherrod*

➤ **Personal probability** is assessed based on past information or intuition. If you apply formal laws of chance to personal probabilities you'd be referred to as a *subjectivist* or *Bayesian* (based on Bayes's theorem probabilities).

Introducing the Classic Theory of Probability

Much of statistics as a branch of mathematics is grounded in the classic theory of probability. You can observe the basics of classic probability theory when you flip a coin or play cards. For instance, if you flip a coin, what are the odds that it will come up heads? Almost everyone knows the answer to this—the odds are 1 to 1 or 1:1, as it is formally expressed.

How likely is it that you will pull a card of the hearts suit if you pull one card from a thoroughly shuffled deck of standard playing cards? "Well," you're probably saying, "Everyone knows that!" The odds are about 1 out of 4 or 1/4. If you put the last card you pulled out back in the deck, what is the probability that you'll randomly select an ace from that same shuffled deck of 52 cards? You got it! The probability is 1/52 or .077 (if you express it as a decimal fraction).

> **Statistical Wisdom**
>
> The quest for certainty blocks the search for meaning. Uncertainty is the very condition to impel man to unfold his powers.
>
> —*Erich Fromm (1900–1980), Man for Himself (1947)*

If you understand these examples, you're ready to take on probability—and its relationship to making more important predictions in your business research and analyses.

The Classic Formula

Now, here's one that might seem a bit harder. What are the odds of tossing a quarter twice and coming up with two heads in a row? If you intuitively answered one in four, you're right. But why isn't the answer one in two, as the first toss of the coin has no effect on the probability of the next toss? In other words, if you flip a coin once it has absolutely no bearing on the result of your second flip. The events are entirely independent. *Independent events* are defined as outcomes that aren't affected by other outcomes.

Well, it is true that the probability that the second toss alone would be one in two. However, to get two heads in a row requires a little calculation. The classic calculation for determining the probability of an even *t* (such as tossing a head, which I'll call H for the example) equals the number of times you'll get a favorable outcome (in this case, a head) divided by the number of possible events there are (in this case, there is one event favoring H and one event (a tail) not favoring H.

The formula is pretty simple, where P equals probability and A equals the desired outcome:

$$P(A) = \frac{\text{Number of favorable outcomes (one head)}}{\text{Total number of possibilities (One head and one nonhead)}}$$

Or in this case of one coin toss:

1/2 or .5

Formally stated, the probability of that head appearing on one toss is equal to the number of ways getting that event (1) divided by the total number of possible outcomes (2). A *probability variable* (such as the P shown in the previous expression) is an algebraic entity that expresses a degree of confidence that something will happen or that some statement or concept has an amount of certainty associated with it. It is customary to express a probability variable by a letter of the alphabet when its value is not precisely known. If its value is known or calculated, it must be a number in the range of 0–1.

Think of the probability as a *proportion,* also called a *ratio.* That ratio is 1/2 or .5. Both of these numbers mean the same thing, but in statistical analysis the probability usually is expressed as a decimal fraction (which is equivalent to the ratio) and ranges from a low of 0, indicating absolutely no chance whatsoever, to a high of 1 (100 percent certainty).

The classic theory discussed thus far assumes that all outcomes have an equal probability of occurring. Nothing is affecting the probability of a head or a tail landing when you make a toss of the coin. The probability also is symmetric; that is, the probability that you will get a head is exactly the same as the probability you'll get a tail. Each toss of the coin in this way also is an independent event.

> **Statistical Wisdom**
>
> To play there are two pleasures for your choosing—the one is winning, and the other losing.
>
> —Lord Byron (1788–1824), British poet

When the Stakes (or Numbers) Are Bigger

You probably figured out the first coin toss question on your own; now consider that you are playing a coin tossing game in Las Vegas and your adversary has tossed 46 heads in a row. What is the probability that the next toss also will be a head? Well, in general, if you tossed a coin *n* times (and *n* is a large number), you'd most likely get a number of heads equal to *n*/2 or a number close to .5.

This effect is called the *relative frequency theory of probability*. This theory states that if you repeat an experiment (or exclusive event) an extremely large number of times, and if an outcome consistently occurs an observed percentage of the time, that percentage is close to the probability of that percentage. This type of theory can be applied directly to business questions.

In this case that didn't happen. And you intuitively know that it would be highly unlikely to get 46 heads in a row. Your adversary obviously is very lucky. Remember: On the next individual toss of the coin, the probability of getting a tail (or a head) on that 47th toss is still .5 or 1 in 2—that is if the coin is not weighted in some fashion.

Figuring the Odds of 46 Heads in a Row

How probable is it that you also would be able to toss 46 heads in a row? Let's start out small. Consider four coin tosses. On the first toss, there are four places for the head. We'll call the first head H1. Here are the sixteen possible outcomes on four tosses of the coin:

H1	T	T	T
T	H1	T	T
T	T	H1	T
T	T	T	H1

There are two possibilities for the first toss, two possibilities for the second, two possibilities for the third, and two for the fourth, for a total of

$$2 \times 2 \times 2 \times 2 = 2^4 = 16$$

possible outcomes. By the way, if you flip a coin 12 times, there will be 212 possible outcomes, which equals 4,096 possibilities of total possible outcomes.

Each outcome of either head or tail is equally possible on each individual toss. You can see in the previous table, there are four places for the first toss of the first head (I'll call it H1). Now if you get a head on the first toss, your probabilities for the second toss will change. Given our chart, there are three possibilities for the second H (I'll call it H2):

H1 H2 T T	H1 T H2 T	H1 T T H2
H2 H1 T T	T H1 H2 T	T H1 T H2
H2 T H1 T	T H2 H1 T	T T H1 H2
H2 T T H1	T H2 T H1	T T H2 H1

As you can see, now there are 12 possible ways to arrange the Hs. However, because it doesn't make any difference which is H1 and which is H2, you must divide by 2 to avoid double counting the duplications. Thus, you end up with six possible ways to get two heads:

HHTT, HTHT, HTTH, THHT, THTH, TTHH

The results of the possibilities of four flips of these coins would look like this in a probability table:

Number of Heads (h)	Number of Outcomes with h Heads	Probability that h Heads Will Appear
0	1	1/16 = .0625
1	4	4/16 = .2500
2	6	6/16 = .3750
3	4	4/16 = .2500
4	1	1/16 = .0625

The possibilities are symmetric—the possibility that you will get h heads is exactly the same as the possibility that you will get h tails. You also will see that the total of all the probabilities will add up to 1. If the total of the probabilities doesn't add up to 1, you've made some error in your calculations. (Of course, in large probability tables based on large numbers of possibilities, there might be a minor error due to rounding of decimal fractions.)

Figuring Out the Possible Outcomes

So now you need to figure out how to determine the possible outcomes that have h heads in n (the number of) tosses. In this case, you're interested in getting 46 heads in 46 tosses. You need to figure out the number of ways you can write n capital Hs on n blanks in the table. For such a large table, this would be extremely tedious—so a little math (and a good calculator and computer) makes it easier to figure out.

Here's how the algorithm works. For the first h we put in the table, there are $n - 1$ places left for the second h, and $n - 2$ places for the third, and so on down to $n - (h - 1)$, which equals $(n - h + 1)$ (if you remember basic algebra). Altogether there will be

$n \times (n - 1) \times (n - 2) \times (n - 3) \times \ldots \times (n - h + 1)$ ways of writing down every h in the table.

After doing that, you must divide by all possible h combinations:

$h \times (h - 1) \times (h - 2) \times (h - 3) \times \ldots \times 3 \times 2 \times 1$

This division eliminates the double counting (duplications) caused by the different ordering of the outcomes. Therefore, if you flip a coin exactly n times, the number of possible outcomes that have exactly h heads will be:

$$\frac{n \times (n - 1) \times (n - 2) \times (n - 3) \times \ldots \times (n - h + 1)}{h \times (h - 1) \times (h - 2) \times (h - 3) \times \ldots \times 3 \times 2 \times 1}$$

Well, this calculating is really a lot of work. But, it does turn out in probability that there are a number of times when you need to calculate the product of all the numbers from 1 up to a target number. Remember, this quantity is called the *factorial* of the number, and is symbolized by an exclamation mark (!).

Calculating Factorials

Here are some examples to make factorials easier to understand:

$1! = 1 \times 1 = 1$

$3! = 3 \times 2 \times 1 = 6$

$10! = 10 \times 9 \times 8 \times 7 \times 6 \times 5 \times 4 \times 3 \times 2 \times 1 = 3,628,800$

Factorials become large numbers very fast. You also should know that there are some calculations in which you need to find $n!$ when $n = 0$. By definition, $0! = 1$ so the formulas will work out.

Remember the big algorithm before all this for calculating the possibility of obtaining n heads on h tosses? Using the factorial notation in the denominator for the number of combinations with h heads as:

$$n \times (n - 1) \times (n - 2) \times (n - 3) \times \ldots \times (n - h + 1)h!$$

And, the numerator can be expressed, after dividing the numerator by $(n - h)!$ as:

$$\frac{n!}{(n - h)!}$$

Well, now it's possible to write the formula, using factorials, in a very compact form as:

$$\frac{n!}{h!(n - h)!}$$

Of course, it's best to calculate this factorial-based algorithm with a good calculator or even a computer program that has been developed to calculate factorials.

So, now that you know the general rule, what is the probability of you tossing those 46 heads in a row just like your adversary did?

Well, there's still one more formula:

$$\left[\frac{n!}{h!(n - h)!}\right] 2^{-n}$$

The 2^{-n} is equivalent to $1/2^{n}$. The 2^{n} is in the denominator because there are a total of 2^{n} possible outcomes when the coin is tossed n times.

To check out whether the formula works, try it with 4 heads in a row:

$$Pr = 4!/4!(4-4)! \times 1/2^{4} = 24/24(1) \times 1/16 = 1/16 = 0.0625$$

So, to get four heads in a row is a 1 in 24 probability. Now we're finally ready to find out the probability of getting 46 heads in a row on 46 tosses of the coin.

Pr = 46!/46!(46 – 46)! × 1/2^{46} = 46/46(1) × 1/70368744177664
    = 1/70368744177664

or 1 probable outcome of 46 heads tossed in a row out of 70,368,744,177,664 attempts—that's less than 1 chance in more than 70 trillion tries of tossing 46 coins in a row. Your adversary was luckier than you can imagine. Keep this in mind if you ever try to repeat it on your own—or in Las Vegas.

Sampling with Replacement

Consider another type of experiment that can teach you more about probability. Consider that you have three blue blocks in a box. Each block has a different number on it: one has the number 1, one block the number two, and the third block the number 3. Your job is to pull a block from the box, record its number on a paper, and then return the block to the box. Then you'll pull another block from the box and record its number. That's all you have to do.

Now you're going to answer the question, "How probable is it I will draw two blocks in a row that will add up to either 2, 3, 4, 5, or 6?" Let's start answering the question of probability by first counting all the possible outcomes of pulling blocks numbered 1, 2, or 3 from the box. The table would look like this:

Outcomes starting with 0	0,0	0,1	0,2	0,3
Outcomes starting with 1	1,0	1,1	1,2	1,3
Outcomes starting with 2	2,0	2,1	2,2	2,3
Outcomes starting with 3	3,0	3,1	3,1	3,2

There are sixteen possible outcomes listed in the preceding table. If you think about it, the probability of picking out any one of these pairs is equally probable to picking out any of the other pairs. So, the probability of picking 3,1 is 1/16, just as the probability of picking out 1,1 is 1/16. Now let's take this analysis to another level. Let's produce a frequency distribution showing the probabilities of different sets of numbers that can help us answer the preceding question about the probabilities of totals of 0, 1, 2, 3, 4, 5, or 6.

Sum	Set	Frequency	Probability
0	0,0	1	.0625
1	0,1 1,0	2	.125
2	0,2 1,1 2,0	3	.1875
3	0,3 1,2 2,1 3,0	4	.2500
4	1,3 2,2 3,1	3	.1875
5	2,3 3,2	2	.125
6	3,3	1	.0625

Again, the total probability for all the possible totals is 1.0. Because the probabilities are stated in decimal fractions in the table, it's relatively easy to create a probability histogram based on the possible replacement samples of two numbers pulled from a box of four blocks.

The Addition Rule

The last experiment brings us to the *addition rule*. If you want to find out the probability that any pair you draw from the box will total 5 or less, you can simply add the frequencies: .124, .1875, .2500, .1875, and .0625, which equals .8125; this means you'll get a combination that is 5 or less 81/25 percent of the time.

In the experiment you saw that it is okay to add probabilities from the organized frequency table as long as the events are mutually exclusive. This example shows how the addition rule works. If any two (or more) probabilities (X and Y for instance) are mutually exclusive, the total of probability X and probability Y is equal to the probability of obtaining either one of them (X or Y).

When using the addition rule in a nonmutually exclusive situation, it is important to realize you actually are double counting. As a simple example, consider the number of possibilities on two tosses of a coin. If you use the addition rule to determine the chance of getting at least one head on two tosses, you'll get the following result:

$$\frac{1}{2} + \frac{1}{2} = \frac{1}{1}$$

or 100 percent probability, which is absurd.

First Toss		Second Toss
head	+	head
head	+	tail
tail	+	head
tail	+	tail

There actually are four total outcomes in trying to get at least one head on two tosses. Three of the outcomes have heads within at least one of the two tosses. To calculate the probability correctly, just as you did with the factorial example with the large number of tosses, subtract the event that double counts (the two head + tail combinations). In this nonmutual case you'd get

$$\frac{1}{2} + \frac{1}{2} - \frac{1}{4} = \frac{3}{4}$$

or .75 percent probability that you'll get a head from two tosses of the coin.

To account for mutually exclusive and nonmutually exclusive events, the addition rule reads like this: The probability of at least one of the events X or Y equals the probability of X plus the probability of Y, minus the probability of their joint occurrence, which is notated as P(XY).

The equation is simple; it looks like this:

P(X + Y) = P(X) + P(Y) – P(XY)

If the events are mutually exclusive, the rule is simply:

P(X + Y) = P(X) + P(Y)

where the joint occurrence of X and Y, P(XY), is 0.

Dependent Events and Probability

The coin toss and numbered blocks from the box examples are based on entirely independent events. However, sometimes random events are affected by other events that have happened before. Consider again a well-shuffled deck of cards. There are four aces in the deck of 52 cards. You'll recall that your probability of pulling an ace is 4 out of 52. If you randomly pull an ace out on the first try, you have 51 cards in the deck but only 3 aces. So, your probability of pulling an ace on the second try, if you don't put the first ace back in the deck, is only 3 out of 51.

If you didn't pull an ace the first time, the number of favorable events would remain the same (4 aces)—but there would be only 51 cards left. So, your odds on the next pull for an ace actually would go up to be 4 out of 51. In either case, the second attempt at pulling an ace would be dependent on the first card you pull. This second pull then is called a *dependent event,* because the results are impacted by the first pull of the card.

Understanding the Probability of Joint Occurrences

Let's consider another kind of probability problem using coins. You have a penny, a nickel, and a dime. You want to compute the probability that all three tossed coins will land as tails as a series of three separate events. First flip the penny; then flip the nickel; then flip the dime. Will the probability of getting three tails still be .125 or 1/8 as you'd expect, based on what we've learned thus far? Well, the multiplication rule can be used to compute the probability of two or more independent events, all occurring together, known as a *joint occurrence.*

For the example, the probability of the penny landing tails is 1/2 or .5 as you've learned already; the probability for landing a tail for the nickel and a tail for a dime are exactly the same. So, you actually can multiply the individual probabilities to determine the probability of getting three tails from the coins on independent tosses. Here's how the multiplication rule works for the example:

$.5 \times .5 \times .5 = .125$ or 1/8

The formal way of notating the multiplication rule is

$P(AB) = P(A) \times P(B)$

where P is the probability of each result. It reads like this: The probability of A and B both happening is equal to the probability of A times the probability of B.

You also can use the multiplication rule to determine the probability of drawing those two aces from a deck of cards, without returning the first drawn card. You know that the first probability is 4/52 and the second draw (if you get an ace the first time) is 3/51. For both aces to be selected from the deck, you can know that the probability of doing this is

$4/52 \times 3/51 = 12/2652 = .0045$

You know this to be true because you actually are computing probability for favorable outcomes for both pulls out of the deck; in this case pulling an ace each time.

Using Conditional Probability for More Informed Judgments

In some cases when determining probability, you might know more about the cases; thus are able to make more informed judgments regarding the probabilities of some occurrence or outcome. Let's consider an example from the battery business: There are 100 batteries in a box; there are 60 12-volt batteries and 40 batteries with 12 volts or less. Twenty of the 12-volt batteries have double connections; 5 of the batteries of less than 12 volts have double connections.

Batteries in a Box	12 volts	< 12 volts	Totals
double connectors	20	5	25
single connectors	40	35	75
	60	40	**100**

What is the probability that a battery selected at random from that box will be 12 volts? Well that's easy; the probability is 60 percent. Now, what is the probability that a battery selected that is 12 volts will also have a double connector? The question is different from the first, as the probability of being 12 volts now is conditional because the battery in question has double connections. Because the number of batteries with double connections and twelve volts is 20/60, the probability of selecting such a battery is 1/3, given that the battery selected was first a 12-volt battery. This is a conditional probability and is determined with this formula:

$$P(A|B) = AB/B = P(AB)/P(B)$$

$$P(A|B) = 20/60 = P(20)/P(60) = 1/3$$

The probability of A given B equals the proportion of the total of A and B to the total of B. The vertical bar in A|B is read *given that* or *given*.

Exploring Normal Curves and the Binomial Scale

Before understanding distributions and curves with probabilities, you must know the difference between a discrete versus a continuous variable. The number of heads (or tails) when tossing a coin can be counted only as whole numbers (integers). Even the number of aces drawn from a deck of cards can be counted only as integers. These countable numbers are known as *discrete variables*. Nothing in between the variables is possible. For example, there is no such thing as a 2.6 of a coin toss.

A discrete variable that can result in only one of two variables is called a *binomial*. Tossing a coin is a binomial variable; drawing a number for a box with 1,000 different numbers is not. If a machine is successful or unsuccessful in meeting the product specification that result is a binomial variable; either a perfect product or an imperfect one.

However, in the previous chapter you learned that you could measure variables, including weight, distance, temperature, and length using fractions or decimals. For example, you might get measurements such as 67.45, 87.22, 21.99, and so on. These numbers are known as *continuous variables*. The normal curves in the previous chapter all are based on continuous variables.

Determining the Success or Failure of an Outcome

Binomial experiments are conducted to determine the number of favorable outcomes of identical, but mutually exclusive and independent events. The outcomes are labeled *successes* and *failures*. The probability of a success is equal to some percentage, which is called *proportion*. Given all these criteria, a formula, called the *binomial formula,* can be applied to any *x* number of favorable events and any number of events (*n*).

However, to avoid all the calculations of the binomial formula, and because it is important in statistics, you can use a binomial table instead to get the answer you need. For example, in a binomial table you will be given an n = 10, s = 5, and = .5. As you read across the table, you'll see that the probability is .2461.

In statistics, the so-called *binomial distribution* describes the possible number of times that a particular event will occur in a sequence of observations. The event is coded as binary; it may or may not occur. The binomial distribution is used when a researcher is interested in the occurrence of an event; not in its magnitude. For instance, an employer might want to know whether a person is ambitious. Here, the binomial distribution describes the number of ambitious persons; not how ambitious they are (and not the magnitude of the person's ambition).

The binomial distribution is specified by the number of observations (*n*) and the probability of occurrence, which is denoted by p. The classic example I've used often to illustrate concepts of probability theory, is the tossing of a coin. If a coin is tossed 4 times, we can obtain 0, 1, 2, 3, or 4 heads. We also can obtain 4, 3, 2, 1, or 0 tails; however, these outcomes are equivalent to 0, 1, 2, 3, or 4 heads. The likelihood of obtaining 0, 1, 2, 3, or 4 heads is, respectively, 1/16, 4/16, 6/16, 4/16, and 1/16.

Thus, in the example discussed here you are likely to attain 2 heads in 4 tosses, because this outcome has the highest probability. Other situations in which binomial distributions arise are quality control, customer opinion surveys, industrial research, and insurance problems.

Using the Poisson Limit

If the probability P is small and the number of observations is large the binomial probabilities are hard to calculate. In this instance it is much easier to approximate the binomial probabilities using *Poisson* probabilities. The *Poisson distribution,* derived by the French mathematician Poisson in 1837, was first applied to describe the number of deaths by horse kicking in the Prussian army.

The binomial distribution approaches the Poisson distribution for large n and small P. When you increase the number of observations from 1 to 50, the parameter P in the binomial distribution remains 1/10. The results show that the degree of approximations to the binomial curve improves as the number of observations increases.

Some events don't happen that often. For instance, car accidents are the exception rather than the rule. Even so, over a period of time, you can say something about the nature of rare events. An example is the improvement of traffic safety: The government wants to know whether seat belts reduce the number of death in car accidents. Here, the Poisson distribution can be a useful tool to answer questions about benefits of seat belt use. Other phenomena that often follow a Poisson distribution are the number of errors in the assembly of a car or the number of earthquakes each day in one area.

The *Poisson distribution* is a mathematical rule that assigns probabilities to the number of desired occurrences. The only thing you have to know to specify the Poisson distribution is the mean number of occurrences. Let's say you want to understand the possibility of an accident. You start with a probability of 1/2 as you are driving slowly, and the probability of no accident ($x = 0$) is large. In time things change; the mean indicates you are driving faster and the probability of no accident decreases dramatically. Looking at it this way, if you drive very fast you probably will end up in a car crash.

The Poisson distribution resembles the binomial distribution if the probability of an accident is very small. However, if you want to use the binomial distribution, you have to know both the number of people who make it safely from A to B, and the number of people who have an accident while driving from A to B, whereas the number of accidents is sufficient for applying the Poisson distribution. Thus, the Poisson distribution is cheaper to use because the number of accidents usually is recorded by the police department, whereas the total number of drivers is not.

Getting to the Heart of the Probability Theory

The central limit theorem is one of the most remarkable findings in the theory of probability. It was briefly mentioned in Chapter 6 if you remember. The theorem is considered the heart of probability theory (and statistics), although a better name might be *normal convergence theorem*. In its simplest form, the theorem states that the sum of a large number of independent observations from the same distribution has, under certain general conditions, a nearly normal distribution. Moreover, the approximation to normal steadily improves as the number of observations increases.

For example, suppose a coin is tossed 100 times and the number of heads is counted. This is equivalent to scoring 1 for a head and 0 for a tail, and computing the total score. Thus, the total number of heads is the sum of 100 independent, identically distributed random variables. By the *central limit theorem*, the distribution of the total number of heads will be, to a very high degree of approximation, normal. This can be illustrated graphically by repeating this experiment many times and creating a frequency histogram of the results. The percentage computed over the number of experiments is arranged along the vertical axis, and the total score or the number of heads is arranged along the horizontal axis. After a large number of repetitions a curve appears that looks exactly like the normal curve you learned about in the previous chapter.

The phenomenon (results) of flipping a coin for a large number of times, say 100,000, is predicted by the *large number theory,* which states that say 100,000 coin tosses likely will bring the ratio of heads to the total number of tosses to closely approximate .5—the same number predicted by probability. Thus the tendency of real-world experiments to move closely approximate the predictions of probability is predicted by the law of large numbers. It has been empirically observed that various natural phenomena, such as the heights of individuals, follow approximately a normal distribution. A suggested explanation is that these phenomena are sums of a large number of independent random effects; hence they are approximately normally distributed as stated in the central limit theorem.

The standard normal curve (you read about in the previous chapter) and the binomial curve are thus closely related. For moderate values of P, the binomial distribution approaches the normal distribution if the number of observations is large. This is an example of the *central limit theorem.*

Thus, you can use *z*-scores to find the area that lies at or beyond the *z*-score, just like you learned to do in Chapter 6, "Solving Problems with Curves and *z*-Scores." The probability of the occurrence is equal to the area at or beyond the *z*-score. This is a one-tail probability. The binomial curve that is equivalent to a standard normal curve can lend itself very well to probability problems.

You also can use the normal curve to examine probabilities that are either above or below the mean. (Consider asking how many people are either below an IQ of 40 or over an IQ of 130. This is called a two-tailed probability value, because the total probability is the sum of probabilities at two opposite ends of the probability curve.

Try Some of Your Own

1. Try tossing a quarter 50 times. Count the number of heads and tails. How close was the result to the probability predicted by classic probability? If it wasn't close, explain why.

2. If you role a set of dice, what are your chances of getting (a) 8, (b) 2 or (c) either a 7 or an 11?

For answers see Appendix A, "Answer Key."

There is a lot more to cover about probability than I've been able to put in this chapter. However, as you read on about inferential statistics and forecasting in the chapters that follow, you'll meet your friend "probability" again and again.

The important thing to remember is that using probability is a better way than simply guessing everything about your business. If it's more probable that you'll make your sales forecast based on past history, that's a good thing to know. If your production line is likely to produce more unusable products than quality ones this week, that's another thing you can learn from statistics and probability—and something you'll need to take action on to improve the probability that you'll do better next week.

As you learn more, you'll see how probability and the rest of statistics go hand in hand to help you avoid the most risky decisions and ultimately make better choices for your enterprise.

The Least You Need to Know

➤ The probabilities of any casino are always based in the laws of probabilities.

➤ In probability you predict the outcomes of the process. In statistics you don't know the process; instead you observe the outcomes to learn more about the process.

➤ There are three generally accepted kinds of probability: classical, relative frequency, or personal (subjective).

➤ Classical probability assumes that events are independent (that is, nothing from the outside is affecting them).

➤ The relative frequency theory of probability is very much like the large number theory.

➤ The binomial curve as a representative of a normal curve can be used to determine the probabilities.

➤ The Poisson distribution, a mathematical rule that assigns probabilities to the number of occurrences, approaches the binomial distribution for large n and small P.

Chapter 8

Forecasting Your Business Results

In This Chapter

➤ Understanding the components in time series data

➤ Forecasting movement in the economy

➤ Determining a data trend by calculating moving averages

➤ Determining a cyclical value of data in a time series

➤ Finding business time series data

When you have measurements for the same variable information for several consecutive time periods, you have *time series data,* which can be used for forecasting and predictions. Much of the data used in business is time series data, including the quarterly *GDP* (*gross domestic product*), the *monthly unemployment rate,* and the *weekly money supply figures.* All these important predictors and more are based on data collected over a certain time period.

This data can be analyzed to see future trends and forecast what is expected to happen. In the battery business we've been discussing, forecasting sales, production over the year, and employee turnover rates are just a few ordinary types of time series data (not government produced) that can be effective in forecasting significant trends or seasonal changes in your business.

Forecasting future events and trends is an important asset in the business world—especially when you need to know the amount of sales you can expect, the overall demand for your product, and the investments you should make to take advantage of the economic conditions anticipated for the future. Time series data can be manipulated to reveal business and economic secrets that otherwise would remain concealed.

Introducing the Components of Time Series Data

Time series analysis consists of breaking down a sequence of observed data into its components: *the trend component, seasonal variation, cyclical variation,* and *irregular variation.* After breaking a *time series model* into its components, the picture can be further clarified with the help of *smoothing techniques.* The goal of these time series manipulations of the data is to give an unambiguous picture of the performance of the time series data that is not distorted by random, irregular, or seasonal fluctuations. The following list will help you sort out all the key terms in time series analysis as you assess your own business data or the standard economic data that might affect your business:

➤ **Time series** A collection of data over several periods of time. These time periods can vary in length; you can collect data over days, weeks, months, or years. Time series data contain at least one of the four components of a time series: trend, seasonal variation, cyclical variation, and irregular variation. Time series analysis is used to assist in forecasting or predicting future events (based on past performance).

➤ **Naive method of forecasting** Naive forecasting is used when data exhibit no upward or downward trend, but change direction suddenly. This method uses the most recent observations to predict or forecast the next observation.

➤ **Secular trend** This trend, which is one of the (less frequently mentioned) time series components, is the protracted behavior of a variable over an extended time period. Examples: Increase in the number of people using our brand of batteries or decline in the domestic use of tobacco over the last 25 years.

➤ **Seasonal variation** Another of the primary components of time series analysis is seasonal variation. Seasonal changes are those patterns that occur regularly over a particular time period. Data that is available for only one year really has no seasonal component; you need at least two full years to be able to see a clear seasonal component in time series data. Seasonal variation is very important in quarterly, monthly, and weekly time series analyses for long periods of time (over one year). For example, the sales of heaters, the sales of air conditioners, and the sales of champagne will vary seasonally.

➤ **Cyclical variation** Cyclical variation, the third of the four major components of time series analysis, occurs over a long period of time. Generally these variations include four phases: the upswing or expansion; the peak, at which point activity levels out; the downturn; and the trough, or the lowest point. Examples include enrollments in U.S. colleges and universities or the performance of the gross domestic product (GDP).

➤ **Irregular fluctuation**   The last of the time series components, irregular fluctuations are random and completely unpredictable. The irregular component is included because there is always some movement up or down in time series data that cannot be explained by the other components, such as trend or cyclical variations. For example, irregular fluctuations can occur after unusual events such as wars, floods, hurricanes, and political upheaval in a top leadership.

➤ **Smoothing technique**   Smoothing techniques use math formulas to remove random fluctuations, or other variations that confuse the picture, from a time series model providing a truer view of the behavior of the variable of interest. These smoothing calculations are best done with a computer program.

➤ **Moving averages**   Used to smooth out large variations in a set of time series data. These averages are computed by averaging the observations in the time series over a certain number of time periods. The same number of time periods is used in each successive average, dropping the oldest observation and picking up the next observation from each average. It is the estimate of the long-run average of the variable.

➤ **Exponential smoothing**   This method of forecasting bases the forecast on a weighted average of current and past values. This technique is used when data do not have a clear trend pattern.

➤ **Decomposition**   This procedure is used to isolate the four components of a time series; decomposition can be used to identify the impact each component has on the time series.

➤ **Ratio to moving average**   Computed by dividing the original time series data by the moving average, this average contains the S (seasonal) and I (irregular) components.

➤ **Deseasonalized values**   Computed by dividing the time series data by their seasonal indexes.

Now for Something Trendy

Often series data will show definite trends, up or down, if you follow the data for a long time. You can study the GDP for a 10-, 20-, or even 100-year period, for which charts are available on many economics and financial sites on the World Wide Web, or in newspapers such as the *Wall Street Journal*. When you see the data, you'll observe that the GDP generally rises from year to year over a long period. If you predicted the next year's GDP, you'd probably say it would rise and continue to follow the same upward trend. For the past few years, the GDP has grown at a rate of about 3 percent per year; however, your prediction of 3 percent growth might not be correct. Some years the GDP grows faster or slower than the trend.

The trend component of time series data most often is calculated with the moving average method. For example, if you calculate the average of 5 years of the GDP closest to 1991 (1989, 1990, 1991, 1992, and 1993) you'd be calculating a *moving average*. In the following table you'll see an example of 5-year moving averages and the real GDP for each year. Along the right side of the table you'll see the ratio of the real GDP to the moving average. The ratio (real GDP/5 year moving average) enables you to see the trend value as a percentage—either below or above the trend.

Average Growth of the Gross Domestic Product

Year	Real GDP	Five-year Moving Average	Ratio of Real to Moving Average
1982	4623.60	4781.70	0.967
1983	4810.0	4925.2	0.977
1984	5138.2	5078.2	1.012
1985	5329.5	5283.2	1.009
1986	5489.9	5493.8	0.999
1987	5648.4	5678.2	0.995
1988	5863.9	5840.1	1.004
1989	6060.4	5957.9	1.017
1990	6138.7	6077.1	1.010
1991	6079.0	6181.3	0.983
1992	6244.4	6290.0	0.993
1993	6383.8	6410.4	0.996

As you can see in the chart, the year 1993 shows that the GDP for that year is below the trend at only 96.7 percent of the trend value. This type of data for the five years in question shows that things really improved in 1989 after some down years; then slowed down again in 1991—a likely depression in the economy.

You can't really calculate a moving average for two years or less. It wouldn't be able to show a trend. In the previous example, I chose five years (which is commonly used by economics). However, you might want to try a larger number of years (say 10 for example) for the moving average to make sure you also can identify the basic components of cyclical and irregular variations. If you choose too long a period for the moving average, you might lose too many data at the beginning and end of the series.

Economists (and even business people interested in finance) often explore time series trends with different lengths of moving averages to see the trend data from multiple perspectives. They also might graph the data to compare the real value of the GDP and its trend value to see the real direction the data is going in over time (it's easier to see with a graph). If you have some graph paper, try it with the data you have in the preceding table. It would be a good practice in developing graphs and understanding the concept of a trend.

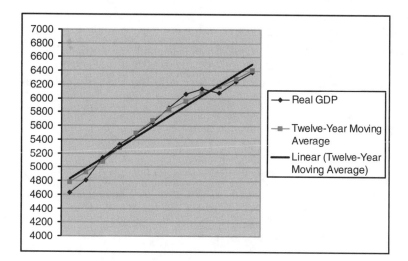

Trend graph of the GDP.

The Cyclic World—What Comes Around Goes Around

The next thing you'll probably want to look at in time series data is the *cyclical variation*, if one exists. The cyclical variation of time series data is determined by comparing the real or actual value with the trend value. There are two general ways to find the actual value of a real GDP with time series components added. The first is the *additive model*, which would look like this if you were working with the GDP as the time series data:

GDP = trend value + cyclical variation + irregular component

Now you calculate the deviation from the trend by subtracting the trend value from the real value, which is known as the cyclical component (the calculated value that adjusts for the cyclical variation).

Statistical Lingo

The **gross domestic product (GDP)** is estimated for each quarter of the year—and then summarized as yearly calculations—and then even further analyzed and processed. The process of analyzing this data is called *national income accounting.*

The other method is called the *multiplicative model.* The real time series GDP is determined like this:

GDP = trend value × cyclical variation × irregular component

Suppose the cyclical value and irregular component value are represented by 1 (as an average) and you calculate the deviation by dividing the actual value by the trend value, as you did in the previous table. The previous plot is exactly a plot of those ratios. The movement in the preceding plot away from the trend line is attributed to either cyclical factors or irregular factors.

Reduce the Risk

The other way to determine the important trend component in time series data is the use of *regression.* You'll learn more about regression in Chapter 15, "Recognizing the Relationships of Business Variables," which shows you how to draw a trend line for a set of data (time series or otherwise).

Another way to forecast time series values (especially when a trend isn't immediately obvious) is the use of *exponential smoothing.* As you advance in statistics, you'll learn how to forecast a new actual value of a time series value for this year, even when the trend for the data is unclear. You then can derive a new forecast value for the next year.

In advanced statistics, you'd learn about techniques known as *Fourier analysis,* which would enable you to determine the real values of the cyclical and irregular components in a time series. However, for now it's important that you understand only the concepts of cyclical and irregular components as factors in predicting the next value on the plot.

What About Adjusting for the Season?

The seasonal adjustment becomes very important (as you might remember from earlier) when you're working with monthly or weekly data. The actual calculation for seasonal adjustment factors is difficult, especially if you employ the complicated procedures used by the government agencies (the Labor Bureau, Federal Reserve, or

Bureau of Economic Analysis.) However, for your own company data, there is a relatively simple procedure.

In many ways, adjusting seasonally is similar to finding a trend using the moving average method for annual data. For seasonal data you'll be using the *ratio to moving average* method. To see how it works, look at the following table, which shows five months of sales data for the batteries we've been discussing in the book.

Statistical Wisdom

I don't try to describe the future. I try to prevent it.

—*Ray Bradbury, U.S. writer of science fiction*

The previous table shows the five-year moving averages for each month. To calculate these I started with the actual monthly sales data and then calculated a one-year moving average for each month of sales. It is a little bit harder to calculate moving averages with even numbers—for each entry you have to calculate two moving averages:

➤ The average of the *six* months of preceding data elements and the *five* months of following data elements for that month and year.

➤ The average of the *five* months of preceding data elements and the *six* months of following data elements for that month and year.

Actual Yearly Sales Data in Thousands

	1997	1998	1999	2000	2001
Jan	117000	118100	119800	122400	124300
Feb	115000	118000	120000	122700	124500
Mar	114000	118200	120400	122900	124600
Apr	115000	118200	120400	123200	124800
May	116000	118300	120700	123400	124900
Jun	116000	118400	120700	123650	124900
Jul	118000	118500	120900	123900	124800
Aug	119000	118600	121100	123900	124100
Sep	117500	118800	121300	123700	124500
Oct	118700	119000	123000	123900	126100
Nov	121000	123000	131000	137000	142000
Dec	122000	124000	131000	136000	147000

In this five-year example, you can't calculate a moving average for the first six values or the last six values, because you don't have enough data to do it.

Monthly Moving Average and Trend Ratio

	1997		1998		1999		2000		2001	
	Mov. Avg.	Ratio	Mov. Avg.	Ratio	Mov. Avg.	Ratio	Mov. Avg.	Ratio	Mov. Avg.	Ratio
Jan	x		119780.00	1.03	130711.67	0.96	131018.33	0.91	133675.00	0.93
Feb	x		119958.33	1.04	131088.33	0.88	131286.67	0.90	135385.00	0.93
Mar	x		120210.00	0.96	130513.33	0.91	131756.67	0.92	136750.00	0.88
Apr	x		120485.00	0.98	129998.33	0.93	132023.33	0.94	136725.00	0.90
May	x		119626.67	1.01	130473.33	0.95	131420.00	0.94	137850.00	0.95
Jun	x		119893.33	1.03	130931.67	0.95	130770.00	0.90	139350.00	0.98
Jul	119656.67	0.96	120123.33	1.04	131306.67	0.90	130981.67	0.91	x	
Aug	119780.00	0.99	120385.00	0.96	130906.67	0.91	131426.67	0.92	x	
Sep	119958.33	1.00	120643.33	0.98	130383.33	0.93	131690.00	0.94	x	
Oct	120210.00	1.02	119861.67	1.01	130795.00	0.95	131296.67	0.95	x	
Nov	120485.00	1.03	120241.67	1.03	131265.83	0.95	130991.67	0.91	x	
Dec	119626.67	0.95	120445.00	1.04	131605.83	0.90	131470.00	0.91	x	

After calculating the moving averages for your sales, you can calculate the ratio between each real sales value and the corresponding moving average value. I've done this for you so you can see the performance of the months based on the average one-year period surrounding the month and year in question. This ratio is called the *monthly trend ratio*. (Obviously, all these calculations are a lot easier with a computer!)

If there is seasonal variation in the sales, in the following plot you will easily see that a month that is below its moving average one year will tend to be lower than its moving average value every year. If you calculate the average of the five years you'll get the average moving average for each month; if you add the total of all these averages you get 7356989.24.

It is interesting to note that the total of the sales and the moving average total of the monthly trend averages add up to almost exactly the same number. Both numbers are nearly, but not exactly, 7356750 (the total real sales). If you average all the monthly trend ratios you get a total of almost exactly 11.44, which will be used in the following table to calculate the standardized average *seasonally adjusted* (actually deseasonalized) ratio.

You can calculate each seasonally adjusted average by simply multiplying the standardized average ratio by each month of sales and derive the seasonally adjusted values for each month of the five years in question. (This is a lot of work by hand.) The results are shown in the following table. You'll see that the *standardized average adjusted ratio* (which is the seasonal adjustment factor you can use to calculate the seasonally adjusted value for each month) is about 11.42—not an impressive difference from that moving average ratio. However, if you divide the sum of the moving average ratios and the sum of the standardized averages you get a seasonal adjustment factor (called the *standardized average*) of about 0.999, which isn't very much for all the trouble.

Standardized Average Monthly Trend Ratios

Jan	0.95
Feb	0.94
Mar	0.92
Apr	0.94
May	0.96
Jun	0.97
Jul	0.94
Aug	0.94
Sep	0.96
Oct	0.97
Nov	0.98
Dec	0.95

The standardized average total ratio = 11.42 (rounded down). Seasonal adjustment amounts to 11.44/11.42 or .099.

If you graph the actual sales numbers compared to the seasonally adjusted numbers you'll see the adjusted numbers as a straight line and the actual sales as peaks and valleys. However, be careful how you graph the data: if you plot the vertical scale of the plot near the lowest point in the data and end near the highest point you'll exaggerate the seasonal variation. It is better to start the vertical scale at zero, so you can see the nondistorted view of the seasonal variations.

In the following plotted example, you don't see too much seasonal sales difference, except once in a while in November/December. (In the battery business this makes sense because at the holidays during those years people were buying the super-hot battery-operated toys.) However, the trend isn't consistent, so you'd probably have to look at the sale forecasts for battery-operated toys (at least based on this fictional data) to really make a good seasonal forecast each year.

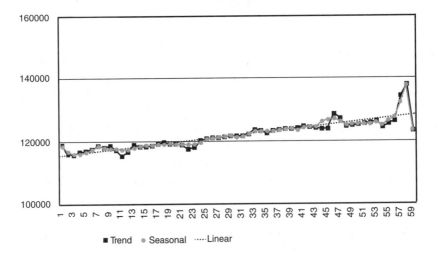

Plot of seasonal trend data.

Working with Precalculated Business Data

Most of the major time series data you'll be working with is calculated for you by the government—except for simple examples shown in the previous sections, which can be used for time series data for sales, expenses, and other general business analyses. Many important economic statistics are available in the form of time series data. The most common statistics for measuring the level of production in the entire economy, for example, is the GDP, which we've already discussed in this chapter.

Reduce the Risk

You should take cautions when using the GDP as a measure of the economy when making plans for your own business. The GDP is not intended to measure the national welfare. Quite simply, all the total goods or services produced can be counted. Therefore, the GDP is not always an accurate predicator.

Nonmarket activities such as work performed by housekeepers should be included in the GDP, but much of it isn't because no one records the pay. Additionally, the GDP doesn't take into consideration the value of leisure time or the impact of harmful things such as pollution or major floods. If you want to look at the average services and goods available to American people, you'd want to look at the per capita GDP rather than the total GDP. (Of course, the Department of Commerce is nice enough to calculate both of these values for us.)

Price Indices and the Role of Inflation

It's logical to think that if the production of everything in the country remains the same and the prices go up on everything, the value of the GDP also goes up. However, the GDP, which is supposed to measure national production, is affected by general or overall price increases to consumers and businesses (associated with inflation). Thus, the effects of general price increases must be separated from the GDP to get a better picture of what's really happening in the economy.

There are many other reasons economists need to measure the average size of prices (called the *price level* or *inflation rate*). Determining the price level is very difficult, but you can understand how it is developed by understanding a quantity known as a *price index*. There actually are many price indexes (commonly called indices in the newspaper) used in national income accounting, including the GDP deflator (which allows the GDP to be adjusted for inflation or deflation), the consumer price index (which can measure how inflation affects you personally), and the producer price index (based on the cost of a specific market group of goods used by firms in production of goods).

Taken together, these indexes can be used to get a more accurate picture of the national economy. There are even more indexes and analyses based on time series data for international economic trends and performance. To find data on the Web for most governmental agencies visit http://www.stat-usa.gov. The site will point you to a wealth of economic, domestic, and business data.

At this point you've seen why time series analysis is important to forecasting basic business trends and in understanding the national, and even international, economic situations. In the next chapter we will discuss projecting your business future and making business decisions using statistics.

The Least You Need to Know

➤ Many important economic and business statistics are available as time series data, which consist of variable observations of over several consecutive time periods.

➤ The four key components of time series data are the trend component, the cyclical component, the irregular component, and the seasonal component.

➤ The ratio to moving average and the centered moving average play an important role in the forecasting process.

➤ Trends in the data, either up or down, have impact on the results of time series analysis.

➤ You can use moving averages and exponential smoothing (both easily done with a computer) to make a forecast.

➤ The deseasonalized data you calculate from time series data can help you determine the true value of a month's sales.

➤ Government agencies can provide a wealth of time series data to help you understand the economic conditions that affect the performance of your business.

Chapter 9

Making Decisions That Count

In This Chapter

➤ Discover the basics of decision theory

➤ Use decision trees for important choices

➤ Know that in business there is always an expected payoff

➤ Recognize that your own expertise and experience will impact every decision

---

In life and business, you're always confronted with decisions—what to wear, where to go, which product to make and how to make it, who to hire and who to let go, and so on. Every decision is a gamble—will your decision be a good one or could it have been better? If you decide to wear a red shirt instead of a green one, the consequences probably aren't too important (unless of course you're marching in a St. Patrick Day's parade). However, in business, most important decisions have equally important consequences. The consequences can affect the very core of the operation—it's financial survival. For this reason, savvy businesspeople try to make their decisions in a systematic, thoughtful way—and statisticians have created some rules, called *decision theory,* which can help when the risk and potential impact of a decision are high.

Statistical Lingo

Decision theory consists of the study and rules that go into making decisions that will help you reach specific objectives. Decision theory is a body of knowledge and related analytical techniques designed to help a decision maker choose from a set of alternatives in light of their possible consequences. The theory usually assumes that you'll be working in conditions of uncertainty—meaning you don't really know the probability of the outcome before you start your analysis. Decision theory shares characteristics with game theory (related to probability theory), but the "opponent" is reality, not another player or players.

Understanding the Key Decisions

When you make decisions, whether in business or in life, you want them to be the best decisions possible. Statisticians have come up with three types of decisions on which to use their magic formulas. The types of decisions are already familiar to you because you make them every day—even without the formulas:

➤ **Decisions under conditions of certainty**   When you make this type of decision you already have all the information you need to determine the best results. With the data in hand, you can calculate the precise outcome of every alternative choice you can make. This doesn't mean you know exactly what to do; however, it does mean that you can choose an appropriate algorithm such as *linear programming,* to analyze the data. Because you may have more data than you can comprehend by looking at it alone, you'll still likely need to use a computer to make the calculations. But, the choices, once calculated, will be obvious. For the purpose of statistics, I won't go into more detail on these types of decisions. If you want to learn more about linear programming, you might want to refer to an advanced management science textbook. In most everyday business decisions of certainty, you can review the data and weigh choices on your own (a *decision tree,* which you'll learn about in this chapter, can help you along the way).

➤ **Decisions under uncertainty** Many business decisions must be made in an environment of uncertainty. In this type of decision, under a curtain of chance outcomes, you consider the probability that things will happen without considering the competition. Intuition and random chance are your bedfellows when you're making these decisions. You'll likely base your decisions on past performance and long-range forecasting (which is another term for guessing in most cases). However, the field of decision theory reduces the guessing by replacing your speculation with rational choices. You also can use decision trees to help with these decisions, as you'll learn later in this chapter.

➤ **Decisions under conflict** When you need to consider professional competition, you are making decisions under conflict. If you have a strong background in management, a penchant for sport in general, and a love of mathematics, you might use *game theory* (an advanced offshoot of the basic probability theory you've read about already) to help you make your decisions. However, this advanced type of decision making really is beyond the scope of this book. When you must assess the impact of a product introduction by your competitors or an unknown price decrease by industry cronies, you'll have to rely on your intuition and experience again (and some of the tricks you'll learn in this chapter).

Charting a Decision Tree

Before making any important decisions in business, you should examine all of the possible choices and their potential outcomes. One technique that can make this easier and more specific is the use of a *decision tree* (also called *classification trees* in other discussions of statistics). A decision tree is a special kind of diagram that illustrates all of the possible consequences of different decisions in different possible states of reality. The diagram is called a "tree" because it vaguely looks like the branches of a great oak when it is completed.

Decision trees are best used when a process consists of making a series of decisions one after the other, with a subsequent decision based on the outcome of an activity, or when a series of outcomes might occur before a payoff can be determined. Decision trees are excellent tools for making financial or number-based decisions in which a lot of complex information must be taken into account. They also help you to form an accurate, balanced picture of the risks and rewards that can result from a particular choice. The following diagram shows what a decision tree looks like (without named branches).

A simple decision tree without named branches.

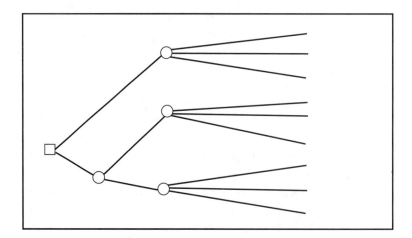

There are many other statistical techniques you can use in decision making; however, as an exploratory technique or a last resort when traditional statistical methods for decision making fail, many researchers consider decision trees to be unsurpassed.

Learning by Example

Decision trees are readily displayed graphically, helping to make them easier to interpret than a strict numerical interpretation. As an example of the usefulness of a decision tree, let's use it to consider whether to develop a new line of battery products or keep our existing product line as it is. Here goes.

List Your Options

A decision tree starts with a decision that needs to be made; in this case, a choice of product development. This decision is represented by a small square (usually placed toward the left of a large piece of paper). From this box, draw out lines towards the right for each possible solution, and write that solution along the line. Keep the lines as far apart as possible so that you can expand your thoughts.

At the end of each solution line, consider the results. If the result of that decision is uncertain, draw a small circle. If the result is another decision that needs to be made, draw another square. Squares represent decisions; circles represent uncertainty (known as *random factors in statistical literature*). Write the decision or factor to be considered above the square or circle. If you have completed the solution at the end of the line, just leave it blank.

In the example we'll be working with, pretend you have two choices: creating a new product line and keeping the existing product line. For each of the two choices, there are different possible outcomes. The different outcomes are called *states of nature* in decision tree theory. A state of nature is a chance result that often is unpredictable because of unknown events and changes in the marketplace, weather, political climate, the plant burning down, or whatever.

Starting from the new decision squares on your diagram, draw out lines representing the options. Draw out lines from the circles representing possible outcomes. Again mark a brief note on the line saying what it means. Continue this until you have drawn down as many of the possible outcomes and decisions as you can see leading on from your original decision. The various states of nature are labeled as additional branches on the tree with labels as shown in the following diagram.

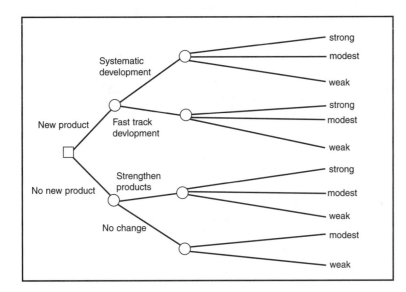

Decision tree with states of nature labeled.

The manufacturing processes might even have more options to deal with, so you have additional decisions to make. These would be added as branches to the decision tree. The branching of a decision tree can be carried out as far as you want or need—but don't get silly; you can't predict everything. Concentrate on those aspects of the decision that are most likely and most important.

Once you have listed out all the options, review your tree diagram. Challenge each square and circle to see if there are any solutions or outcomes you have not considered. If there are, draw them in. If parts of your tree are too congested or untidy, redraft it. You now should have a good understanding of the range of possible outcomes.

Statistical Wisdom

Every decision is liberating, even if it leads to disaster. Otherwise, why do so many people walk upright and with open eyes into their misfortune?

—Elias Canetti (1905–94), Bulgarian-born British novelist philosopher

Evaluate Your Options

When your decision tree is done to your satisfaction, you can calculate the decision that has the greatest worth to you or your business. You can start by assigning a cash or numeric value to each possible outcome. In our example, we use sales as the value (also called an *objective variable,* which we'll discuss later). Next look at each circle (representing an uncertainty point) and estimate the probability of each outcome. If you use percentages, the total must come to 100 percent at each circle. If you use fractions to indicate probability, these must add up to one. If you have data on past events you might be able to make rigorous estimates of the probabilities; otherwise write down your best guess. When you're done, you'll have a tree that looks something like the following.

Decision tree with values and probability estimates.

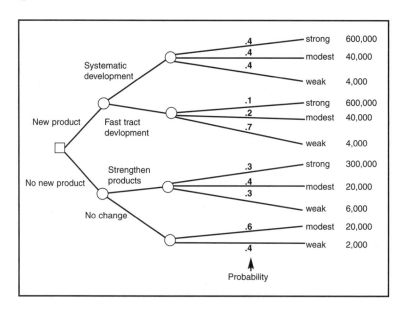

Calculate the Benefits of Your Decisions

Once you have worked out the value of the outcomes, and have assessed the probability of the outcomes of uncertainty, it is time to start calculating the values that will help you make your decision. Start on the right side of the decision tree and work back toward the left. As you complete a set of calculations on a node (decision square or uncertainty circle), all you need to do is to record the result. All the calculations that lead to that result can be ignored from now on, and effectively that branch of the tree can be discarded. This is called "pruning the tree."

You can assess the value of uncertain outcome (circles on the diagram), by multiplying the value of the outcomes by their probability and noting the result. The total value of that node of the tree is gained by adding these together. In the preceding example, the value for "new product, systematic development" is as follows:

0.4 (probability strong outcome) × $600,000 (value) = $240,000

0.4 (probability modest outcome) × $40,000 (value) = $16,000

0.2 (probability weak outcome) × $4,000 (value) = $800

If you add these up, the total is $256,800. This is shown across the example tree in the following diagram. Note that the values calculated for each node are shown in the boxes in the diagram.

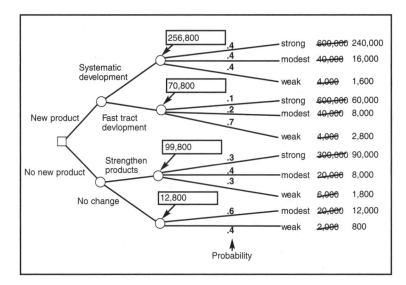

Decision tree with states of nature labeled.

When you are evaluating a decision node, write down the cost of each option along each decision line and subtract the cost from the value of the outcome you have already calculated. This value represents the benefit of that decision. Sunken cost or amounts already spent do not count in this analysis. When you have calculated the benefit of each decision, select the decision that has the largest benefit; this is the decision made and the value of that node.

Incorporate the Cost of the Decision

Before you can really make a decision, even though you know the calculated benefit of each decision you must consider the cost of each choice. The benefit you calculated for "new product, systematic development" was $256,800; you calculate the cost of this approach as $105,000. This offers a net benefit of $151,800. The benefit of "new product, fast-track development" as labeled on the decision tree was $56,000.

On this branch you choose the most valuable option, "new product, systematic development." This value is allocated to the decision node.

By applying the decision tree technique, you can see that the best option might be to develop a new product. The decision tree analysis shows something you might not have otherwise appreciated: It is worth much more to you to take your time and get the product right than to rush the product to market. In fact, it is better just to improve our existing products than to botch a new product through rapid development, even though it costs less. The following diagram shows the calculation of decision nodes in our example, incorporating the cost of each decision about battery products. Ultimately, you can easily see that the thorough development of the product is the best decision.

Final choice using the decision tree calculations.

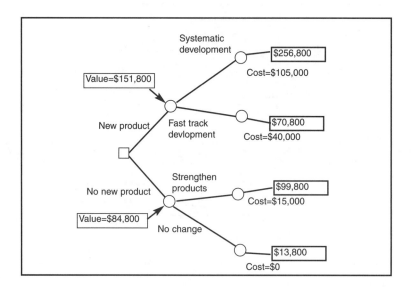

Always Use Objective Variables

When using decision trees to make a decision, it's important to always use objective variables. Objective variables enable you to clearly and understandably compare outcomes in a decision tree. An objective variable is one that everyone can agree upon. For example, sales volume, as used in the decision tree example we've been discussing, is an objective variable. If the nickel cadmium batteries consistently sell more than the alkaline batteries, this is an objective fact—no matter who reads the sales report. Profit per product, production volume, and battery life when installed in a specific device also are objective variables. No one can argue with these numbers (if you have the data).

Now consider a new battery product you want to develop. You want to color the batteries blue instead of red because you like blue better. You are only guessing (or hoping) that blue batteries will sell better than red ones. Thus, your color preference for batteries is not an objective variable for making the decision. When choosing variables in your decision trees, you are trying to maximize or minimize that variable. You can't maximize or minimize the color blue—unless you have some objective research (not just a personal preference) on which to make the decision.

Statistical Wisdom

As with all decision making methods, decision tree analysis should be used in conjunction with common sense. Decision trees are just one important part of your decision making tool kit.

Select the Right Path with the Payoff Table

To figure out which objective variable should have the most or least influence in a decision tree choice, you can use something called a *payoff table* instead of a decision tree. The payoff table enables the decision tree example. A payoff table lists the payoff (the value of the objective variable) that is estimated for each possible decision and each possible state of nature.

In the simplest decision trees you would have one level of choice and one level of states of nature, and for each choice, the same states of nature to consider. When this is the case, you can use a simple payoff table to represent your decision tree.

Payoff Table Example

Choice	B1 More Competition	B2 Less Competition	B2 Same Competition
A1 China	50,000	80,000	50,000
A2 Europe	45,000	90,000	50,000
A3 Africa	25,000	35,000	35,000

In this table you are trying to decide which new market to open for your new product. You have three choices:

➤ A1: Sell in China

➤ A2: Sell in Europe

➤ A3: Sell in Africa

The states of nature are the sales levels:

➤ B1: Increased competition

➤ B2: Decreased competition

➤ B3: Competition remains the same

If you examine the table, the total payoff (the amount of sales realized by this combination of choice and state of nature) is estimated and shown in the intersection of that row and column. Notice that some of the options are automatically eliminated (these choices are termed *inadmissible* in decision theory); these are choices that should not be made because there are always other choices in the table that are better. For example, the choice of going to Africa always equals fewer sales than the other two choices. Therefore, the A3 (Africa) choices are inadmissible across the grid.

Watch Out!

Risk! Risk anything! Care no more for the opinion of others, for those voices. Do the hardest thing on earth for you. Act for yourself. Face the truth.

—*Katherine Mansfield (1888–1923), New Zealand-born British author*

To really determine the best choice, you must estimate the probability for each of the states of nature (B1, B2, and B3). Even though the estimates are estimates, you can still take the expected values of the objective variable (in this case sales) for a given choice. Yes, this is based on estimation. However, for this type of decision making that's about the best you have—unless you have facts from other sources that substantiate your probabilities for each state of nature.

In this example, you're only going to guess, based on other competitors' experience. You estimate that the probability that B1 will occur is .50 and the probability of B2 is .2 and B3 is .3. Based on these probabilities, you would choose option A1 (China) for your new location, because it provides the most probable choice for the highest sales numbers. However, if the probabilities were different—say B1 is .10 and B2 is .6 and B3 is .3—you'd be better off choosing A2 (Europe) as your new sales location, because there is more probability of less competition and the higher predicted sales numbers in Europe.

To further justify the choices I've just described based on the probabilities of the states, you can use the same type of calculation we used with the decision tree example. It really is the same type of decision, except you use a table instead of a tree diagram.

For the first set of probabilities, you'd get these totals .5 × 50,000 = 25,000 plus .2 × 80,000 = 16,000 plus .3 × 50,000 = 15,000, or a total of 56,000 for A1 (China). For A2 (Europe), using similar calculations, you'd get a total of only 55,500; for A3 (Africa), you'd get a total of only 37,000. Thus, A1 is the obvious choice given the predicted probabilities in the first example.

In the second example for A1 (China), using these calculations you'd get a total of only 62,000, whereas you'd get a total of 73,500 for A2 (Europe). This would make Europe the best choice, if the probabilities have any validity in the second example. A3 (Africa) is again out of the running, as it loses on all states of nature in both cases.

Devising Strategies for Decision Making

The type of decision making we've been discussing here is based on the maximum expected payoff. This is a helpful criterion for making the decision. However, sometimes other factors must be considered. Thus, the costs of getting into the marketplace and the long-term potential for other products might affect your decision—even though the initial maximum payoff might lie somewhere else. Further, your choices might be affected by your confidence in the probabilities you have assigned to the states of nature. The more confidence you have in these probabilities, the more useful the maximum payoff calculation will be.

There are other strategies you can use to make decisions when you don't know the likelihood of each of the states of nature or events. Here are four general decision making criteria you should be aware of when this is the case:

➤ **Optimistic decision criterion (maximax)**
Choose the strategy that gives the greatest possible payoff, no matter what the risk of a large loss.

➤ **Pessimistic decision criterion (maximin)**
Choose the strategy that gives the best possible result when the worst occurs.

➤ **Equal likelihood decision criterion**
Assume each event is equally likely and choose the strategy with the best expected return.

Statistical Wisdom

I see it all perfectly; there are two possible situations—one can either do this or that. My honest opinion and my friendly advice is this: do it or do not do it—you will regret both.

—Soren Kierkegaard, (1813–55), Danish philosopher

Reduce the Risk

Caution has its place, no doubt, but we cannot refuse our support to a serious venture which challenges the whole of the personality. If we oppose it, we are trying to suppress what is best in man—his daring and his aspirations.

—Carl Jung (1875–1961), Swiss psychiatrist

➤ **Minimum regret criterion**   Choose the strategy for which minimum regret is most likely. (This is similar to selecting the choice with the least risk.)

Try It On Your Own

At this point, you're ready to try developing a decision tree on your own. Suppose you are an onion grower who can set up a shop in the city or at the vegetable markets close to your fields. Your daily supply of onions is 20 pounds. If you sell in the city your demand will be either 5, 15, or 25 pounds of onions. However, if you sell at the markets, you might encounter competition, in which case demand will be 0, 10, or 20 pounds of onions. Assume onions cost $2 a pound, and sell for $5 a pound. Remember that there is no return credit or benefit for any onions unsold at the end of a day. You can't sell them tomorrow, because they'll rot in the evening dew.

To decide what you should do, draw a decision tree and explain what will offer the maximum payoff for your decision. Assume that the probability of the sales in the city is .60 and the probability of the sales in the markets is .40. (Remember: The total probabilities must add up to 1.0 or 100 percent of the probability.) You'll find the answer to this exercise in Appendix A, "Answer Key."

Now you've completed the section of chapters on probability and forecasting. In the next section, you're going to take on research in business and the ways you can test your own hypotheses about the way things work (or don't) in your business. It's going to be an exciting exploration of the world of inferences and conclusions. Hold on to your hat—there are a lot more statistics coming your way!

The Least You Need to Know

➤ Decision trees are an effective decision making method because they clearly lay out a problem so that all choices can be viewed, discussed and challenged.

➤ Decision trees provide a framework to quantify of the values of outcomes and the probabilities of achieving them.

➤ Even though people often are uncertain about what state of nature will occur, you still can estimate the probability of one particular state occurring opposed to another.

➤ Before making an intelligent decision, you must have all of the most likely choices and their outcomes charted with a decision tree or assembled in a table.

➤ Use your best estimates of the probability of outcomes when making your decisions and use other credible, published data to substantiate your estimates.

Part 3

Using Business Research and Inference

Congratulations! You've made it through the core concepts in statistics and probability. It wasn't as hard as you thought, was it? Now you're ready to move on to developing research, and then making statistical inferences from your research data to guide your methods and decisions regarding products, staff, customer relations, advertising, and much more.

Inferential statistics is all about drawing conclusions from the statistics obtained from sample data. This enables you to ask a few customers about your new product ideas and predict what the rest of your customers will likely do when the product is released. Or you can take a few samples of your products from the production line and understand the overall quality of what is being made. In business, these questions and samples are all a part of the research required to gather the data necessary for statistics to do their work.

The power of business research and the inferential statistics used to test your research hypotheses is almost limitless. From testing whether your sample truly represents the customer base to understanding if the output of two different production facilities are really the same, research and inferential statistics can help answer your questions. In this section you'll get an idea of what is possible—and what you need to know to make it work.

Chapter 10

Using Research in Your Business

In This Chapter

➤ Knowing when research is the best way to decide on a course of action

➤ Understanding the types of research and their uses

➤ Defining the steps in the scientific process

➤ Understanding the difference between research and evaluation

➤ Stepping through a research model

You have to make many decisions in business. In the previous chapter (which introduced decision theory), you learned that you could graph out the options and probabilities related to a decision in the form of a decision tree or payoff table to help you decide on the best course of action. However, to actually make the decision using a decision tree or payoff table, you still have to use your judgment.

Many decisions in business require the application of knowledge and common sense—together, I call this the *application of judgment* in making the decision. For example, numerous day-to-day decisions such as determining the number of manufacturing shifts to run to meet your production goals or deciding on the placement of the employee information bulletin board depend more on judgment and experience than formal decision theory.

However, some business alternatives potentially will consume a great deal of time and resources, and something even more robust than a decision tree is required before a final choice is made. Business questions of this sort include those about strategic changes, new product introductions, and other major dilemmas that could have crucial impact on the enterprise. These types of questions call for *research.*

Please note, because this is a book on business statistics and not research design, the specific, detailed implementation of various types of research studies are beyond the scope of this volume. I'm only going to cover the statistical tests used to evaluate the data you've gathered through research. For more information on research design— and there's a lot of it out there—you should get your hands on a book that specifically focuses on research methodologies.

Deciding When to Use Research

Research is essentially a systematic and unbiased way of solving a problem or answering questions. Research, which usually employs the use of statistics, takes more time and money than the use of judgment alone. Because of this, research isn't always the best choice for answering questions about your business. However, if you can answer "yes" to most of the following six questions, research probably is a superior course of action:

1. **Is the issue important enough for research?** If the cost of the decision is small in terms of time, impact, or money, research probably is not worth the effort. Use your judgment or a well-constructed decision tree instead.

2. **Is information from other sources inadequate?** Sometimes there are other sources of information or studies of similar questions that can provide enough information for you to make a decision without additional research. Asking someone who has already done related research usually is cheaper and faster. However, if these sources of information are not adequate, research probably is a good alternative.

3. **Is there enough time to do the research?** If the research would take too long, the results might have no value. Remember, great research studies are worthless if they are completed too late to influence the decision you have to make.

4. **Is there enough money for the research?** Your business needs the financial resources to be able to support the research. If it doesn't have enough funds, the research won't be feasible (and could negatively impact the organization's operations).

5. **Are there skilled research professionals available to complete the research?** Good research requires people who understand how to design and interpret research. Research is a skill that is learned through training and experience. If

affordable, skilled researchers aren't available to help you, research probably is not the best course of action. Don't just wing it on your own unless you have someone who can evaluate what you're doing.

6. **Would research impact your judgment on the question?** If the answers from research could change your mind, and the other options also point to research, you probably need to undertake some research to make sure your preconceived notion isn't leading you in the wrong direction.

If you answer "no" to two or more of these questions, you probably should use your best judgment and available information resources to help you make the decision. However, for other types of important business choices, you'll need to learn more about research and the statistics used to analyze the data gathered during research.

Developing a Basic Research Methodology

Research, based on the *scientific method* or a similar discovery method, is considered the most reliable way to move from biased perceptions and opinions to facts or tentative truth. The scientific way of solving problems goes back to Aristotle. In the early twentieth century American philosopher John Dewey created an easy-to-understand formulation of the scientific methodology, which helped bring it back into the mainstream of contemporary thought for social (and business) research. Dewey's *theory of cognition* identifies the basic elements of the *inductive-deductive process,* which is central to scientific research methods and other problem solving approaches.

Dewey's theory of cognition applies aptly to many business research issues. The paraphrased steps in Dewey's schema are as follows:

1. An indeterminate or puzzling situation exists that requires a decision, choice, or answer.

2. The problem is further defined or clarified so it can be considered further.

3. A hypothesis (usually starting as an intelligent guess or set of assumptions) is formed in an attempt to answer the problem or question.

4. Data collection, organization, and analysis are undertaken to help understand the question and the validity of the hypothesis. (This is where statistics come in to play.)

Statistical Wisdom

The hallmark of the researcher is not the sophisticated equipment nor the shiny laboratory, but a way of thinking and tackling a problem.

—*Gerhard Lang and George D. Hess, A Practical Guide to Research Methods, 1994, University Press of America*

5. All possible conclusions and decisions are formulated.

6. The consequences of the hypothesis are tested in specific situations and the hypothesis is verified, rejected, or modified. Again, you'll probably need statistics to help you do this for most questions. Ultimately, the best hypothesis becomes the answer to the question being asked, which leads to the best logical course of action for the business.

There are other methods of applying logic and observation to problem solving in business. However, most methods will apply the various steps and parts of the system as described in the preceding, although they might use a different vocabulary to describe the processes or add steps for solving particular types of problems. It's important that the definition of the research process not be too rigid—otherwise it impedes on the creativity with which researchers and businesspeople go about gathering data to answer important questions.

Identifying Appropriate Research Projects

There are almost unending legitimate, ethical uses of research projects in business. For example, research can be used to help design safer products or help find ways to diminish the use of natural resources in the production process. Research also can be used to determine the effectiveness of a product in various applications; for example, paint could be tested outdoors, indoors, and in severe weather conditions to determine the best way to market it to consumers. This type of research also would reveal the limitations of the paint in various applications.

You might want to compare your products to those of other companies or determine consumer preferences for certain functionalities or features associated with your products. If you're an ethical businessperson, you'd never want to use research to justify or legitimize products that are unsafe, dangerous, or otherwise defective. This would mean you had purposively "skewed" the research to put a poor product in a good light.

You should never feel pressured when conducting research to produce the "right" answer to please your boss or other stakeholder. Good research is objective by definition—this means you are looking for truth; not political acceptance. The ethical researcher in business has obligations to the public and the subjects involved in the research to be professional, truthful, fair, and unbiased.

Understanding the Levels of Research

The various types of research often are referred to as a *hierarchy of research levels.* These levels of research apply to business and science in general. The first level in the hierarchy, generally called *action research,* involves solving a problem of limited or local interest. For example, you might wish to compare the efficiency of two different layouts of the office furniture or try two different organizational structures. Another action research project might involve improving relations between two departments in your company.

Many of the immediate questions in business are suited to this type of research. This category of research does not extend to situations outside the current question or predict outcomes beyond the current enterprise. Further, action research generally is the least rigorous; the problems action research addresses are limited in scope and application.

At the other end of the research hierarchy is *basic* or *pure* research. This type of research is designed to develop theories and principles that will increase humankind's overall knowledge. Sometimes this type of research has little immediate or practical application, especially if performed by researchers in academic institutions. The research often is done solely for the sake of knowledge.

In most cases, businesspeople (unless they're a part of a research lab or company-sponsored think tank) don't have time for pure, broad research. This is left to the academicians who need to prove one management approach over another, understand the principles governing economic exchange on a global scale, or establish that their general theories are justified.

Research that is most relevant to the significant questions in an operational business is called *applied research;* it shares many characteristics of basic research including sampling techniques, statistical tests, and the drawing of inferences about a larger population from the sample results. However, applied research is designed to solve immediate problems such as improving a product or enhancing a production process.

Statistical Wisdom

There does not exist a category of science to which one can give the name "applied science." There are science and the applications of science, bound together as the fruit of the tree which bears it.

—*Louis Pasteur (1822–1895), French scientist*

Watch Out!

Almost all scholarly research carries practical and political implications. Better that we should spell these out ourselves than leave that task to people with a vested interest in stressing only some of the implications and falsifying others. The idea that academics should remain "above the fray" only gives ideologues license to misuse our work.

—*Stephanie Coontz, American social historian*

In addition to the hierarchy of research approached (action, applied, and pure), there are three broad categories of research available to help you answer your questions. These include the following:

➤ **Historical-documentary research** generally addresses a present question by analyzing past documentation. This type of research is easy to conduct, but valid only if enough data related to your question is readily available.

➤ **Descriptive research** typically deals with questions by the analysis of data gathered by interviews, observations, and questionnaires. The statistics used in this type of research always include the descriptive statistics you've been reading about in this book already, although other statistical analyses, which you'll read about later, might be involved.

➤ **Experimental research** typically is focused on the future, and involves carefully controlled conditions and robust statistical analysis. Experimental research typically answers questions worded as "What will happen if ...?"

Sometimes it is necessary to use all three types of research to answer a question. However, it's important to focus on the type of research that is the most relevant and the most advantageous for answering the specific question at hand. For example, if you can readily answer the question with historical-documentary information, there is no reason to gather additional descriptive research. If a descriptive study will gain the answers you need, you needn't design a complex experimental research schema, because it probably would waste both time and money. However, when you need to discover the limitation of your products in application in the real world, you probably will need some experimental research to garner the answers you need.

Comparing Research with Evaluation

It's important as a businessperson to understand the differences and similarities between research and evaluation; in business you do both. Both are systematic processes for gathering data and both use at least descriptive statistics in the decision making process.

Evaluation typically is associated with making an immediate, direct decision about the performance or effectiveness of a person or program in business. In evaluation, unlike most research, you're not trying to limit your data to one or two variables or techniques best suited to answering a specific question. Evaluation is more a naturalistic or holistic process. The evaluator tends to gather as much information as possible to make an informed judgment (the evaluation) of the subject.

Typical evaluation questions include, "Should this employee be promoted, retained, or moved to another department?" or "Is this program worth keeping, or should it be changed or eliminated?" Employee reviews are a good example of evaluations in business. To complete the evaluation, you must supply a subjective rating to a person's overall performance over the last period being evaluated. Hopefully, this rating is based on specific data along with good judgment. Conversely, research typically tends to answer more specific questions or respond to the validity of explicit hypotheses about the performance of some aspect of the business or a product.

If the difference between research and evaluation seems a bit vague, that's because it is. A robust evaluation that includes questionnaires, measurement scales, and direct observations is not much different from a robust applied research project—the difference actually is the type of question being studied.

Developing Your Research Literacy

To conduct appropriate research in business, you need to possess something known as *research literacy*. Research literacy assumes that you will be able to ask cogent questions pertaining to the problem at hand, select the appropriate research tools (statistical measures and tests) for gaining answers to the problem, and analyze the data appropriately. At the very least, you should be able to evaluate a formal report on a research study related to your business. Answering the following questions will prove helpful in your evaluation of research before you make any major decisions based on the results:

Statistical Wisdom

After all, the ultimate goal of all research is not objectivity, but truth.

—*Helene Deutsch, American psychiatrist*

1. Does the title of the research convey the content of the study?

2. Is the problem significant or important enough to warrant the research?

3. Is the question or problem that warrants the research clearly stated?

4. Is the purpose of the study clear and precise?

5. Is previous or related research presented in the report? Is this research relevant and meaningfully summarized?

6. Are the hypotheses to be tested clearly stated, important, and in a form that permits them to be tested?

7. Are the assumptions underlying the study explicitly stated? Are any implicit assumptions made that should have been made explicit?

8. Are all the key concepts and definitions clearly defined and meaningful?

9. Are the definitions of the population and sample clear? Is the sampling method indicated? (You'll learn more about this aspect of research in Chapter 11, "Eliminating the Bias in Your Research.")

10. Are the research design and techniques fully described, including research instruments such as questionnaires?

11. Are the tests and techniques used reliable, valid, and appropriate for the collection of the data?

12. Can the study be replicated? If it can't, it's not really scientific research.

13. Are the results and conclusions intelligibly and logically reported based on the data presented?

14. Are the limitations of the research recognized and discussed? Are suggestions for further research made?

15. Is the research adequately and fairly summarized, with the major findings, generalizations, implications, and limitations succinctly summarized?

You should be able to answer the preceding questions on any adequate report of research related to your business. As you learn more about the statistical tests used in research, these questions will make even more sense.

Understanding Validity and Reliability in Research

To be useful in making decisions, research in business should meet two important criteria: *validity* and *reliability*. Validity is the extent to which a research tool, such as a questionnaire, interview script, rating scale, or test, actually measures what it intends to measure. For a research instrument to be valid, it must at least meet the criterion of *face validity*. This type of validity is apparent when the questions being asked or the rating scale being used seem to be important in answering the research question you're focusing on. Face value is simply based on common sense.

Statistical Wisdom

Fools make researches and wise men exploit them.

—*H. G. Wells, British writer*

Even better, the research instrument should meet the criterion of *content validity*, which pertains to the number and subject matter of the questions. To have content validity, the types of items in the research instrument should reflect the emphasis on the questions being asked and the scope of the program or process being evaluated.

On the other hand, reliability denotes the consistency in which the research tool results in similar responses or results. Thus, if you try the questionnaire or rating scale on two similar audiences or research samples, you should get similar results. If not, there is something wrong with either the sample (it actually might represent a different population of individuals) or the construction of the research instrument. As you develop your research or review the research of others, always ask if the research is both valid and reliable; if it's not, it's not worth using.

Developing a Model for Your Research

To use statistics in your business research, you should understand the concept of a *research model*. The goal of research models is to produce simple rules that will explain how things work in business. Some samples of models include the model of the time value of money espoused in finance, the model of supply and demand used in economics, and the model of relativity used in physics. Models are created from three general things: data, concepts, and the hypotheses that form theories:

➤ **Data** include the measurements and records of activity or events. Hopefully, this data is accurate and free of bias. The data also should be valid and reliable, as mentioned previously.

➤ **Concepts** in your model are the abstract ideas relevant to the questions you are trying to answer in your research. For example, customer satisfaction and quality are typical concepts used in business research. These abstract ideas relate directly to the data you've gathered. Because abstract ideas can't be measured directly, you must define them operationally as some piece of data you can actually record or observe. Thus, your research model will require *operational definitions*—the specific data used to define your abstract concepts. It is important that the operational definitions are valid (meaning the data actually measures the concept you're trying to quantify).

➤ **Hypotheses** are the statements that explain the relationships between concepts. A set of related hypotheses go into making up a *theory* about your business problem or question. For example, you might hypothesize that "customer satisfaction increases with lower prices for our product." For another question you might hypothesize that "employees will produce more widgets if they make more money per widget." By stating a theory (a group of hypotheses) or a single hypothesis, you are structuring your analysis of the problem.

To make your hypotheses and theories clear you need to express them in a way that can be translated into statistical tests. *Functions* are one such way to state your hypotheses or theories about a question being studied. Functions are stated as equations. For example, here is a function for a hypothesis that equates employee productivity to the combination of pay, training, management, and working hours:

productivity = f (pay, training, management, working hours)

Each of the concepts in this functional equation needs to be operationally defined as a specific type of data to measure them with research. *Variables* are the elements of functions that can change or vary when they are measured. Independent variables are values that determine the value of other variables. In the preceding functional equation, *pay*, *training*, *management*, and *working hours* all are independent variables.

Dependent variables can be predicted or are affected in some systematic way by the independent variables. In the example functional equation, *productivity* is a dependent variable. According to the function, productivity is dependent on a combination of the independent variables of pay, training, management, and working hours.

The research problem or question determines how many variables are needed. Specific problems require only a few variables to arrive at a conclusion. Complex problems will likely have more variables involved. For example, if your problem is to learn which product color is preferred by your customers, only two variables are involved: the color and the preference. However, if you want to study the reasons for this preference, you might have to add variables for age, education, income level, and cultural background, among others.

Three Steps to Prepare for Statistical Analysis

When preparing your research for statistical analysis, you'll have to complete three steps related to the research model I've just been discussing. These steps are always necessary before you can conduct any meaningful statistical analysis regarding your business problem or question:

1. Define the problem or question as a hypothesis or a theory (a number of related hypotheses). Describe the hypothesis as a function that includes a variable for each concept.

2. Review each variable in your functional equation and make sure the variables reflect the dependent/independent relationship you're trying to understand.

3. Develop a specific operational definition (a piece of data that can be measured) for each variable in the functional representation of your hypothesis.

If you always complete these steps before you start a research project, you'll at least be able to conduct appropriate statistical analyses, because you'll be asking the right kinds of questions and gathering appropriate types of data to answer those questions.

This chapter has introduced only a few important research concepts so you can see how statistics and research go hand in hand. You'll be working with these concepts throughout the rest of this book. In the next few chapters you'll learn some basic statistical techniques related to research in general, as we've been discussing here. These techniques include establishing the sample for your research, statistical analyses focused on proving or disproving a hypothesis, and considering the reliability (and confidence) of your statistical analyses.

The Least You Need to Know

➤ Research is a good idea if you don't have enough related information to support a choice based on judgment and decision trees alone.

➤ Good research is systematic, objective, valid, and reliable.

➤ Research categories include action research for local problems, applied research for significant problems, and pure research to find out about general truths in business.

➤ Within these types of research, you can design your research program to be historical-documentary, descriptive, experimental, or a combination of these.

➤ Research and evaluation are closely related; however, research is more specific whereas evaluation is more holistic in its approach to data analysis.

➤ Concepts in research are the abstract ideas relevant to the research problem.

➤ To be used in research, abstract concepts must be defined operationally as a specific type of data that can be observed or measured, because abstract concepts cannot be measured directly. These concepts become the variables (independent and dependent) that form the basis of your hypothesis.

➤ Hypotheses and theories explain the relationships between operationally defined concepts (also called variables).

➤ Hypotheses can be stated as functional equations. These equations demonstrate the relationship among the independent and dependent variables in your research.

Chapter 11

Eliminating the Bias in Your Research

In This Chapter

➤ Using representative samples in research and statistics

➤ Understanding the importance of sampling in making accurate statistical inferences

➤ Selecting samples at random

➤ Looking at standard sampling techniques that are considered acceptable

One primary purpose of statistical methods is to draw general conclusions about populations using data from samples. I discussed the concepts of population and sample way back in Chapter 1, "Statistics and Business Go Hand in Hand," as you might recall. The proportion of people in a sample with a particular characteristic is used to estimate the proportion of people in the population with the same characteristic. You might recall from Chapter 4, "Predicting Profits with Measures of Central Tendency," that the population characteristic is called a *parameter*; the *statistic* is the characteristic measure of the sample.

For example, almost every public opinion poll involves selecting a representative sample of the public at large, obtaining data on or from the individual cases in that sample, and then making conclusions (called *inferences* in statistics) about the population's opinion from the data drawn from the sample *cases*. A sample is made up of data drawn from individual cases that represent the population.

Individual cases are used to populate the data files used in research. The definition of a case (who or what you study) is determined by the definition of the population you'll be making inferences about; the population is determined by the research problem or question. A case does not necessarily represent a person. In business research, a case could be a customer, a vendor, a production lot, a fiscal year, or other instances that can be studied.

Watch Out!

The discovery of truth is prevented more effectively, not by the false appearance things present and which mislead into error, not directly by weakness of the reasoning powers, but by preconceived opinion, by prejudice.

—*Arthur Schopenhauer (1788–1860), German philosopher*

The Infinite Population in Applied Statistics

Some populations are finite and can be measured in their entirety. For example, the population of the employees in your company or your customers might be a number of cases small enough that you can gather data from every member of the population. However, typically this is not practical. Because it is seldom practical to study an entire population, most researchers use samples of representative cases instead.

For most research purposes, populations are assumed to be infinite, not finite, in size. Most applied statistical techniques are based on the assumption that an infinite population is being sampled. Thus, if the population is large and the sample from the population constitutes only a small proportion of the population (say less than 5 percent), the fact that the population is not actually infinite is of little concern. The statistical analyses that assume an infinite population generally still will be valid.

The Importance of Random Sampling

To select a sample of cases from the population, you'll have to ensure that your sample is truly representative of the population. It makes a big difference how the sample is selected, because the values of the mean of a particular parameter will depend on exactly who or what is in the sample.

You must determine a good system for choosing the sample so that it will be representative of the population as a whole. You can't simply start asking friends or talking to only those customers who happen to call that week. You can't just mail out postcards and ask people to return them. The people who return the cards might have entirely different attitudes or opinions than a truly representative sample. To accurately represent your population you must use *random sampling*.

The validity of statistical inference depends on how representative the sample is of the population. In fact, the representative nature of the sample is more important than the size of the sample. In all major textbooks on statistical methods, great emphasis is given to simple random sampling as a legitimate way of selecting representative samples from a population. The concept of random sampling is closely related to probability, which I discussed in Chapter 7, "Playing the Probability Game."

Statistical Wisdom

The method used to select the sample is of utmost importance in judging the validity of the inferences made from the sample to the population.

—*Gene V. Glass and Kenneth Hopkins,* Statistical Methods in Education and Psychology, *Second Edition, 1984*

In simple random sampling, all individuals (cases) in a population have an equal and independent chance of being selected. If a sample truly is drawn randomly from a population, it is representative of the population in all respects. If a sample is indeed random, a statistic gathered from the sample differs from the actual parameter (the population measure) only by chance on any variable. Through the "magic" of statistical theory, the degree of this difference between the statistic and the actual parameter of the population can be estimated. This difference, known as the *error due to chance* (sampling error), is an important feature of a random sample.

Choosing the Appropriate Sampling Methods

Let's say you have 5,000 customers on your customer list. If you were simply to take the first 50 names from your customer list as a sample for your research into future purchase plans, the sample would not be random. It would be impossible to estimate the actual future sales volume per customer based on this convenience sample. The sample is not representative in unknown ways and to an unknown extent.

Random Sampling

However, if 50 customers were randomly selected from your customer list, it would be possible to answer questions such as, "How likely is it that a sample of 50 customers randomly drawn from all customers on the customer list will have a mean projected purchase amount that differs by less than $500 from the mean projected purchase amount?" If you could answer this question using only 50 randomly selected customers, instead of the population of 5,000, you can see the immediate advantages of properly constructed random sampling.

One common way to construct a random sample is to use a table of random digits and then select the sample based on the numeric place of the customers on your list in relationship to the random digits. There are tables for random digits available in advanced books on statistics and on the World Wide Web. If you own a computer, most computers have a built-in function for generating random numbers. The following table is a subset of random numbers from a larger random number table generated by a computer. In the complete table, there are many more combinations of 25 random numbers to choose from. You can use these random number tables to choose samples of your own. For example, you could choose the customers who match the random number on the table based on their position on a list of customers.

Reduce the Risk

Accidental or *convenience sampling* is an inappropriate, although often used, method of obtaining a sample. Don't do it yourself! Haphazard collections of observations usually are of little use in measuring parameters (actual values of the variables in a population). Further, it is not possible to estimate the error with accidental and other nonrandom sampling methods because they contain unknown types and degrees of bias.

A classic example of a misused convenience sample was the research done for Shere Hite's book, *Women and Love*. Shere sent out 100,000 questionnaires. Unfortunately, only 4.9 percent of the questionnaires were completed and returned. Thus, the "results" reported in the book were based on a biased sample of women who, for whatever reason, were highly motivated to complete the questionnaires. Consequently, all the conclusions in the book are questionable at best.

A Simple Table of 25 Random Numbers

60	36	59	46	53
83	79	94	24	02
32	96	00	74	05
19	32	25	38	45
11	22	09	47	31

Systematic Sampling

Pure random sampling is the most appropriate type of sampling, but often it is infeasible. Another technique used to obtain an appropriate sample is called *systematic sampling*. For example, you could select a single random number from a table of random numbers between one and thirty and then pick the customer corresponding to that number. Then you could pick every twentieth or thirtieth customer from that first random selection.

A systematic sample of this type is easier to obtain than pure random samples based on random number tables or computer-generated lists of random numbers. The good news is that results from systematic samples tend to be slightly more accurate than results from simple random samples—although the difference in accuracy is inconsequential in most cases. The orderly sampling process presents less opportunity for sampling error. The primary disadvantage is that there is no satisfactory way to determine precisely how accurate the estimates are in the long run.

Watch Out!

Without randomized design, there can be no dependable statistical analysis, no matter how it is modified. The beauty of random sampling is that it "statistically guarantees" the accuracy of the survey.

—Larry Gonick and Wollcott Smith, The Cartoon Guide to Statistics

In most cases, samples using systematic sampling will differ little from simple random sampling. And unlike accidental sampling, a systematic sampling, properly employed, is not biased and produces generalizable results (within a given margin of sampling error) to the parent population.

Cluster Sampling

Cluster sampling often is used in major opinion polls and other research that covers a huge population that is geographically diverse. In cluster sampling, the population is divided into different clusters and the sample is taken only from selected clusters. In this method ideally each cluster would be representative of the entire population. However, in practice usually clusters are selected geographically. Typically, some regions are selected at random, then some subregions, and finally the individual cases (people, households, customers, or whatever) are selected.

Statistical Wisdom

Artists use frauds to make human beings seem more wonderful than they really are. Dancers show us human beings who move much more gracefully than human beings really move. Films and books and plays show us people talking much more entertainingly than people really talk, make paltry human enterprises seem important. Singers and musicians show us human beings making sounds far more lovely than human beings really make. Architects give us temples in which something marvelous is obviously going on. Actually, practically nothing is going on.

—*Kurt Vonnegut Jr., American novelist*

Stratified Sampling

Another viable sampling method is called *stratified sampling.* This method is used when a population can be grouped into subgroups that all consist of individuals who are very much alike. You can obtain a representative sample by interviewing a random sample of people in each group. This type of sampling can produce very accurate results but it works only when the population can be accurately divided into homogenous groups (*strata*).

How Big Should the Sample Be?

Normally, the bigger the sample, the more accurate the results—as long as the sample is representative of the population as a whole. When the number of cases in the samples is more than 30, you can use some statistical tools that can't be used with smaller sample sizes. (There also are some special tests for use with small sample sizes [less than 30] that help make the inferences more credible.)

Sometimes researchers use a pilot study to determine how large the sample should be. You also can refer to more advanced statistics textbooks for learning ways to estimate the necessary sample size using various assumptions and formulas.

In Chapter 12, "Being Confident About Your Sample," you'll learn how to calculate the sampling error based on various sample sizes. This can help you determine how large you want your sample to be, based on the accuracy you require for your results.

Now that you understand the importance of a representative sample of the population you want to study, you'll need to know how to calculate the confidence you have in your sample and its results. You're going to learn how to do that in the next chapter. Beware—it's going to take some math and you'll need to recall all the information we talked about earlier related to normal and binomial distributions.

Reduce the Risk

Never take a quick sample for expediency's sake without ensuring that your sample cases will represent the parameters of your population within an acceptable margin of error (typically 5–10 percent). If you prioritize the speed and ease of sampling over its representation of the population, you're simply wasting the company's time, money, and resources—and any conclusions you make on such sloppy work could point you toward disaster instead of profitability.

The Least You Need to Know

➤ It is expensive to survey everyone or everything in a population being studied, so samples are used instead.

➤ Most applied statistical techniques are based on the assumption that an infinite population is being sampled.

➤ Random samples are the most accurate—but sometimes they are difficult to obtain. For this reason, other sampling methods are used, including systematic, clustered, and stratified.

➤ The most important aspect of a good sample is that it truly represents the populations being studied. This representative structure is even more important than the size of the sample.

Chapter 12

Being Confident About Your Sample

In This Chapter

➤ Estimating the mean of a population by studying a sample

➤ Figuring the standard sampling error

➤ Calculating the confidence interval for your observations

➤ Understanding how the Central Limit Theorem makes all this possible

---

Let's say we're back at the old battery factory again. Your boss just asked how many defective batteries are being produced on the new production line. Each new battery produced has some probability I'll call p of being defect free. (Remember probability?) Knowing this, how can you determine how accurately a sample of the batteries is in estimating the true number of successes and failures on the production line?

Knowing what you know about sampling a population (in this case, the population is "all the batteries being produced") you know that you have to take a random sample of the batteries to estimate how many batteries are actually defective. How accurate will that random sample really be? That's what this chapter will help you determine.

In this chapter, you'll see a lot of math. If math frightens you, just try to follow the logic—and then go to the end of the chapter to learn the least you really need to know.

Conducting Bernoulli Trials

Each time you select a battery for testing, you are conducting a repeatable experiment called a *Bernoulli trial*. A Bernoulli trial has these important properties:

1. The result of each test or trial can be either a success or a failure.

2. The probability (*p*) of success is the same for every trial.

3. The tests or trials are completely independent, which means the outcome of one test or trial has no influence on the later tests or trials.

When you do this, you can build a new random variable, called a *binomial random variable*, by repeating the Bernoulli trial and adding up the results. That variable can help you determine how accurate your sample of batteries tested is in representing the defects (and successes) in the production of batteries as a whole. In statistical terms, each battery test, X (the binomial random variable) is the number of successful (nondefective) batteries (*k*) found in *n* repeated trials with probability *p* of success.

What is the probability distribution for any probability (*p*) and number of trials (*n*)? A probability calculation provides the answer: The probability of obtaining *k* good batteries (successes) in *n* trails is

$$\Pr\left(X = k\right) = \binom{n}{k} p^{k} \left(1 - p\right)^{n-k}$$

To interpret this equation, read the binomial coefficient $\binom{n}{k}$ as "*n* choose *k*," which is the binomial coefficient. This counts all possible ways of obtaining *k* successes in *n* trials. This binomial coefficient is equal to the equation you learned in Chapter 7, "Playing the Probability Game," in a different format:

$$\binom{n}{k} = \frac{n!}{k!\left(n - k\right)!}$$

where $n! = n\,(n-1) \times (n-2) \times \ldots \times 1$. (Remember, that 0! is equal to 1 in this equation.)

As an example, here's how it works:

$$\binom{4}{2} = \frac{4!}{2!\,2!} = \frac{24}{4} = 6$$

> ### Statistical Wisdom
>
> One of the advantages of living in a capitalist society is that we are all free to spend our hard-earned cash on nearly any type of product we may choose regardless of whether it is moderately dangerous or simply a waste of money.
>
> —*Jefferson Hane Weaver,*
> *Conquering Statistics: Numbers*
> *without the Crunch, 1997*

Back to the Sample

If you're comfortable with all the math you've just seen you'll remember that each battery for testing is an example of a Bernoulli test. However, because you don't know what p is at the onset—and because you need to find out—you take a random sample of n batteries and find out that x of them are nondefective (successful tests).

The proportion of successes (good batteries) in this random sample should be somewhere close to the actual p of successes. There is an equation for this (naturally) that looks like this:

$$\hat{p} = \frac{x}{n}$$

$\hat{p}$, which is (pronounced "p-hat"), is the number of successes (x) in the sample divided by the sample size n. (By the way, capital $\hat{P}$ is the actual random variable of the population; little $\hat{p}$ is the value for a particular sample.)

Suppose the real p (for probability) is .92, meaning there is a 92 percent actual probability that the batteries are good. Now assume you take a sample of 100 batteries and 93 of the batteries are good. This would make $\hat{p}$ = .93. This is a number close to .92. However, what does this really mean, given that you still don't really know that the true value of p is .92? At this point you need to find out how confident you are that .93 is close to the actual value of p.

The Confidence Interval

To understand the confidence interval, you must ask another question that statistics can answer: If you take many samples of the batteries and observe $\hat{p}$ successes for each sample, how will those values of $\hat{p}$ be distributed around the actual value of $\hat{p}$?

When you look at the data this way, the $\hat{p}$ values look like a random variable (and in fact are such), and the sample n actually is a random experiment, with the value of $\hat{p}$ being an observation called a *numerical outcome*.

Ultimately, you'll get a binomial distribution of the values of $\hat{p}$. This binomial distribution and the normal distribution you learned about in Chapters 6 and 7 are, for general purposes, considered the same in this analysis. Thus, for a large n, the values of $\hat{P}$ is approximately a normal distribution. Not surprisingly, the observed (sample) values of $\hat{P}$ will be centered around $\hat{P}$ (the actual probability of successful battery production).

The more samples you take, the smaller the spread around the actual values of $\hat{p}$. Thus, the larger the sample (assuming the sample is random), the more accurate the values observed from the sample. The distribution of $\hat{P}$ for a large number of samples is approximately normal. Because the distribution of $\hat{P}$ is approximately normal, we can conclude that approximately 68 percent of all estimates will fall within one standard deviation of the true value of p, and 95 percent of all estimates will fall within two standard deviations of the true value of p. (Refer to Chapter 6, "Solving Problems with Curves and z-Scores," if you don't remember what a normal distribution looks like.)

Larger Sample Means Smaller Spread

The size of the standard deviation will be directly affected by the sample size, meaning that the spread between the observed and the actual values of p will be smaller for larger sample sizes.

You can derive the standard deviation of $\hat{P}$ with this equation:

$$\sigma\left(\hat{P}\right) = \frac{\sqrt{p(1-p)}}{\sqrt{n}}$$

Statistical Wisdom

Who would not rather trust and be deceived?

—Eliza Cook, English poet

Remember, σ is the symbol for a population's standard deviation. A sample's standard deviation usually is referred to as s. However, for purposes of the example, I will treat them as being the same. If you go back to the example you'll get the following specifics:

$$\sigma\left(\hat{P}\right) = \frac{\sqrt{.93(.7)}}{\sqrt{100}} = \frac{\sqrt{1.302}}{10} = \frac{1.14}{10} = .114$$

This means 68 percent of the sample observations would fall in the interval of $92.886 \leq p \geq 93.114$, and 95 percent of the sample observations would fall in the interval of $92.772 \leq p \geq 93.228$. Notice that the actual value of $p(.93)$ is within this range, and that's a good thing.

So it's really pretty simple. The standard deviation of a sample binomial $\hat{p}$ is a measure of the sampling error—and this sampling error will tell you how accurate the sample is in obtaining that actual number of successes (and failures). Simply stated, the sampling error is inversely proportional to $\sqrt{n}$. This means the spread in the error of the mean of an observed sample is proportional to $\sqrt[1]{n}$. Thus, increasing the sample size by a factor of 4 reduces the spread of the standard deviation of $\hat{p}$ by 2.

Here's a table that shows how it works for binomial variable sample sizes where $p = .85$:

n	1	4	16	25	100	10,000
$\sqrt{n}$	1	2	4	5	10	100
$\sigma(\hat{p})$	.357	.1785	.089	.071	.0357	.0036

What About Interval and Ratio Samples?

You should notice at this point that the calculations I've been talking about work only with binomial observations, which have only two possible states: They are either successful or unsuccessful. What about other sorts of measurements and experiments in business in which the data are ratio or interval in nature?

Well, there's good news. The types of analysis you can do with binomial probabilities is similar for data where you have to deal with the mean values obtained for ratio and interval measures. For example, scores on a customer questionnaire, the average length of time your batteries last, or the number of batteries produced each day. (If you don't remember what ratio and interval measures are, return to Chapter 2, "Understanding and Organizing Business Data," to refresh your memory.)

Let's pretend you want to know about purchase amounts your customers intend to make next year. Just for purposes of example, the actual mean purchasing forecast for the entire population is $27,875—of course you wouldn't know this unless you asked all 25,000 customers on your list, which is something you don't really want to do. Instead you need to take a sample of the customers' purchase forecasts.

You call 100 customers selected at random. All 100 customers answer your question. When you average the amounts the customers say they'll purchase next year, you get a sample mean ($\overline{X}$) of $27,800. Now, you repeat the experiment again. This time, you get a sample mean of $26,454. Do this 8 more times; you end up with the following ten sample means:

$27,800	$26,545	$28,407	$27,684	$27,809
$28,527	$28,827	$27,904	$28,102	$27,195

The average of these 10 sample means is 27,880. You can see that the first sample mean is not a bad estimate of the actual sample mean—but the average of the ten sample means is even better. The more sample means included in the sampling distribution, the more accurate the mean of the sampling distribution becomes as an estimate of the population mean. In fact, each sample mean is a random variable, the numerical outcome of a random experiment.

You already know from the last section based on a binomial random variable obtained as the outcome of a random experiment, that the sample probability distribution of $\hat{p}$ was almost normal. But what about a sample mean as an estimator of a population mean? It turns out that the distribution of the sample $\overline{X}$ also is approximately normal because of a great statistical truth called the central limit theorem, which I discussed briefly in Chapter 6; it probably will make more sense to you now.

The central limit theorem states that the mean of a sampling distribution of means is an unbiased estimator of the population mean. In statistics symbols, this looks like this equation:

$$E_{\overline{X}} = \mu \text{ also represented by some as } \mu_{\overline{X}} = \mu$$

Here E stands for the unbiased estimator, $\overline{X}$ is the average of sample values, and the Greek letter μ (called mu) stands for the mean of a random variable's distribution. Similarly, the standard deviation of a sampling distribution of means, like the ten samples we just discussed, is represented by this equation:

$$\sigma_{\overline{X}} = \frac{\sigma}{\sqrt{n}} \; .$$

This is similar to the equations discussed earlier. The spread of sample means is again proportional to

$$\frac{1}{\sqrt{n}}$$

which is a sort of magic number in sampling! Based on the observations in the previous example regarding customers' forecast purchases for next year, you'd get the following results:

The sample mean

$$\overline{X} = 27,880$$

and the standard deviation of the 10 sample means is 662. (Calculate it yourself if you want to.) The total number of cases is 1000, derived from 100 cases times 10 samples. This is the formula:

$$\sigma_{\overline{X}} = \frac{662}{\sqrt{1000}} = \frac{662}{100} = 6.62$$

The standard deviation of a distribution of means (in this case 6.62) in a sample also is called the *standard error of the mean*. Every statistic has a standard error of the mean (also called simply a *standard error*), which is a measure of a statistic's random variability.

Another remarkable thing about the Central Limit Theorem is that regardless of the shape of the original distribution, the measurement of averages from a sample results in a normal distribution.

Determining a Confidence Interval

Now that you know how to get the standard errors of the mean for the mean sampling value, you still need to determine a confidence interval—a range of numbers that indicates how confident you are in this sample estimate as a predictor of the actual mean value. For example, let's say you want to be 95 percent confident that your confidence interval contains the actual population mean. To do this, you use the z-tables you learned about in Chapter 6. Here's how it works:

1. Calculate the standard error of the mean. This is equal to the equation you just learned, which is

$$\sigma_{\overline{X}} = \frac{\sigma}{\sqrt{n}}$$

   or stated using the sample symbols for standard deviation,

$$\sigma_{\overline{X}} = \frac{\sigma}{\sqrt{n}}$$

   which for our purposes are approximately equal. In the current example regarding forecast customer purchases this number is 6.62.

2. If you remember, per the normal standard tables you learned about in Chapter 6, the critical point (z-score) for 95 percent of a value is 1.96 standard deviations. Using the following formulas, you can calculate the range of values within ±1.96 standard errors of the mean of x.

-1.96 standard deviations

$x = (z * std.error) + \overline{x}$

$x = (-1.96 * 6.22) + 27,880$

$x = 27867.81$

-1.96 standard deviations

$x = (z * std.error) + \overline{x}$

$x = (-1.96 * 6.22) + 27,880$

$x = 27892.19$

Watch Out!

Don't confuse a confidence level with a confidence interval. The confidence level is the percentage of estimated accuracy (95 percent or 99 percent, for example) in your confidence interval. The confidence interval is a range of values between the lowest and highest values that a given estimated parameter, such as the mean, could realize at a given confidence level.

Notice that instead of the sample standard deviation (which you used to calculate values in Chapter 6 using *z*-scores) you are using the standard error of the mean to obtain this range. This is an important difference for calculating confidence intervals.

For this example, you can be 95 percent confident that the true, actual population mean of forecast sales per customer is somewhere between $27,867.81 and $27,892.19. Because this is an example—not the real world—you already know that the actual mean is $27,875; this range is a pretty valid confidence interval for the experiment. In fact, the 95 percent confidence level is the most commonly used confidence interval in business research. The 99 percent confidence level also is commonly cited in research.

Confidence levels indicate the probability that the confidence interval will contain the real value for the population—stated in terms of a percentage of confidence. Try it on your own. Here is a table of values. Given the discussion in this chapter thus far, you should be able to calculate the missing values in the table using an ordinary calculator. The answers are provided in Appendix A, "Answer Key."

Mean ($\bar{X}$)	Standard Deviation (*s*) Standard Error of the Mean	Number of Cases (*n*) Confidence Interval of 95%
100	10	30
500	50	65
50	5	37
20	2	40

It Won't Work with Small Samples

All the calculations you've learned thus far will work just fine if your sample size is more than 30. However, for small sample sizes (those less than 30) you'll need to use the *t* distribution instead of the *z* (standard normal) distribution to calculate your confidence intervals. To use the *t* distribution in this way, you should be able to presume that the original distribution is roughly bell-shaped.

The only difference in using the *t* distribution for calculating the confidence interval is that the standard error is larger; thus the range of values (the confidence interval) at a specific confidence level also will be larger. Further, we plug in values from the appropriate *t* distribution instead of using the *z*-scores, which would be appropriate for the normal distribution of a larger sample.

To obtain a *t*-value you also need to know the degrees of freedom associated with your sample. By definition, the degrees of freedom for a sample mean is

$(n–1)$

Statistical Wisdom

The number is certainly the cause. The apparent disorder augments the grandeur.

—Edmund Burke (1729–1797), British philosopher and statesman

When you look up *t* values in statistical tables, you'll see that there are a two-tailed *t* distribution and a one-tailed *t* distribution. Obviously, for this test, you'd want to use the former table; not the latter. The following is a selection of values from a *t* table that demonstrates the *t*-values for levels of significance. These values are appropriate for two-tailed tests (such as determining the confidence interval, which is ± the value for *t*).

Degrees of Freedom $(n–1)$	Value of t 0.05 significance level	Value of t 0.01 significance level
5	2.57	4.03
10	2.23	3.17
20	2.09	2.79

Now, let's examine the example calculation, but assuming that the sample size is only 6 (instead of the 1000 used before). According to the formula you've already learned, the standard error of the mean would be equal to

$$\sigma_X = \frac{662}{\sqrt{6}} = 270.26$$

Then you'd use the following formulas to determine the appropriate confidence interval based on the *t* distribution values for 95 percent confidence level:

$$x = (t * std.error) + \bar{x}$$
$$x = (-2.57 * 270.26) + 27,880$$
$$x = 27185.43$$

$$x = (t * std.error) + \bar{x}$$
$$x = (2.57 * 270.26) + 27,880$$
$$x = 28574.57$$

As you can see, the range of the values is much larger than for a confidence interval based on a much larger sample. Even so, the actual mean for the population (27,875) still is within this range. So you're pretty lucky using such a small sample size.

Watch Out!

Sometimes the actual mean value of your population won't be contained in your confidence interval. If you use a .05 level of significance (which is equivalent to a 95 percent confidence level), you still have a chance of error and that implies your sample mean could be misrepresentative of the actual value you're trying to estimate. This chance for error (accepting a value that actually is a false representation, which you'll learn more about in the next chapter) should always be considered; especially when your sample is very small, but also when the sample is large. Always remember: Statistical estimators are only approximation—not absolute fact. And sometimes they're downright wrong.

There is a lot more math involved to prove what we just discussed for large and small samples; I'm not going to cover all that here. You can find detailed proof and explanations in larger textbooks on statistics if you want to know more. For now it's most important that you understand the meaning of the important terms, these being sampling error (standard error of the mean), confidence level, and the confidence interval).

With these terms in mind, and if you think you're ready to go on, I'm going to use the concepts you've learned in this and previous chapters to actually test a hypothesis made in your business research. It's all waiting for you in the next chapter.

The Least You Need to Know

➤ A confidence interval is the range of values that a population parameter (for example, the mean) could take at a desired level of probability.

➤ In business, and social sciences in general, it is common to calculate confidence intervals that have a 95 percent chance of containing the true population value.

➤ Confidence intervals enable you to estimate population means from sample means.

➤ Statistical inference techniques, such as estimating a population mean from a sample, are not valid with nonrandom samples.

➤ A confidence level is the degree associated with a confidence interval; it also is the probability that the confidence interval will contain the actual value of the parameter in question.

➤ The standard error of the mean is the standard deviation of the sample mean in question.

➤ The accuracy of a statistic from a random sample depends on the size of the sample; not the size of the population.

➤ All statistics have a standard error associated with them.

➤ When a sample is smaller than 30 cases ($n<30$) and the distribution is assumed to be bell shaped, you must use special statistics (the t distribution) instead of the standard normal distribution z-scores to estimate your confidence intervals.

Chapter 13

Testing Your Hypothesis

In This Chapter

➤ Stating your hypothesis

➤ Understanding the role of the null and alternative hypotheses

➤ Reviewing the standard steps for testing a hypothesis

➤ Using z-scores (again) to reject of accept the null hypothesis

---

In Chapter 11, "Eliminating the Bias in Your Research," I discussed a great deal about research in business and its importance. One of the most common uses of research in business is to answer questions that can help you make better decisions. And for statistics to be useful in interpreting the data you gather in your research, it helps if you phrase your questions in terms that relate to statistical tests by using specific variables and quantities.

Using the Normal Distribution to Answer Questions

If you want statistics to be truly useful in answering your research questions, your questions can be worded like this: What percent of (some variable) lies beyond (or between or ahead of) some value? Many questions in business can be formulated in this manner. Here are some examples:

➤ As a percentage of production, how many batteries are coming off the production line that are within the 12-volt specification, plus or minus .1 volts? Alternatively, what percentage of batteries produced are defective?

➤ How many new employee applicants will qualify for the jobs by passing our initial entrance examination with a score of 75 or better?

➤ What percentage of the customer population will respond favorably to the new product packaging?

➤ What percentage of the potential customer population will find our product superior to that of our main competitor?

As you've learned already, you can answer these types of questions using the standard normal curve and the associated z-scores—if you know the mean of the responses and the standard deviation. As you might recall, the process involves these steps:

1. Translate critical values into z-scores.

2. Look up critical areas on a table of standard normal z-scores.

3. Come to a conclusion based on the value of the variable.

Here's an example to refresh your memory: How many applicants will pass the entrance exam by a score of more than 75? This is a one-tailed analysis—because we aren't looking at the people who get less than 75. You know from calculating the averages of all past applicants that the mean score on the entrance exam is 70 and the standard deviation is 5.

The critical value to answer this question is 75. This value must be translated into a z-score so you can look it up in a standard normal table (such as the one at the end of the book). To convert the score of 75 into a z-score, subtract the mean from that value; then divide by the standard deviation. Here's the equation:

$$z = \left(x - \bar{x}\right) / s$$
$$z = \left(75 - 70\right) / 5 = 1$$

A z=1 means that 84.13 percent of the applicants taking the test will get 75 or less and 15.87 percent of the applicants would score more than 75. The following figure shows a standard curve that represents this answer.

You also could have done a two-tailed test to answer a different question. Suppose you wanted to know how many people will get scores of less than 65 and more than 75? The average (mean) still is 70 and the standard deviation still is 5 for this example.

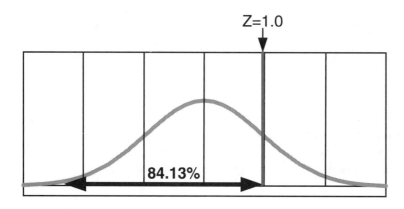

*One-tailed test for em-
ployees with scores above
75.*

Here's how you'd figure it out:

$$z = (x - \bar{x}) / s$$
$$z = (75 - 70) / 5 = 1$$
$$z = (65 - 70) / 5 = -1$$

Thus, 15.87 percent of the people taking the test would get more than 75, based on a
z=1; 15.87 percent would get less than 65 on the entrance exam based on a z=1. The
following figure shows the standard curve for this distribution.

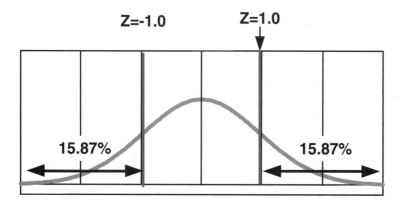

*Two-tailed test for em-
ployees scores under 65
and over 75.*

All this means is that when data is ratio or interval, the frequency distribution for the data variable is symmetrical or bell-shaped. Further, the percent of total cases within 1, 2, and 3 standard deviations of the mean data value corresponds to the standard normal curve. The use of the normal distribution is a good model for understanding the frequency distribution of the variable.

For most frequency distributions of a large number of cases (more than 30), the normal distribution is assumed when you're answering questions about a frequency distribution, as was done in the above examples. This generally is a good assumption, because the results of statistical testing are not significantly affected by slightly skewed (nonnormal) data (at least most of the time).

Stating Hypotheses to Test Assumptions

Sometimes you're not asking simple questions such as those we've been talking about. Instead, you're testing an assumption about a population parameter; this is called a *hypothesis,* as we've previously discussed. For example, you might have a hypothesis that the mean monthly commission for your regional sales force is $3,000. Because the cost of locating and interviewing every salesperson in the regions would be exorbitant, instead you select a random sample from the population (as discussed in the last two chapters) to test the validity of your hypothesis ($\mu =$ $3,000). You calculate simple statistics and then, based on certain decision rules, either accept or reject the hypothesis.

Statistical Wisdom

The terms *hypothesis testing* and *testing a hypothesis* are used interchangeably in statistics books.

Testing scientific hypotheses in this way is one of the more common uses of statistics. The process, as you just saw, and in the steps you'll learn in the following, is very similar to the steps we used for answering the preceding questions using the z-scores as a test statistic.

Using a Five-Step Procedure for Testing a Hypothesis

To test a hypothesis, generally there is a five-step process used by most businesspeople and researchers that systematizes the testing of the hypothesis. When you get to step five, you are ready to reject or accept the hypothesis. However, know that hypothesis testing does not prove that something is absolutely true. It is not like the proofs that mathematicians use. Instead, accepting a hypothesis proves only that the conclusion is "proof beyond a reasonable doubt."

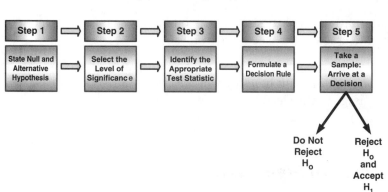

Five Steps for Testing a Hypothesis

Testing a hypothesis with five standard steps.

Step 1: State the Null and Alternative Hypothesis

First determine a research hypothesis that states an expectation or assumption to be test; then derive a statement that is the opposite of the research hypothesis. This statement is called the *null hypothesis.* In notation the null hypothesis is represented like this: H_o. The capital H stands for hypothesis and the subscript zero implies *no difference.* The null hypothesis often works like this: "There is no significant difference between ..." or "The mean strength of the steel is not significantly different from ..." There usually is a "not" or a "no" term in the null hypothesis.

It is the null hypothesis that actually is tested; not the research hypothesis or the assumption. The null hypothesis is developed only for testing. You either reject or fail to reject the null hypothesis. If the null hypothesis can be rejected, that is taken as convincing evidence in support of the *research hypothesis.* Remember that the research hypothesis is the hypothesis that you actually want to prove or disprove.

The research hypothesis also is called the *alternative hypothesis.* In notation, the alternate hypothesis, noted as H_a, where H still means hypothesis and the subscript a means alternative. It also is

Statistical Wisdom

The null hypothesis is a statement that is not rejected if the sample data fail to provide convincing evidence that it is false.

written as H_1 and pronounced as "H sub-one." At first this might seem confusing but you'll get used to it. You're actually trying to reject the null hypothesis to strongly support the alternative hypothesis.

Here is a simple hypothesis in H_0 and H_1 notation:

➤ **The research (alternative) hypothesis:** The 12-volt batteries last an average of 14 hours in full-time usage in the electric train toy.

In notation: $H_1 : \mu_1 = \mu_2$

➤ **The null hypothesis:** The 12-volt batteries will not last for an average of 14 hours in full-time usage in the electric train toy.

In notation: $H_0 : \mu_1 \neq \mu_2$

Step 2: Select a Level of Significance

The level of *significance* is the risk level you are taking of rejecting the null hypothesis when it really is true. The level of significance is designated by the Greek letter alpha (α). There is not one level of significance applied to all tests. The researcher makes a decision to use the .05 level (often stated as the 5 percent level), the .10 level, the .01 level, or any other level between 0 and 1. It is traditional to use the .05 level for consumer-related research, .01 for production quality assurance, and the .10 level in political polls. The level of significance must be decided *before* you begin collecting sample data.

Watch Out!

Because individual tests rarely are conclusive, usually it is not stated that a research hypothesis as been "proved"; only that is has been strongly supported.

The level of significance is important because it indicates the risk of either rejecting the null hypothesis when it is true, or accepting the null hypothesis when it is false. When you reject the null hypotheses, H_0, when it is true, you might make incorrect decisions based on the alternative hypothesis, H_1, which actually is false. This is called a *Type I* error. The probability of a type one error also is represented by the Greek letter alpha (α). This means you rejected a true hypothesis. If you accept the null hypothesis when it is false, this is called a *Type II* error. The Type II error is designated by the Greek letter beta (β).

A related concept is *power*—the probability that a test will reject a null hypothesis when in fact it is false. Power is simply 1 minus the Type II error rate; high power is desirable. However, like β, power can be difficult to estimate accurately, although increasing the sample size always increases power (assuming the sample is random, of course).

The following table helps you keep the Type I and Type II errors clear in your mind.

Null Hypothesis	Researcher	
	Accepts H_o	Rejects H_o
H_o is true	Correct decision	Type I error
H_o is false	Type II error	Correct decision

Because researchers cannot study every item, case, or individual in a large population, there is always a possibility of two types of error—a Type I error when the null hypothesis is rejected incorrectly and a Type II error when the null hypothesis is accepted incorrectly.

There are several ways to refer to the significance level of a statistical test; it is important to be familiar with all of them. The following statements pertaining to significance level all are equivalent in meaning:

➤ The result is significant at the .05 level.

➤ There is 95 percent certainty that the result is not due to chance.

➤ The *p*-value is .05.

➤ The Type I error rate is .05.

➤ α =.05.

➤ The alpha level is .05.

➤ The confidence level is 95 percent (Do you remember this from the last chapter?).

Step 3: Compute the Test Statistic

Now that you have the null and alternative hypotheses and a level of significance, you need to compute the *test statistic*. There are many test statistics; for this chapter we'll use z from the z-test for the test statistic. However, in the following chapters you'll learn other test statistics, such as *t, F,* and chi square (x^2).

In testing a hypothesis test that is testing for the mean (μ), the test statistic z is computed like this:

$$z = \frac{\overline{X} - \mu}{\sigma / \sqrt{n}}$$

Statistical Lingo

A **test statistic** is a value derived from sample information and used to determine whether to reject or accept the null hypothesis.

To use the z–value to test the mean in this way, the sample mean ($\overline{X}$), is assumed to be normally distributed, and reasonably large, where $\mu_{\overline{X}}$ is equal to μ, and a standard deviation of $\sigma_{\overline{x}}$ is equal to $\sigma / \sqrt{n}$. Thus, you can determine whether the difference between μ and $\overline{X}$ is statistically significant by finding the number of standard deviations $\overline{X}$ is from μ, using the previous formula. (I'll provide an example of how this is done a little later in this chapter.)

Step 4: Formulate the Decision Rule

You must state a rule that specifies the conditions under which the null hypothesis is rejected and the conditions under which the null hypothesis is not rejected. Again we use a standard normal curve to help illustrate the area of rejection and the critical value used to determine that value. This area of rejection defines the location of all the values that are so large or small that the probability of their occurrence under a true null hypothesis is extremely remote.

The following diagram illustrates a sample distribution for the statistic z, with a one-way, right-tailed test at the .05 level of significance.

Sampling distribution for the z statistic; right-tailed test at .05 level of significance.

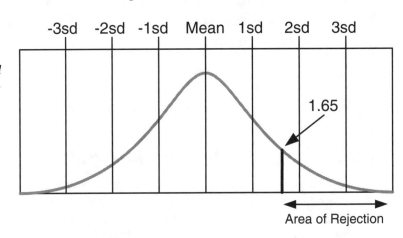

You should notice some important aspects of the diagram:

➤ The sampling distribution of the z statistic is normally distributed.

➤ The .05 level of significance, which determines the z statistic being used (in this case 1.65), is selected.

➤ The area of rejection is to the right of 1.65 standard deviations.

➤ The area in which the null hypothesis is not rejected is to the left of 1.65 standard deviations.

➤ This is a one-tailed test that is interested only in values above a certain point of probability. You already know the difference between a one-tailed and a two-tailed test (as used in the example provided at the beginning of this chapter).

Step 5: Make Your Decision

Finally, you have the information you need to make your decision. This is the final step in hypothesis testing. If you look at the preceding diagram, based on sample information, pretend the z statistic is calculated to be 2.34. At the illustrated .05 level of significance, the null hypothesis would be rejected (meaning the alternative hypothesis has a very good chance of being correct). It is very unlikely that a value this large is due to sampling variation (random chance).

However, if the z-value is calculated to be .083, the null hypothesis will not be rejected. It would be reasoned that such a small computer value could be attributed to chance; thus the value is not significant at the .05 level.

As you read formal reports that use hypothesis testing, you'll note that some researchers prefer to phrase the decision of accepting the null hypothesis like this: "We fail to reject the H_0," or "We do not reject H_0," or "The sample results do not allow us to reject H_0." This is a way of covering your conclusion because of the possible error when H_0 is accepted incorrectly. (Yes, it sounds like waffling, but because statistics is not a perfect science, many researchers prefer to make the possibility of error in judgment very clear from the onset.)

Statistical Lingo

You may have heard the term **critical value** in general discussions about business performance, but it's important to emphasize the meaning of the term here as it pertains to hypothesis testing. The critical value in hypothesis testing is the dividing point between the region (on a standard curve) where the null hypothesis is rejected and the region where the null hypothesis is not rejected.

Understanding the p-Value in Hypothesis Testing

The statistical significance you choose for the test of your hypothesis is the likelihood of obtaining a given result by chance. The concept has already been introduced many times using the terms *probability, area of the curve,* and *Type I error rate.* Another common representation of significance is the p for probability, which you saw in the previous chapter when we examined testing the validity of samples. The p-value also is a number between 0 and 1, like the statistical significance mentioned earlier.

But another value for p, called the p-value, is not exactly the same as the significance level. Instead, it is a comparison of the significance level with the probability of observing a sample value as extreme as, or more extreme than, the value observed in a test result, assuming that the null hypothesis is true.

In testing a hypothesis, you compare the test statistic to a critical value. This critical value allows you to make a decision to either reject or accept the null hypothesis. In recent years, because of the availability of computer software for statistics, additional information often is reported on the strength of the rejection of the null hypothesis—this is the *p*-value. This is a value that answers how confident you were in rejecting the null hypothesis.

A *p*-value is a way to express the odds that H_0 is not true (even when you assume it is). I'm not going to cover the calculation of the *p*-value here, but it is important to know that if the *p*-value is less than the significance level, you should reject H_0. If it is greater than the significance level, do not reject H_0. If you use the *p*-value in your testing in addition to the critical value of the test statistic, here are some guidelines:

If the *p*-value is less than ...

.10 you have some evidence that H_0 is not true.

.05 you have strong evidence that H_0 is not true.

.01 you have very strong evidence that H_0 is not true.

.001 you have extremely strong evidence that H_0 is not true.

Testing a Hypothesis

Let's discuss hypothesis testing for a large sample when the population standard deviation is known. This can only be done when the population is small enough to be able to calculate an actual population mean. Here are the types of questions you'd answer that involve a population mean:

➤ Is the mean voltage of the batteries being manufactured at least 12.1?

➤ Is the mean amount of credit owed to us by our customers more than $5,000?

➤ Is the mean monthly production of batteries at the Pittsburgh factory 2000?

Here's the scenario: The vice president of production opened the Pittsburgh plant 15 months ago. She measured the production rate over the first 3 months and found the monthly average production to be 2000 with a standard deviation of 21. Now she wants to know whether the mean production level at the Pittsburgh plant is different from 2000 at the .01 significance level for the last year, not including these first three months. Let's use the five-step hypothesis testing process to answer the last question in the preceding list:

1. The null hypothesis is "The population mean is 2000." The alternate hypothesis is "The mean is different from 2000" or "The mean is not 2000." These two hypotheses are written:

$H_o : \mu = 2000$

$H_1 : \mu \neq 2000$

This is a two-tailed test because the alternate hypothesis does not state a direction about the mean being either greater than or less than 2000. The vice president of production wants to find out only whether production is different from 2000.

2. The vice president has already stated the level of significance that should be used (as is common with production research). This is the .01 level of significance. This is α, the probability of committing a Type I error (the probability of rejecting a true hypothesis).

3. You decide to use the z statistic for this type of problem (and correctly so!). Transforming the production data to standard z-values permits the hypothesis to be tested.

4. The decision rule is determined by finding the critical value of z from a z-table (as you've done before for other problems). There is a z-table at the back of this book in Appendix C, "Sample Statistical Tables," for you to use. Because this is a two-tailed test, half of .01, or .005, is in each tail as the region of rejection. Using the table, you'll find that this equals 2.58 and –2.58. The decision rule can be worded like this: You can reject the null hypothesis and accept the alternative hypothesis if the computer value of z does not fall in the region between –2.58 and +2.58 standard deviations from the mean value of monthly production. You should not reject the null hypothesis if z falls between –2.58 and +2.58 standard deviations of the mean value of monthly production.

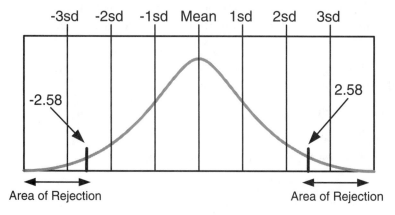

Regions of rejection at the .01 significance level for a two-tailed test.

5. Now take a sample from the monthly production rates. In this case you can sample all 12 months. Then compute z and arrive at a decision based on the rule you established in Step 4, to reject or accept H_o.

You find that the mean production numbers for the 12 months are these:

2005, 2212, 2015, 2065, 2013, 2056, 2012, 2104, 2145, 2002

The average for production over the 12 months is 2070. The standard deviation for production is 72. We then can use the formula for calculating the Z-statistic:

$$z = \frac{\overline{X} - \mu}{\sigma / \sqrt{n}} = \frac{2070 - 2000}{72\sqrt{12}} = \frac{70}{20.78} = 3.369$$

In this case the Z-score is 3.369 and you reject the null hypothesis. (By the way, you also could have used the confidence interval approach from the last chapter. The conclusion about production would have been the same.) Assume that the alternate hypothesis is correct and production is not 2000, but in this case it is greater than 2000 each month.

Technically, what you did in this hypothesis test was fail to prove the null hypothesis at the .01 significance level. This is not the same thing as proving the null hypothesis false or the alternate hypothesis true; it's just that the probability points to the alternate hypothesis being true.

Try One on Your Own

Why not try testing a hypothesis on your own? Here are the facts for the questions that follow. You have learned that the mean annual turnover rate of cases of 12-volt batteries is 6, meaning the cases of 12-volt batteries turn over 6 times a year. The standard deviation is 0.5. You need to know whether the turnover has changed and is not still 6.0—as this would affect your production needs one way or the other. The significance level you choose to solve this problem is .05.

You have gathered the following data already: A random sample of cases of the 12-volt batteries showed a mean turnover of 5.84 for this year.

Now, solve the following problems:

1. State the null and alternative hypotheses.
2. What is the probability of a Type I error, given the .05 significance level?
3. Give the formula for the appropriate test statistic.
4. State the decision rule you'll use.
5. Should you reject the hypothesis that the population mean is 6.0? Interpret the result.

Have fun! The answers are in Appendix A, "Answer Key."

Now you know what hypothesis testing is all about. You'll be learning more examples of statistics that can be used in hypothesis testing in the next few chapters. Starting in the next chapter you're going to learn a new statistic called chi square—another test you can use with the five-step hypothesis testing process you've just learned.

The Least You Need to Know

➤ The objective of hypothesis testing is to check the validity of an assumption or statement about a population parameter.

➤ There are five steps in hypothesis testing.

➤ The level of significance, designated by the Greek letter alpha (α), is the risk level you are taking by rejecting the null hypothesis when it really is true.

➤ The z-test can be used in testing hypotheses, especially those involving means; however, there are many others used for other types of hypotheses tests.

➤ A p-value is the probability that the value of a test statistic is as large or larger than that gathered when the null hypothesis is true.

Chapter 14

Learning from Contingency Tables

In This Chapter

➤ Knowing the difference between a parametric and a nonparametric test

➤ Understanding how contingency tables can be used to represent data

➤ Discovering relationships between nominal variables

➤ Recognizing contingency tables that show positive, negative, and no relationship

➤ Using the goodness of fit test

➤ Using the chi square statistic to test your hypothesis

Until now we've discussed making inferences with ratio and interval data; however, not all hypotheses use these types of data. Some use data that is nominal or ordinal in nature. Tests of hypotheses concerned with nominal or ordinal data are called *nonparametric* or *distribution-free* tests. The latter term implies that the results are free of the assumptions about distribution of the parent population, which we've discussed so much in this book. In general, these distribution-free tests are relatively easy to perform; likewise, the computations are relatively simple.

To better understand nonparametric data and distribution-free tests, it helps to start by understanding how contingency tables can be used to represent nominal data.

How to Create a Contingency Table

To develop a *contingency table* you must have two or more nominal variables (remember these from Chapter 1, "Statistics and Business Go Hand in Hand"?), and more than 10 expected cases for every possible combination of values in the table. When you think of contingency tables, visualize a spreadsheet. The rows represent values of one variable; the columns represent the values of another variable. Each *cell* (as it's called in a spreadsheet) is the interaction of a row and a column.

Statistical Lingo

A **contingency table** is a statistical table that displays the observed frequencies of data elements classified according to two variables. The rows indicate one variable; the columns indicate the other variable.

You can use contingency tables to discover relationships between concepts. For example, you might want to test whether the eastern region has small, medium, or large orders compared to the western region. Note that you are coding the information in nominal terms for the table; not numeric ones. Another example you might want to test is whether specific types of your batteries are always associated with the sales of another product such as a toy, home improvement tool, or lighting devices such as flashlights. You could classify the batteries as Battery 1, Battery 2, and Battery 3, and code the products as Toy, Home Tool, and Lighting.

To find the significance of these relationships, you'll use a test statistic called *chi square* (pronounced "kye" square), also called the *goodness of fit test,* which is positively skewed in general. Not surprisingly, as the number of degrees of freedom increases, the distribution begins to approximate the normal distribution. You don't really need to understand this now; instead let's look at some example contingency tables.

Statistical Lingo

The **chi square test,** also called the **goodness of fit test,** was developed by Karl Pearson in the early 1900s. It can be used for any level of data but commonly is used to test the significance of equal expected frequencies. The goodness of fit test is one of the most commonly used nonparametric tests.

A Positive Relationship Example

The following contingency tables are based on customer satisfaction with four of your new product proposals and the internal marketing staff's satisfaction with each of the four new product proposals. There is a contingency table for each set of evaluations. It's easy to do; all you have to do is count the number of cases for each set of values. For the following examples, imagine you have asked 70 customers and 70 members of your marketing staff about their satisfaction with the new product designs. Each person can give one of two answers: high satisfaction or low satisfaction.

The following table shows you the various responses from the customers and the marketing staff totaled in a contingency table. Notice the strong predictive power of responses on the high and low values.

Product 1 Contingency Table

Staff's Satisfaction with the Product	Customer's Satisfaction with the Product		
	Low	High	Total
Low	30	7	37
High	13	90	103
Total	43	97	140

There is a strong positive relationship in this contingency diagram because knowing either variable (from the customer or the marketing staff) enables you to predict the other variable. In other words, when the marketing staff satisfaction is high, the customer satisfaction also is high. The key to understanding this is to recognize when rows and columns do or do not show the same proportions as total rows and columns.

A Negative Value Contingency Table

Here's an example for Product 2; the relationship now is negative. If the value of one variable is known, the other will be the opposite relative value. Notice that the totals of the rows and columns are the same as in the positive example.

Product 2 Contingency Table

Staff's Satisfaction with the Product	Customer's Satisfaction with the Product		
	Low	High	Total
Low	13	90	103
High	30	7	37
Total	43	97	140

Contingency Examples with No Relationship

When the value of one variable in a contingency table really doesn't help you predict the value of the other variable, your contingency table has *no relationship* among the variables. Here are two examples of such tables with no relationship, at least not a strong, obvious relationship. In the following table the number of cases in each cell is exactly as predicted. Exactly the same number of marketing staff and customers has low and high satisfaction with the product.

Product 3 Contingency Table

Staff's Satisfaction with the Product	Customer's Satisfaction with the Product		
	Low	High	Total
Low	35	35	70
High	35	35	70
Total	70	70	140

In the following table, you can't really predict the value of one variable from the other. The relationship is not obvious, if there is one, so this still is a table with no relationship.

Product 4 Contingency Table

Staff's Satisfaction with the Product	Customer's Satisfaction with the Product		
	Low	High	Total
Low	35	35	70
High	35	35	70
Total	70	70	140

How Confident Are You in These Conclusions?

Of course in some contingency tables, such as those for Products 1 and 2, it's easy to say that strong predictive power exists. How strong is that power? In the table for Product 4, it isn't really clear whether there is no relationship at all. To find out whether your results are significant or how significant they are, you'll need to do some calculations. (I bet you knew *that* was coming.) Here are the steps:

1. Develop a contingency table for the data. You know how to do this after reading the previous section.

2. Create a table containing the expected number of cases, as if there were no relationship between the two variables. This is quite simple: The row, column, and table totals will be the same. (The example for Product 3 is an example of such a table.) Here is the calculation if you can't do it in your head (and often you can't when the numbers are large):

$$\text{expected \# of cases} = \frac{\text{row} \times \text{column total}}{\text{table total}}$$

Remember: The expected number of cases is important. You must calculate it for each cell in the table based on your sample observations (such as row total and column table). If the number of expected cases in any cell is less than 5, using chi square analysis (which is what we'll be doing) is inappropriate. Also, if any cell in a 2×2 contingency table has an expected value of less than 10, you should refer to a more advanced book for the corrections required to the chi square formula. In both cases you can reclassify the data into fewer categories, increase the number of cases in your sample, or do both things to improve the validity of your analysis.

3. Calculate a test statistic called chi square ($x2$). Chi square is a measure of the difference between the number of cases you observed and the number of cases you expected to observe if there was no relationship between the variables. This is a comparison of the first table in Step 1 and the table created in Step 2.

    Here is the formula for calculating chi square. The formula says to subtract the actual number of observations from the expected number of observations, square the result, and divide by the expected number. Total this figure for all the cells: that's what the capital sigma (Σ) means at the beginning of the equation.

$$x^2 = \Sigma \left(\frac{\left(\text{actual} - \text{expected}^2 \right)}{\text{expected}} \right)$$

Watch Out!

When calculating the values to be used in calculating chi square, don't use the row, column, or table totals—only the cell values and cell expectations.

The larger the chi square statistic, the more likely there is a strong relationship between the variables. You must examine the table to understand the direction of the statistic (positive, negative, or none).

4. After calculating the chi square statistic, you'll need to determine the degrees of freedom. This is related to the number of rows and columns in the table. Quite simply you multiply the number of columns minus 1 by the number of rows minus 1. The calculation looks like this:

degrees of freedom = (number of columns – 1) × (number of rows – 1)

The examples thus far all are 2×2 tables, so the degrees of freedom are always $(2 - 1) \times (2 - 1)$ or 1.

5. Look up the probability in a chi square distribution table. The chi square table will show the probability associated with the value and degrees of freedom you have calculated. If the probability you found for your results are 5 percent or below, the results will be considered statistically significant. (This is just like the statistical significance we talked about in the last chapter when hypothesis testing.)

Here is a sample of a chi square distribution table. You can find more complete tables in larger statistics books or on the Internet.

Rows	Columns	Degrees of Freedom	Critical Value at .05 Significance Level (.95 probability that chi square is less than this number)	Critical Value at .01 Significance Level (.01 probability that chi square is less than this number)
2	2	1	3.84	6.64
3	2	2	5.99	9.21
3	3	4	9.49	13.3
4	4	9	16.9	21.7

If you think about a very large population you're working with, such as all the people who buy batteries in the United States, you're probably selecting your table relationships from a random sample. If you think about taking many such samples from your population, you'll be able to create a frequency distribution of the chi square values for all your individual sample observations. This frequency distribution would show

how often you'd find a relationship—even when there isn't one—based on the sample you selected for your observation. (All this should sound pretty familiar by now, because it's similar to selecting means from a sample and then drawing the frequency distribution.)

Based on this hypothetical frequency of all your chi square tests, there is a probability that your chi square number would be a big or even bigger number. In this case, "statistically significant" means it is highly unlikely that the particular cases you happened to select in your sample caused the results. Another way to look at it is that you are 95 percent confident that the usual variation between samples taken would cause a difference such as the one you calculated less than 5 percent of the time, if there truly was no difference. Alternatively, you are 95 percent confident that the contingency table indicates an association between the variables based on the test statistic (chi square) you calculated.

A Real Example of How It Works

There's no doubt that it's easier to use statistical software to determine the significant results (or lack thereof) for large, complicated contingency tables. After all, there are contingency tables that can have many more than two row and two columns. But, to give you a flavor of the actual calculations, let's consider the customer's and marketing staff's evaluation of yet another product, Product 5.

In this example, we'll again use the goodness of fit test (chi square) to show whether an observed set of frequencies could have come from a hypothesized discrete (unique) distribution. In other words, the frequencies are not accidental; they are related to the relationships being compared.

Contingency Table for Product 5

Staff's Satisfaction with the Product	Customer's Satisfaction with the Product		
	Low	High	Total
Low	55	20	75
High	15	50	65
Total	70	70	140

Now you calculate the expected number of cases, assuming no relationship among the variables. The formula is

$$\text{expected \# of cases} = \frac{\text{row total} \times \text{column total}}{\text{table total}}$$

for each cell in the table.

Let's calculate the expected cases in the cell where customer equals high and staff equals high as an example.

$$\text{expected \# of cases} = \frac{\text{row total} \times \text{column total}}{\text{table total}} = \frac{65 \times 70}{140} = 32.5$$

Note that you are using the row total (65 cases) and column total (70 cases) labeled "high" in this calculation divided by the total number of cases, which is 140. Now we do this for each cell and get the following expected values for each cell in the table (shown in italic).

Expected Staff's Satisfaction with the Product	Expected Customer's Satisfaction with the Product		
	Low	High	Total
Low	*37.5*	*37.5*	70
High	*32.5*	*32.5*	65
Total	70	70	140

The next step is to calculate chi square. To do this, subtract the actual value from the expected value. Here's how the table looks after that calculation:

Expected Staff's Satisfaction with the Product	Expected Customer's Satisfaction with the Product	
	Low	High
Low	8.17	8.17
High	9.42	9.42

The chi square calculation then becomes the total of all the differences, as follows

$$8.17 + 8.17 + 9.42 + 9.42 = 35.18$$

Now, the degrees of freedom for this example equal 1, which I explained earlier; this is true for all 2 × 2 tables. If you look up the critical value for degrees of freedom for chi square with 1 degree of freedom (abbreviated as DF) at the 5 percent level, you'll see that the value is 3.8. Because the value is only 1.01, you can see that the relationship among the variables is significant beyond the .05 level. (Note that the values here have been rounded to make them simpler to understand.)

In fact, this result is significant at the .01 level (with less probability of error based on chance). The critical value for chi square with one degree of freedom at the .01 level of significance is 6.64. This means there is a probability of .99 that a chi square random variable with 1 degree of freedom will be less than 6.64. You can see that 35.18 is much larger than that. Thus, when customers think the product is good, so does the marketing staff—and vice versa. Unfortunately, this tells us that neither group agrees on their satisfaction with the product (customers or marketing staff). In this case, the information isn't very helpful in determining what to do with the product. Some additional testing will be required.

Watch Out!

If there is an unusually small expected frequency in a cell, chi square (if applied) might result in an erroneous conclusion. This can happen because the expected frequency appears in the denominator of the equation, and dividing by a very small number makes the quotient quite large. If there are only two cells, the expected frequency in each cell should be five or more. For more than two cells, χ^2 should not be used if more than 20 percent of the expected frequency cells have values of less than 5.

Using Chi Square for Other Expected Frequencies

You can use tables other than contingency tables to illustrate expected frequencies. You also can use the chi square distribution to test for a goodness of fit between expected and observed frequencies for these tables. You'll find a lot of uses for chi square tests like the one you've just seen.

When Expected Frequencies Are Equal

Here is an example of a table in which the expected frequencies are the same for all the people on the list. In this case it is expected that all of the salespeople will sell exactly 20 boxes of our batteries each day. The actual boxes sold is represented by the symbol f_0; the expected number to be sold is represented by f_e.

Salesperson	Boxes of Batteries Sold (f_0)	Expected Number Sold (f_e)
George	13	20
Sally	33	20
Fred	14	20
Marion	7	20
Kim	36	20
Sangeeta	17	20
Total	120	120

To use the chi square test statistic to test your hypothesis, this formula is easier to use than the one we used for the contingency tables. The formula looks like this:

$$X^2 = \Sigma \left(\frac{(f_0 - f_e)}{f_e} \right)$$

where k is the number of categories (so there are $k - 1$ degrees of freedom). We didn't use the number of categories (k) in the previous chi square calculation because we were using contingency tables. You can obtain the chi square statistic from Table 3 in Appendix C, "Sample Statistical Tables.". The following table presents the χ^2 calculation for the previous example.

Salesperson	Boxes of Batteries Sold (f_0)	Expected Number Sold (f_e)	$f_0 - f_e$	$(f_0 - f_e)^2$	$\dfrac{(f_0 - f_e)^2}{f_e}$
George	13	20	–7	49	2.45
Sally	33	20	13	169	8.45
Fred	14	20	–6	36	1.80
Marion	7	20	–13	169	8.45
Kim	36	20	16	256	12.80
Sangeeta	17	20	–3	9	0.45
Total	120	120			$\chi^2 = 34.40$

Because there are six categories, there are $6 - 1 = 5$ degrees of freedom. If you want to determine at the .95 level of significance that the boxes sold are within the probability of the expected number to be sold by the salespeople each day, you'll get a critical value of 11.1. This means you'll need a value equal to or less than 11.1 to accept the null hypothesis and a number greater than this to accept the alternative hypothesis. If you accept the null hypothesis your reasoning should be that the differences between the observed and expected sales per salesperson probably are due to chance.

Statistical Wisdom

Here are some things to know about chi square: (1) Chi square is never negative, because the difference between the observed and expected frequencies is always squared; (2) There is a family of chi square distributions, one for each degree of freedom; 3) The chi square distribution is positively skewed, but as the number of degrees of freedom increases, the distribution begins to approximate the normal distribution.

However, in the example calculation the value of chi square is 34.40, which puts the statistic in the rejection region beyond the critical value (11.1) at the .05 level. This means it is unlikely that the sales of battery boxes are the same among the six salespeople. (Of course this is obvious in the example—but it does show how chi square works in affirming these observations.)

Unequal Expected Frequencies and Chi Square

Often frequencies in a table are not equal. Here's an example in which chi square can help determine whether the expected but unequal frequencies are on target or out of range. Let's suppose the same salespeople had different expected sales forecasts. The following shows how the table might look.

Salesperson	Boxes of Batteries Sold (f_0)	Expected Number Sold (f_e)	$f_0 - f_e$	$(f_0 - f_e)^2$	$\dfrac{(f_0 - f_e)^2}{f_e}$
George	13	30	−17	289	1.60
Sally	33	30	3	9	.05
Fred	14	10	4	16	.09
Marion	40	40	0	0	0
Kim	36	50	−14	196	1.09
Sangeeta	17	20	−3	9	0.05
Total		**180**			$\chi^2 = \mathbf{2.88}$

Notice that the χ^2 in this example equals 2.88—much less than the critical value of 11.1. In this case the salespeople are working within their expectations and the null hypothesis is accepted (not rejected).

Try Using a Contingency Table On Your Own

Here is an example of using contingency tables and chi square to prove a hypothesis that you can try on your own: Accountants calculate accounts receivable as "current," "late," and "not collectible." Industry standards show that it is typical for about 60 percent of accounts to be "current," about 30 percent to be "late," and about 10 percent to be "not collectable." You have 500 customers in your company. Three hundred twenty are current, 120 are late, and 60 are not collectible. At the .05 significance level, are your numbers typical based on industry standards? Use the hypothesis testing method and the chi square statistic in your answer. Enjoy! You'll find the answers in Appendix A.

In this chapter, you learned how to use contingency tables and the chi square statistic to determine whether relationships among nominal variables are significant. You're more than halfway through the book at this point; by now you know a lot about representing your business data in statistical terms and testing your assumptions about business data. Congratulations! You've come a long way already.

In the next chapters, you're going to learn more ways that businesspeople can use to understand relationships including correlation, regression, and the use of the t-test. If you're ready for more statistics, just keep reading on.

The Least You Need to Know

➤ Contingency diagrams can be used to display the relationships among nominal variables.

➤ Nonparametric statistics deal with the analysis of nominal and ordinal data.

➤ The goodness of fit test, commonly called chi square, is one of the most frequently used nonparametric analyses.

➤ The value of chi square is never negative.

➤ A goodness of fit test (chi square) will show whether an observed set of frequencies could have come from a hypothesized discrete (also called *unique*) distribution.

➤ Chi square can be used as a test statistic in hypothesis testing (as discussed in the previous chapter) when you have categorized nominal or ordinal data to analyze.

Part 4

Seeing the Industry Relationships

Now that you've garnered knowledge on research, sampling, and inferential testing, you're ready to look at other questions. In business you'll often hear questions like these: Will changes in interest rates affect the demand for our new four-wheel-drive trucks? How does the age of our equipment affect production output? Do customers purchase more products because of their location on the retail shelves?

These questions look at relationships between two quantities or things. To understand how to answer these questions, and then move on to predicting outcomes in the future, you need to understand the concepts of correlation and regression.

You'll also need to solve other dilemmas in business, such as knowing if your customers in different parts of the country have the same or different buying patterns, or if your suppliers in China produce the same quality widgets as those in the United States and Europe. To do these things, you'll need to compare data and analyze the variance in results.

You'll learn how to do all these things in this section. Understanding relationships in business is key to understanding what's going on. However, you can't start understanding the relationships or answering the questions until you get started, so let's do just that.

Chapter 15

Recognizing the Relationships of Business Variables

In This Chapter

➤ Understanding the concept of correlation

➤ Showing the direction of a correlation with a scatterplot

➤ Recognizing positive, negative, and uncorrelated trends in a scatterplot

➤ Using Pearson's product moment coefficient (the correlation coefficient)

➤ Employing simple linear regression to predict the value of a variable

---

In the last chapter you learned about the chi square statistic. You also explored the way variables might have predictive power over the value of another variable. As you recall, chi square is a nonparametric statistic that can be used when assumptions about the normal distribution of a population cannot be met or when the level of measurement is ordinal or less. (Note: Nonparametric tests are less powerful than parametric tests.)

Now let's consider how two index or two ordinal variables might relate to each other—and have predictive power over one another. This means we're back into the world of parametric tests and inferences. Because we're going to be looking at two variables, it's also called *bivariate* analysis. (Bi, as you know, stands for two, like the two wheels an a *bicycle*).

Starting with Correlation of Business Variables

Let's start with a discussion of correlation. Correlation is a word that connotes a relationship between one or more things. Suppose you have observations of the following monthly production numbers on product wrapping machines of various ages as shown in the following table.

Machine	1	2	3	4	5	6	7	8	9	10
Age of Machine	5	10	4	8	2	7	9	6	1	12
Production (in thousands)	5	3	8	3	9	4	5	8	12	2

Well, you might be able to visualize a relationship between the age of the machine and the number of products wrapped if you really look at the numbers. However, it's a lot easier if you plot the data using a scatter diagram (like you learned about in Chapter 3, "Visualizing Profit and Performance").

Production and age of the machine compared.

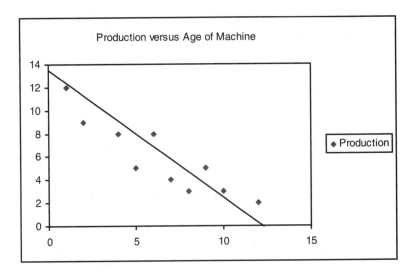

If you display the data pairs (age of the machine and production) in a *scatter plot* as shown in the preceding, you can see a definite trend. The points appear to form a line. The line goes from the upper left to the lower right of the diagram area. As you move along that line from right to left you'll see that the values on the vertical axis (age of machine) get smaller. On the other hand, the values on the horizontal axis (production) get larger. In statistical terms you could say that the two variables are inversely related: The younger the machine, the more production is realized from that machine.

Another way to talk about the two variables is to say that they are *correlated*. Correlation is a statistical measurement of this relationship. Specifically, the variables in the example are correlated in a negative direction, called a *negative correlation*. If two variables are negatively correlated, as the value of one variable increases, the value of the other decreases.

Other Relationships to Consider

You also can have variables that are positively correlated. Consider another example: Suppose you have salespeople with more experience than others. If you compare the monthly sales data with the years of experience the sales people have, you might get a scatter plot that looks like the following. This scatter plot shows a strong positive correlation—meaning that as the value of one increases, so does the value of the other.

Statistical Wisdom

To create a **scatter plot** the vertical axis (Y axis) represents one variable and the horizontal axis (X axis) represents the other. Each case or data value is represented by a dot (or other shape such as a square, triangle, or circle).

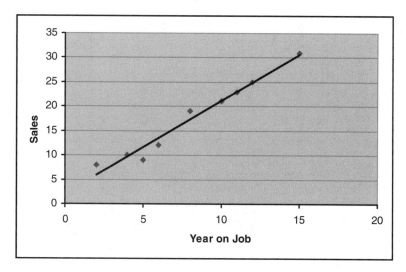

Sales experience and total sales.

If you have a perfectly positive correlation, it will look like the following scatter plot. You'd have a perfectly straight line of values, where each value of x has a perfectly correlated value of y.

Perfectly positive correlation.

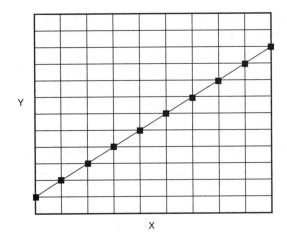

A perfectly negative correlation would have a correlation coefficient of –1.0. It would look like the following graph.

Perfectly negative correlation.

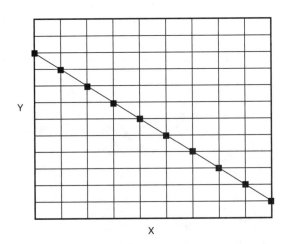

Other than positive and negative correlations, there are scattergraphs that indicate no correlation at all. In this case a pattern or relationship between the variables cannot be determined; the variables are said to be uncorrelated. However, by using statistics you might find that there is some small (and perhaps significant) relationship among the variables. The problem with scattergraphs is they can't always show the subtle correlations; only the most obvious ones.

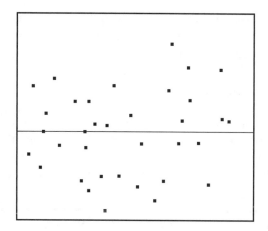

Seemingly uncorrelated variables on a scatter-graph.

Revealing Hidden Relationships with the Correlation Coefficient

To establish the true strength of a potential relationship between two variables, you would use the *correlation coefficient statistic*. Originated by Karl Pearson in 1900, the coefficient of correlation describes the strength of the relationship between two sets of interval-scaled or ration-scaled variables. This statistic is represented by the letter *r*, although often it is referred to as *Pearson's r* or the *Pearson product-moment correlation coefficient*.

The formula for the correlation coefficient is shown in the following, if you really want to know the details, but it is easily calculated with most statistics-capable computer programs, including Microsoft Excel, SPSS, and similar programs. But believe me: it's a lot of work to do it by hand, so let the computers do the work for you.)

$$r = \frac{n(\sum XY) - (\sum X)(\sum Y)}{\sqrt{\left[n(\sum X^2) - (\sum X)^2\right]\left[n(\sum y^2) - (\sum y)^2\right]}}$$

The important thing to know is what the correlation coefficient means. It is used to measure both the strength and direction of a correlation. The correlation coefficient has a value between –1.0 and 1.0. Thus, a perfect positive correlation has a correlation coefficient of 1.0. It would look like the diagram above that illustrates a perfect correlation between two variables.

A correlation is stronger if the data values swarm closely around the straight line that can be drawn through the data to indicate the direction of the correlation. The closer the data points are to forming a straight line, the stronger the correlation and the closer it will be to –.0 or 1.0. Thus, an *r* value of –.23 is considered weak, whereas if

$r = -.87$ it would be considered a strong negative relationship. On the positive side, an $r = .23$ also would be weak; an $r = .87$ considered strong. The strength of the correlation does not depend on the direction (either – or +).

An Example and What It Means

As an example, let's consider the correlation between disposable income and consumption spending, data that is publicly available from the U.S. government. The table that follows summarized both disposable income and consumption spending over a period of eleven years. The values have been rounded to make them easier to deal with.

Year	Disposable Income (in trillions of dollars)	Consumption Spending (in trillions of dollars)
1985	3.00	2.70
1986	3.19	2.89
1987	3.36	3.09
1988	3.64	3.35
1989	3.89	3.54
1990	4.17	3.84
1991	4.34	3.98
1992	4.61	4.22
1993	4.79	4.45
1994	5.02	4.70
1995	5.31	4.92

Following is a scatter plot that shows the relationship between the two numbers. I also calculated the *r* value for these two variables, which is rounded to equal 0.99—an almost totally perfect positive correlation. This obviously is a very strong relationship. In this case it means that as disposable income goes up so does consumption spending.

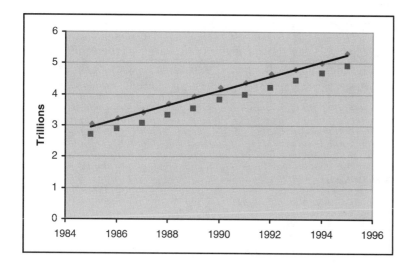

Correlation of disposable income and consumption spending.

The Coefficient of Determination

Another important calculation related to *r* is the *coefficient of determination.* Using terms such as "weak," "moderate," and "strong" is not a very precise way of defining a correlation. The coefficient of determination, equal to r^2, is more easily interpreted. Using r^2, you can say that a percentage of the variation in consumption spending is related to disposable income. In the case of the example, this percentage is about 98. Thus, you'd say that about 98 percent of the variation in consumption spending is accounted for or explained by the variation in the amount of disposable income. (Notice that I didn't use the words "caused by"—you can never assume direct causation in correlation analysis.)

Reduce the Risk

Beware of assigning direct causation to strong correlations—it's usually enough (and safer) to say that the variables are correlated. If there is a very strong relationship (*r* = .90 or more, for example) between two variables, you might be tempted to assume that an increase in one variable will *cause* a change in the other variable. A good example is the strong correlation related to the decrease in the use of donkeys for transporting goods and the increase in the number of doctoral degrees granted each year. Obviously there is no causation between these occurrences. This type of relationship is known as a *spurious correlation.*

Calculating the Significance of r

Another thing that's important to know about *r* is the significance of the result. You might want to know how significant an *r* of .99 is. The formula to test the null hypothesis (there's that hypothesis testing again) that *r* (the population correlation) = 0 is:

$$t = \frac{r\sqrt{n-2}}{\sqrt{1-r^2}}$$

In the example, this works out to:

$$t = \frac{.99\sqrt{10-2}}{\sqrt{1-.98}} = \frac{2.807}{.14} = 20.85$$

The probability of *t* can be looked up in a t table (such as the one in Appendix C, "Sample Statistical Tables") using n – 2 degrees of freedom (in this case df = 8). The probability of obtaining a *t* = 20.85 with 8 df is lower than the lowest listed probability of .0005. (Any number higher than 5.041 will do to meet that level of significance.) Thus, you must reject the null hypothesis and assume that this value for *r* did not occur by chance.

It's always important to evaluate the significance of a correlation coefficient before going any further in your analysis. An insignificant correlation might be only by chance and might not reflect anything other than sampling error.

Going Beyond Correlation to Prediction

Most of the time in business you want to know more than whether two variables are correlated; you want to know how much predictive power exists between two variables. To help you uncover these predictive relationships between two interval or ratio variables, you can use a statistics tool called *linear regression*. Although correlation is not concerned with causation in relationships, often regression is.

How Linear Regression Works

The goal of linear regression is to condense the information in two variables into the mathematical model of a straight line (like we've been talking about in correlation; thus these relationships are often called "linear" in nature). With the formula for a straight line, if you know one variable, you can predict the value of the other.

Linear regression starts with this mathematical model for a straight line:

$$y = (m \times x) + b$$

where:

> *y* = the value of the dependent variable (the one that you're trying to predict)
>
> *x* = the value of the independent variable (the value you know)
>
> *m* = the slope of the line. Based on what you've learned about correlation already, you might know that the slope of the line can be from –1.0 to 1.0. A line that indicates no relationship between the variables will have an value close to zero.
>
> *b* = a constant, which also happens to be the place on the Y axis where the line crosses, also called the *intercept*.

In the next few pages we'll discuss some examples of using linear regression to predict the value of a variable; first it's important to know that nobody does linear regression by hand. Sure, it's possible for simple problems such as those here; however, statistical and spreadsheet programs contain very easy-to-use regression capabilities. You simply need to have data entered on the two variables; then identify the data for each variable by name or range in the software program and run the regression procedures. Most software will produce scatter plots (like the ones you've seen in the preceding) and calculate the values for m, x, and b.

Further, there is a lot more math involved in a detailed linear regression analysis than you'll learn here. I'm covering only the basic concepts, so you'll understand how to interpret the results of regression studies. The regression procedure fits the best possible straight line to an array of data points, thereby providing predicted values for y. If no single line can be drawn such that all the points fall on it, what is the best line, you might ask? The best line is the one that minimizes the distance of all the data points to the line.

The most common method for determining the regression line is using a mathematical method called the *least squares principle*. This method gives what is commonly called the "best fitting straight line. The least squares principle is used by computer programs in calculating regression analysis; it is not complex, but too convoluted to go into here. If you really want to know how least squares calculations are used to calculate the straight line used in regression analysis, look it up in a textbook on basic statistics.

The Goals of Regression Analysis

Regression is another inferential procedure; thus (as you should know by now) it can be used to draw conclusions about populations based on random samples drawn from those populations. In regression analysis, you are specifically trying to predict the value of one variable from another.

Watch Out!

Here are some assumptions underlying linear regression that you should be aware of:

➤ For each group of x values, there is a group of y values. These y values are normally distributed.

➤ The means of the y values all lie on the straight line of the regression.

➤ The standard deviations of these normal y distributions are equal.

➤ The y values are statistically independent, meaning in the selection of a sample the y values selected for a particular x value do not depend on the y values for any other x values.

At this point you might realize that linear regression has similar goals to that of contingency table analysis in Chapter 14, "Learning From Contingency Tables." Both methods try to uncover relationships between two or more variables. However, remember that contingency tables use nominal (and sometime ordinal) data. Regression analysis is performed on interval or ratio data only; therefore regression analysis is a much more powerful analysis and provides a more complete picture of the relationship between the variables.

Try Some Regression Calculations on Your Own

In the following table I've filled in the first two examples of calculating the value of y, using the equation for determining a straight line provided above. Why not try the rest on your own? (The rest of the answers are in Appendix A.)

m	*x*	*c*	$y = (m \times x) + b$	Relationship? Positive or Negative
−2	3	10	4	Positive
4	2	8	16	Positive
−1	1	5		
−4	6	3		
5	3	7		
−5	2	4		

The General Form Equation

Some books and statisticians use other formulas for calculating linear regression. In general, the equations mean the same thing as the line equation you just used to fill in the blanks in the previous table. For example, in other books on statistics you will likely see the following equation used for linear regression, called the *general form* of linear regression:

$$Y' = a + bX$$

where:

Y' (read y prime) is the predicted value of the y variable for a selected x value.

a is the Y intercept. It is the estimated value of y when $X = 0$.

b is the slope of the line, or the average change in Y' for each change of one unit in the independent variable X.

X is the value of the independent variable.

Notice that the symbols are used differently, so it might be confusing, but the equation basically means the same thing as the first equation you learned for plotting a straight line.

Watch Out!

Least squares regression (which was mentioned earlier as the technique used by most computer programs) is sensitive to outliers (data points that fall far from most of the other points). You need to be wary of outliers because they can influence the regression equation greatly. Most good statistics programs on computers have methods available for reducing the influence of stray outliers in regression analysis.

Predicting Business Values

Here's an example of using simple linear regression to predict a value of importance to your business: Let's pretend you're trying to understand the battery sales again.

You've gathered data on 10 salespeople. However, you would specifically like to give the salespeople guidelines about the number of sales calls required to yield an expected sales amount. For this example you've calculated a coefficient of correlation of 0.759 and a coefficient of determination of 0.576. This means 57.6 percent of the variation in the amount of batteries sold is explained by the variation in the number of sales calls made each month.

You also calculated that the *p*-Value for your coefficient of correlation is less than .02, making the results more significant than the minimum .05 significance level you demanded. At this point you must determine the linear regression equation that will enable you to estimate sale of batteries based on sales calls.

Statistical Wisdom

Every worker needs tools. The carpenter needs a hammer and a saw; the surgeon, a scalpel; the dentist, a drill; and the researcher, an array of means by which data may be discovered and manipulated and information made meaningful. The rules of research are merely ancillary to the ultimate goal of research itself; to derive conclusions from a body of data and to discover that which was hitherto unknown.

—*Paul D. Leedy*, Practical Research, *1997*

You use a computer to determine, using the least squares equation, that the line of regression, is $Y' = 18.94 + 1.84X_1$ in thousands of dollars of batteries sold. Based on this equation, you can look at the number of salespersons' expected calls to customers, and estimate the sales (calculated in thousands of dollars) you can expect the salesperson to make next month. For example, if a salesperson makes 20 sales calls, you can expect her to sell $18.94 + (1.84 \times 20) = \$55,940$ worth of batteries next month.

You can use the same types of calculations to forecast future sales based on advertising expenditures, understand turnover rates based on employee characteristics, recognize the predicted earnings rates based on past sales levels, and make many other types of business predictions based on related variables.

The Standard Error of the Estimate

Perfect prediction in business, economics, or statistics is practically impossible. You can approximate closely, but there is always some error—even when variables are almost perfectly correlated. To understand the level of error in a regression analysis, you can use a measure called the *standard error of estimate,* which is similar to the formula for calculating the standard deviation of a sample. The standard deviation is based on squared deviations from the mean, whereas the standard error of estimate is based on squared deviations from the regression line. If the squared deviations result in a small total, the regression line is representative of the data. If the standard error is a large number, the regression line might be representative of the data.

I'm not going to go into the calculations here; however, you should know that the purpose of obtaining a standard error is to predict the range of values within which most of the samples fall. Specifically, this number will tell you how that the sample values for y are within one standard error of the regression line. The more values within this standard error, the better—and the smaller the standard error, the better yet.

The Confidence and Prediction Intervals

Thank heavens for computers, because you need even more calculations to complete a quality regression analysis. The first is the *confidence interval,* which reports the mean value of *y* for a given *x.* The second type of estimate is called a *prediction interval.* This statistic reports the range of values of *y* for a specific value of *x.* Both of these can be easily computed by a good statistics program. The point of both intervals is to look at the actual range of values the *y* can take, given specific levels of confidence such as .90, .95, or .99.

There is an important distinction between a *confidence interval* (which you learned about in Chapter 12, "Being Confident About Your Sample," and a *prediction interval.* A confidence interval refers to all cases with a given value of *x.* A prediction interval refers to a particular (specific) case for a given value of *x.* The prediction interval will have a wider spread of possible values for *y.*

Statistical Wisdom

Every college admission officer knows that applicants with high SAT scores tend to have higher college grade point averages than applicants with lower SAT scores. But the question is how *much* higher? That's what linear regression can predict.

What Happens When You Have More Variables?

The use of one independent variable to predict the dependent variable in correlation and simple linear regression analysis, which we've been discussing, ignores the relationship of other variables to the dependent variable. In more advanced statistical analysis, it's possible to examine the influence of two or more independent variables on the dependent variable. This type of analysis is called *multiple regression and correlation analysis*. If you intend to pursue this type of analysis, you should refer to a more advanced book on statistics or one of the Internet sites recommended in Chapter 21, "Advancing Your Business with Statistics."

There are a lot of pitfalls associated with multiple regression analysis. There is a risk of spurious correlations and misguided conclusions based on small effects from many independent variables that might have statistical significance but no practical importance. For this reason, I suggest that you master simple linear regression and correlation analysis before you attempt more complex, multiple regression models of the data.

In this chapter, I've focused on studying the relationship between variables and developing an equation that enables you to estimate one variable based on another. For example, now you can use statistics to answer questions such as "Is there a relationship between the amount we spend on advertising and our sales levels?" At this point you're ready to look at even more inferential and data comparison techniques, all associated with hypothesis testing, of course. In the next chapter you will read about research based on small samples using the *t*-test. You already know about the *t*-test in verifying the significance of a small sample; now you'll see the t again in some very practical business research applications.

The Least You Need to Know

➤ Scatter plots visually depict the relationship between two variables, indicating a positive, negative, or no observable correlation.

➤ Correlation analysis is a group of statistical techniques used to measure the strength of relationship between variables.

➤ The correlation coefficient is a statistical measure that can range from −1.0 to 1.0 in value. The closer the coefficient value is to either end of this range, the stronger the correlation.

➤ The square of the correlation coefficient indicates the percent of total variation explained by the relationship between the two variables being studied.

➤ Linear regression is a statistical process that uses the standard formula for a line in two-dimensional space as a model for a relationship between two concepts.

➤ The goal of linear regression is to predict the value of a dependent variable based on a known value of an independent variable.

➤ Linear regression works best when the correlation between variables is moderate to strong.

➤ Simple regression and correlation examines the relationship between two variables.

➤ To examine the influence of two or more independent variables on the dependent variable multiple regression analysis is required.

Chapter 16

Estimating the Probability of Success with the *t*-Test

In This Chapter

➤ Understanding the student's *t* distribution

➤ Differentiating between dependent and independent samples

➤ The assumptions for conducting a test of a hypothesis for a small sample

➤ Conducting tests of hypotheses for one and two means

➤ Testing a hypothesis regarding the mean difference between paired observations

---

When I presented the basics about hypothesis testing in Chapter 13, the *z* distribution was used as the test statistic. To use the *z* distribution correctly, you need to know either the population standard deviation or to have a large sample. ("Large" in statistical terms is defined as a sample of more than 30 cases or observations.)

In real practice, often there isn't time to get more than 30 observations to test your hypothesis or the population standard deviation is not known. In these cases, you still can use *s* (the sample standard deviation) to test your hypothesis, but you need to use a different test statistic—the *Student's t*, more commonly known as just the *t* distribution.

Understanding the Student's *t* Distribution

You've already been using the *t* distribution in this book; we just haven't explored how it really differs from the *z* distribution as a test statistic.

Statistical Wisdom

Many small make a great.

—*Geoffrey Chaucer (1343–1400), English poet*

Watch Out!

There is always a tradeoff between the size of the sample and the accuracy with which the sample will approximate the population mean.

Student's *t* distribution (the same old *t* distribution we've been using for sample testing and in correlation analysis) was developed by William S. Gossett, an Irish brew master for Guinness Brewery, at the beginning of the twentieth century. He used the pen name "Student" in his published papers on statistics, thus the name Student's *t*.

Gossett was concerned about the problem of using *s* (the sample standard deviation) as an estimator for σ (the population standard deviation). He was especially worried about using *s* from a very small sample.

The *t* distribution Gossett developed is more spread out than the normal *z* distribution. Like the *z* distribution, it is a continuous distribution, and is bell-shaped and symmetrical. In actuality, there is not one *t* distribution; there is a family of *t* distributions. All have the same mean of zero, but their standard deviations differ according to the sample size. For example, there is a *t* distribution for a sample size 18, 20, 22, and so on. As the sample size increases (approaches 30), the *t* distribution approaches the standard normal distribution.

As a result of the greater spread of the *t* distribution, the critical values for *t* for a given level of significance are larger in magnitude than the *z* critical values at the same level of significance. The following diagram illustrates how this works for a one-tailed test at the .05 significance level. It's important to remember that there are different significance levels for the one-tailed and two-tailed tests.

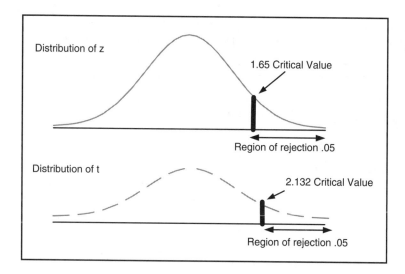

z and t distributions compared at .05 significance level.

Using *t* to Test a Mean

Here is a simple example to show you how the *t*-test can be used to test a simple business hypothesis. The quandary is that the recent production of a case of batteries has been tested and the cost was $57 to produce a case based on randomly testing 26 cases. The standard deviation is $10 a case. In the last test of the cost of a case of batteries, the cost was found to be $60 a case. Should you pass some of the supposed savings on to the customer? Well, to do this you must find out whether the savings is actual, or attributed only to chance and sampling error. To do this, you'd employ the familiar five-step hypothesis testing process:

1. **State the null and alternative hypothesis.** In this case the null hypothesis is that the population mean is at least $60. The alternative hypothesis is that the population mean is less than $60. This is a one-tailed test, because you're interested only in a reduction of cost. Therefore, the region of rejection will be in the left tail of the distribution.

2. **Select a level of significance.** In this case, you select the .01 level to a high degree of significance to avoid the error of reducing prices by mistake.

3. **Select the test statistic.** You will use the *t* distribution because the sample size is less than 30 and the population standard deviation is unknown. The formula for *t* for a one-sample test of mean is

$$t = \frac{\overline{X} - \mu}{s\sqrt{n}}$$

(If you don't recall what these symbols mean, check out Appendix B, "Statistics Formulas," for a description.)

195

4. **Formulate the decision rule.** There is a table in Appendix C for Student's *t* distribution. The leftmost column of the table is labeled *df* for *degrees of freedom*. The degrees of freedom are defined as the total number of observations in a sample minus the number of samples, expressed as *n*–1. For this example, df therefore equals 25.

   Now that you know the degrees of freedom, you can find the critical value by looking in the table at the df – 25 row at the intersection of the columns for the .01 one-tailed significance level. You'll find that the value is 2.485. Because this is a negative rejection (on the left side of the distribution), the value for the area of rejection is redefined as –2.485. A diagram of the rejection region for a *t* distribution at .01 significance level is shown in the following.

One-tailed rejection region, t distribution, .01 significance level.

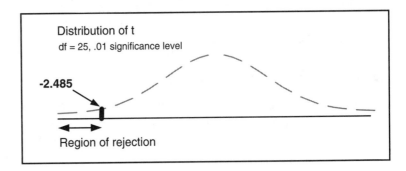

5. **Compute t and make a decision.** The value of *t* is computed as

$$\frac{57-60}{10\sqrt{26}} = -1.53$$

Because *t* = 1.53 lies to the right of the critical value of –2.485, the null hypothesis is not rejected. This means most likely that the decrease in production cost is due to chance and you shouldn't lower the price of your batteries at this point.

Comparing Two Population Means Using *t*

In the preceding example, only a single random sample was used to compare that sample to a hypothesized value of the population mean. However, what if you want to ask another type of question to determine whether two different sample means come from identical populations? For example, you might want to do this if you are comparing the results of two production processes or looking at the attitudes of customers from different parts of the country to determine whether they're the same or different.

To conduct this type of test of two independent samples, you have to make three assumptions:

1. The sampled populations both are normally (or approximately normally) distributed.

2. The two populations are independent.

3. The standard deviations of the two populations are equal.

To use the *t* statistic for this calculation of a two-sample case, pool the sample variances in order to form a single estimate of the unknown population variance. In essence, to pool the sample variances you compute a weighted mean of the two sample standard deviations; then use the value of the standard deviation for the population standard deviation. This is because we have to assume the standard deviations of the two populations are equal. Here is the calculation for *pooled variance* (in case you actually want to do the math by hand, instead of with a computer):

$$s_p^2 = \frac{(n_1 - 1)(s_1^2) + (n_2 - 1)(s_2^2)}{n_1 + n_2 - 2}$$

Using this pooled variance, here is the formula for the *t*-test using a two-sample test of means:

$$t = \frac{\overline{X}_1 - \overline{X}_2}{\sqrt{s_p^2 \left(\frac{1}{n_1} + \frac{1}{n_2}\right)}}$$

Note that the number of degrees of freedom in the test is equal to the total number of *items in the sample* minus the number of samples. Because there are two samples, there are $n_1 + n_2 - 2$ degrees of freedom.

Are the Processes the Same?

Here is a typical application of this *t*-test of two sample means. Suppose you are trying two new production processes in the battery factory. The plant managers want to know which process to use. The processes take different amounts of time when you measure them—or at least seem to at first glance. You get the following results from five tests of Process 1 and six tests of Process 2.

Process 1	Process 2
2 minutes	3 minutes
4	7
9	5
2	8
3	4
2	3
	4

To decide which process is best, you are going to test the null hypothesis that there is no real difference between Processes 1 and 2. There are 9 degrees of freedom in this experiment, calculated by 5 + 6 – 2 = 9. The critical value of *t* at the .10 level of significance you've selected for this test is 1.833. This is a two-tailed test, because you're interested in both faster and slower times.

The t Distribution Calculations

To determine the *t*-test value for this test of two processes, there are three steps:

1. Calculate the sample standard deviations. The standard deviation for Process 1 is 2.9155. The standard deviation for Process 2 is 2.0976.

2. Pool the sample variance. Using the preceding calculation, you'll get a pooled variance of 6.222.

3. Calculate *t* using the preceding formula for 2 samples. The result you'll arrive at is –0.662.

The decision you make based on this value of *t* should be to not reject the null hypothesis. This is because the value of –0.662 falls within the range of –1.833 and 1.833. You should conclude that there is not significant difference between the two production processes. Therefore, you can tell your plant managers that they can use the process their staff prefer.

If you tried to calculate this answer by hand, you're a heartier person than I am! For those who own a copy of Excel, you'll be pleased to know that the program has a procedure called "t-Test: Two Sample Assuming Equal Variances" that is very easy to use and will do all the calculations for you. Of course, other statistics programs have procedures that are similar.

Statistical Wisdom

You might have noticed that in other sections on statistics I conveniently had the value of the population standard deviation available to plug into the equations. This is one of the benefits of being the author of the book. However, it is not always indicative of the situations businesspeople face in the real world.

—*Sunny Baker*

At this point we've tested one independent sample and two independent samples; however, sometimes you'll need to test the difference between the means from two samples that are related. Two related samples also are called a *paired sample;* you'll need to perform a paired *t*-test from the following formula:

$$t = \frac{\bar{d}}{s_d\sqrt{n}}$$

Notice the new symbol in the denominator (S_d). This is the standard deviation of the differences, calculated with a formula similar to the standard deviation formula used for raw data. The exception is that $\bar{d}$, the mean of the difference between paired or related observations, is substituted for $\overline{X}$. Here's the formula for standard deviation of the difference:

$$s_d = \sqrt{\frac{\sum \bar{d}^2 - \dfrac{\left(\sum d\right)^2}{n}}{\left(n-1\right)}}$$

If it seems too complicated, don't dismay. Your computer can handle it for you. For now, it's just good to know that a special calculation for the S_d is required to the paired *t*-test. As with the other *t*-tests you should assume that the distribution of the population of differences is normal.

A Paired t-Test Example

Pretend you're the CEO of the battery factory again. Your chief financial officer wants to establish the value of your ten factories across the United States. He decides to have two expert appraisers provide an estimate of the value of the ten properties. The following table shows the results from the two appraisers.

Factory	Appraiser 1	Appraiser 2
Des Moines	135	128
Chicago	110	105
Philadelphia	131	119
San Jose	142	140
Redlands	105	98
Ontario	130	123
Newark	131	127
Cleveland	110	115
Miami	125	122
Toledo	149	145

You tell the chief financial officer to determine whether there is a significant difference at the .05 level between the two appraisers' estimates. If there isn't, you won't need to hire both of them next time you try to determine property value.

The null hypothesis the chief financial officer must test is that there is no difference in appraised values between the two appraisers. Because there are 10 factories, the degrees of freedom equals $10 - 1 = 9$. The *t*-test should be conducted at the .05 significance level for a two-tailed test because both lower and higher appraisal values are of interest. The critical value from the *t* table is found to be ±2.262. The decision rule the chief financial officer will use is to reject the null hypothesis if the computer values of *t* is less than –2.262 or greater than 2.262.

At this point (using a computer of course) the chief financial officer computes the *t*-value to be 3.305. In this case the null hypothesis is rejected, because the value is more than the right tail value of 2.262. The appraisers have different appraisals of the property; the largest difference regarding the factory in Philadelphia. Perhaps this discrepancy requires further review; maybe it wasn't such a good idea to recommend the use of only one appraiser after all.

Statistical Wisdom

The fun of testing a claim about a mean is that it requires us to stick our toe in the pool of statistical nomenclature and learn some words such as null hypothesis (which will probably not be of much use in serenading a loved one perched on a balcony).

—*Jefferson Hane Weaver*, Conquering Statistics, 1997

By the way, to find the location of the actual *p*-value for *t*, go to the *t* table at the back of the book. Look at the values for a two-tailed test and move along the row for 9 degrees of freedom. For a .01 significance level the value of t is 3.250; for a .001 significance level, the value of t is 4.781. This means the computed values for *t* of 3.305 falls between these two values. Thus, the *p*-value for *t* is less than .01 and greater than .001 level of significance. (For a refresher of *p*-values, review Chapter 13, "Testing Your Company's Hypothesis.")

Understanding Dependent and Independent Samples

It's often confusing when people new to statistics have to determine whether a sample is dependent or independent for the *t*-test or other statistical evaluations. There actually are two possible types of sources for dependent samples: When there is a measurement, then an intervention (such as a new training program or a new procedure), and then a second measurement of the sample population after the intervention; or when a pairing of observations by two different people or at two different times or locations, as in the preceding factory appraisal example.

It's important to know when a sample is dependent, because dependent samples are preferred over independent samples. This is because the variation in the sampling distribution is reduced in dependent paired samples. The standard error in paired sample tests is always smaller. This in turn leads to a larger test statistic and a greater chance of rejecting the null hypothesis. This makes the test more powerful when assessing differences of means at the same levels of significance compared to independent sample tests.

However, there is bad news about paired sample tests: The degrees of freedom are half of what they are in samples that are not paired. In most cases, this is a small price to pay for a more powerful test.

Try Using a t-Test on Your Own

To test your new skills with the *t*-test, here is a simple business problem for you to solve: Pretend you are the production manager in charge of two factories. You have the following daily results in thousands of boxes for battery production from the two plants: 9 observations for Factory 1 and 7 for Factory 2:

Factory 1	72	69	66	98	76	85	79	80	77
Factory 2	76	80	81	78	90	67	81		

At the .01 significance level, is the mean production of Factory 2 higher than that of Factory 1? What will you tell your boss? You'll find the answer in Appendix A.

In this chapter, I've focused on using the *t*-test on small samples to test whether the probability that the mean of a population and the differences between means of two populations or a paired sample are statistically significant. You saw that these inferential tests were used to answer a wide range of different questions in business. You'll likely find that using the *t*-test on small samples becomes one of your mainstays in answering your day to day research questions. Now you're ready to look at some more.

The Least You Need to Know

➤ The *t* distribution is the commonly used name for Student's *t* distribution.

➤ The *t* distribution is a test statistic used in place of the *z* distribution when the sample contains less than 30 observations and the population standard deviation is not known.

➤ The t distribution actually is a family of distributions based on the number of observations in the sample.

➤ The critical areas for the t-test are determined from a t table, like the one in Appendix C, "Sample Statistical Tables."

➤ There are different t formulas used for testing one-sample, two-sample, and paired-sample (dependent samples) observations.

➤ The *t* distribution tests can be applied to a wide variety of research questions in business when large samples are infeasible or difficult to obtain.

➤ Microsoft Excel is one example of a computer program that can do the detailed calculations for the various types of *t*-tests on one, two, or paired samples.

Chapter 17

Are These Customers the Same or Different?

In This Chapter

➤ Working with large samples and the z distribution to test means

➤ Testing the population mean with a known value of the population standard deviation

➤ Testing the population mean with an unknown value of the population standard deviation

➤ Testing two population means using a large sample

➤ Testing one and two population proportions

In many formal research projects in business you'll be using large samples to test your hypotheses, unlike the small samples you learned to test in the last chapter. You'll be collecting large random samples (remember: Large means more than 30 cases or observations) and completing your hypothesis testing based on these samples.

You've already seen some uses of the z statistic to test mean values on large samples in other chapters. In this chapter we'll focus on more ways to use the z-test to compare means and proportions. This way you can start answering questions such as, "Are these two customer groups representative of the same purchase behaviors or preferences or different ones?" These types of questions can be applied to a wide range of business dilemmas; not just customer behavior. For example, you can use these tests for small populations—only with a large sample, your statistical comparisons will be more powerful; thus less suspect.

Testing the Mean, Standard Deviation Known

Let's review what we learned in Chapter 13, "Testing Your Hypothesis." Testing a mean from a large sample might be used to answer questions like: Is the mean production from the Pittsburgh factory really 350,000 units a day? Or are the customers really satisfied an average of 93 percent of the time? Using the same five-step hypothesis testing procedure you learned in Chapter 13, you can transform a known mean value and standard deviation into *z-values*. To compute the *z*-value with a known standard deviation, use this formula:

$$z = \frac{\overline{X} - \mu}{\sigma\sqrt{n}}$$

Statistical Wisdom

Utility is our national shibboleth: the savior of the American businessman is *fact* and his uterine half-brother, *statistics*.

—Edward Dahlberg, The Carnal Myth, 1968

You can use this one sample test of a mean for both one-tailed and two-tailed tests. Simply compare the *z*-score obtained from your test sample with the critical value based on the *z*-score table (provided in Appendix C, "Sample Statistical Tables") for your selected significance level for the type of *t*-test (one-tailed or two-tailed). (Review Chapter 13 if you don't recall how it all works.)

Using z-Tests When the Standard Deviation Is Unknown

In reality, you almost never know the population standard deviation. A population standard deviation can be known, or accurately estimated, only when based on prior studies or assumptions about the sample standard deviation or if the population is small enough to measure in totality. As long as the sample size is 30 or more, there's good news. You can substitute the sample standard deviation for the population standard deviation and come up with results that are almost as accurate. Here's the *z* statistic formula you'd use (and this is the one you'll use most of the time in business research using large samples):

$$z = \frac{\overline{X} - \mu}{s\sqrt{n}}$$

Notice that the only difference is in the denominator, where the sample standard deviation is shown instead of the symbol for the population standard deviation. The rest of the test is the same, so you already know how to use this statistic to test the significance of a mean value from a single large sample. It's exactly the same process used in Chapter 13.

But what happens when you have two means to test? Well, you already know how to do that with small samples. For large samples the process is pretty much that same, only you'll be using the z statistic in place of the t statistic. Here is the z statistic formula you'd use to test the difference between two means:

$$z = \frac{\overline{X}_1 - \overline{X}_2}{\sqrt{\dfrac{s_1^2}{n_1} + \dfrac{s_2^2}{n_2}}}$$

Statistical Wisdom

Here's the rule for bargains: "Do other men, for they would do you." That's the true business precept.

—*Charles Dickens (1812–1870), British novelist*

This formula would enable you to answer questions about two mean values being the same or different. Notice that the formula uses the sample variances (sample deviation squared); not the population variances for the two samples. Let's look at an example to see how it works.

What's the Investment Turnover?

Pretend for a moment that you're a financial analyst. You're interested in the turnover of technology-related stocks compared to so-called blue-chip stocks that aren't technology related. You select 32 blue-chip stocks and 49 technology stocks. The mean turnover rate of the blue-chip stocks is 31.4 percent and the standard deviation is 5.1 percent. For the technology stocks, the mean rate of turnover was calculated to be 34.9 percent; the standard deviation 6.7 percent. At the .01 level of significance, are the turnover rates different for technology stocks?

Because you're asking about a higher or lower difference, this is a two-tailed test. The critical value for a .01 level of significance is ±1.96. The null hypothesis is rejected if $z < -1.96$ or $z > 1.96$. Using the preceding formula, fill in the following values to calculate the z statistic:

$$z = \frac{31.4 - 34.9}{\sqrt{\dfrac{5.1^2}{32} + \dfrac{6.2^2}{49}}} = -2.66$$

Watch Out!

It's easy to misread the standard normal (z) table. Not all standard normal tables have the same format as used in Tables 1 and 2 in Appendix C, "Sample Statistical Tables," of this book. It is important to know what area of the standard normal curve or probability the table presents as corresponding to a given z-score. The area to the right of z (or the probability of obtaining a value higher than z) is simply one minus the tabled probability.

Given this value of z, you'll reject the null hypothesis. There is a significant mean difference between the turnover rates. In this case it looks like the blue chip stocks turn over less frequently.

Working with Proportions and the z Distribution

It isn't always mean scores that you need to test or compare for significance in business. In the z-tests shown for large samples so far we've been using interval or ratio data measurement such as weight income, distances, and ages. However, sometimes percentages, also known as *proportions,* of nominal data are involved. Here are some typical examples:

➤ The human resources director reports that 70 percent of the applicants have degrees related to the jobs they're applying for.

➤ Sales reports that 35 percent of sales are made by repeat customers.

➤ The plant manager wants to know whether there is a difference in the proportion of male and female employees who are willing to move to a new city to gain a promotion.

Sample proportions are a lot like binomial probabilities. The formula for calculating a proportion looks the same:

$$p = \frac{\text{successes in the sample}}{\text{number sampled}}$$

You can test proportions in many of the same ways you test population means that are obtained from sample data. But some assumptions must be made before testing a population proportion. Foremost, these binomial assumptions must be met:

➤ The sample data are the result of counts.

➤ The outcome of an experiment is classified into two mutually exclusive categories: a "success" or a "failure."

➤ The probability of a success is the same for each experiment (trial).

➤ The trials are independent. Thus, the outcome of one trial does not affect the outcome of any subsequent trial.

Electing the New Chairman of the Board

Tests of a single proportion often are used in election predictions. To test a single proportion using the following formula, you must meet the criteria that both $n\pi$ and $n(1 - \pi)$ equal 5 or more. Note that the symbol pi (π) stands for target population proportion; not the traditional value of π in other mathematical calculations. (Okay, this is confusing. But, just substitute a p in your mind when you see pi in a proportion test; it's easier to remember that way.)

> **Statistical Wisdom**
>
> I will stand on, and continue to use, the figures I have used, because I believe they are correct. Now, I'm not going to deny that you now and then slip up on something; no one bats a thousand.
>
> —*Ronald Reagan, 40th U.S. President*

In this case the CEO wants to know what her chances are of obtaining the 80 percent of the 2,000 votes needed to be elected chairman of the board; she's asked you to help. The test can be conducted because both $n\pi$ and $n(1 - \pi)$ equal 5 or more (actually they equal about 1,600 and 400 respectively).

Now apply the same five hypothesis testing steps that should be very familiar to you now. The CEO is concerned only with a π that is less than .80. If the sample proportion is .80 or more the CEO will have no problem being elected chairman. The null hypothesis is that the population proportion is .80 or more. The alternate hypothesis is that the proportion is less than .80. Thus, the null and alternative hypotheses are written as

$$H_0 : \pi \geq .80$$
$$H_1 : \pi < .80$$

Choose a significance level of .05. In proportion testing this is the likelihood that a true hypothesis will be rejected. In this example, the CEO doesn't want to reject the true hypothesis, because she wants to win the election. To find the critical value for z at .05 significance level look at Table 2 in Appendix C. You'll find that the value closed to a .95 probability, equal to a significance level of .05, is 1.65. Remember: this is a one-tailed test because you're interested only in a result less than .80. Thus you determine the critical value to be a negative number; in this case –1.65. The z statistic for testing one proportion is the appropriate statistic to use for your test. Here is the formula you'll use:

$$z = \frac{p - \pi}{\sqrt{\dfrac{\pi(1-\pi)}{n}}}$$

where

π is the population proportion.

p is the sample proportion.

n is the sample size (as always).

σ_π is the standard error of the population proportion, computed by $\sqrt{\pi(1-\pi)/n}$

Reduce the Risk

Statistics will not be completely satisfactory to those who are content with nothing less then complete certainty. Such certainty defeats the purpose of analyzing a sample to draw conclusions about the population from which it is drawn.

—Jefferson Hane Weaver, Conquering Statistics, 1997

You also might see the formula written like this:

$$z = \frac{p - \pi}{\sigma_p}$$

It means the same thing.

Now that you know the formula for the statistic, you're ready to take a sample from the stockholders to see whether the vote will go the CEO's way. Your sample survey revealed that 1550 plan to vote for the CEO. This is a proportion of .775 (calculated by 1550/2000). Is this proportion close enough to .80? Using the preceding formula, you calculate the z statistic. The formula works out like this:

$$\frac{.775 - .80}{\sqrt{.00008}} = \frac{-.025}{.0089443} = -2.80$$

The computer value of z is in the rejection region. This means you must accept the alternate hypothesis. This is bad news for the CEO. It is unlikely that she'll be elected as chairman of the board because it doesn't look as if your sample result is based on chance.

Now you look up the p-value, which is the probability of finding a z-value less than –2.80. By looking at Table 2, Part 1 (included in Appendix C, "Sample Statistical Tables,") you see that the probability of a z-value of –2.80 is .0026—a very low probability. You've verified the preceding conclusion; you need to tell the CEO that it's unlikely she'll be elected.

Testing Two Population Proportions

Yes, you guessed it. If you can test one proportion, you also can test two. For example, you might want to test whether the proportion of different types of customers would like your product equally well. Of course you might need to find out whether two different production lines produced the same proportion of defective parts. Let's look at an example to see how you might conduct a test to answer these types of proportion questions.

Do Customers Prefer the Same Packaging?

In this example you ask whether the proportion of customers on the West Coast and the proportion of customers on the East Coast are equally in favor of the new red packaging for your batteries. Your null hypothesis is that there is no difference between the two customer groups' preferences for the packaging. Because you'll be using large samples for your test, this is the formula for the z-test statistic you should use:

$$z = \frac{p_1 - p_2}{\sqrt{\frac{p_c(1 - p_c)}{n_1} + \frac{p_c(1 - p_c)}{n_2}}}$$

where

n_1 is the number of West Coast customers in the sample.

n_2 is the number of East Coast customers in the sample.

X_1 is the number of West Coast customers who prefer the red packaging.

X_2 is the number of East Coast customers who prefer the red packaging.

p_c is the weighted mean of the two sample proportions.

211

p_c is computed by the following equation (which you'll be happy to know, like the rest of these equations, can be calculated easily with a computer program):

$$p_c = \frac{x_1 + x_2}{n_1 + n_2}$$

This equation for p_c generally is referred to as the *pooled estimate* of the population proportion. This is the best estimate of the proportion of West Coast and East Coast customers who prefer the red packaging. It does not consider whether they are on the West Coast or on the East Coast. Thus, it is a "pooled" estimate (meaning combined).

You decide that the .05 level of significance is appropriate. Because this is a two-tailed test (no direction, because you don't care whether they like the red packaging more or less), the critical values for .05 are –1.96 and 1.96. If the calculated z-value falls in the region between these two numbers, the null hypothesis is not rejected.

Statistical Wisdom

Even when results are *statistically* significant, executives should ask if results are also *practically* significant: strong enough to justify *doing* something different.

—*Terry Dickey,* Using Business Statistics, *1994*

You now take a sample of 100 customers on the West Coast; 20 percent of these customers prefer the red packaging (compared to the current blue packaging). Two hundred customers on the East Coast were sampled; of these, 100 prefer the red packaging (or 50 percent). The pooled proportion, p_c, is calculated to be .40. Notice that this value is closer to the proportion of the East Coast, because more customers were sampled from the East Coast. With these numbers you can calculate the z-value, which works out like this:

$$\frac{.20 - .50}{\sqrt{\dfrac{.40(1 - .40)}{100} + \dfrac{.40(1 - .40)}{200}}} = \frac{-.30}{.06} = -5.0$$

The computed z-value is in the region of rejection; in this case to the left of –1.96. Thus, the proportion of the population on the East Coast that prefers the red packaging is not equal to the proportion of the population in the West Coast that prefers the red packaging. Based on this test, it is highly unlikely that such a large difference in preference (30 percent) is due to sampling.

Note that the probability of committing a Type I error is .05, which is equal to the level of significance used for the test. This indicates a 5 percent risk of rejecting the true hypothesis that the two population proportions are the same. The *p* value for this test is virtually 0, because the probability of finding a *z* less than –5.00 or greater than 5.00 is virtually 0. In this case there is almost no chance that the null hypothesis is true.

Try Solving a Problem on Your Own

Here is an example problem for you to try based on what you've just read. Use the following data to answer the questions; you can find the answers in Appendix A.

A sample of 40 customers is selected from the population of long-term customers. They complete a customer service evaluation and the mean score from the sample is 102, out of a possible 125 points. The sample standard deviation is 5. A second sample is taken from the population of new customers (those who've been buying from the company for less than a year). The sample mean is 99 on the same test; the sample standard deviation is 6., at the .04 significance level.

Answer these questions:

1. Which of the *z*-score formulas would you use?
2. You want to know whether there is any difference between the two customer groups. Is this a one-tailed or two-tailed test?
3. What is the decision rule you'd use?
4. What is the value of *z?*
5. What is your decision regarding the null hypothesis?
6. What is the *p*-value of *z?*

Questions about differences in means can be difficult because usually there will be some difference between the means of any two or more samples. At this point you've learned to compare the means of two small samples and two large samples. However, there is more to learn about comparing means and looking at variance. You can test variances in the means of more than two samples, which is what you'll learn about in the next chapter.

The Least You Need to Know

➤ Regardless of the sampling method selected, it is unlikely that a sample mean will be exactly the same as a population mean.

➤ If the sample size is more than 30, use the *z* distribution and *z* statistic formulas to test your hypothesis.

➤ There are different formulas for calculating *z* statistics for hypotheses regarding a single population mean, two population means, a single population proportion, and two population proportions.

➤ The critical areas for the *z* calculations are determined from a *z*-score table (available in Appendix C).

➤ The *p*-value is the probability that the value of the test statistic is as large or larger than that obtained when the null hypothesis is true.

Chapter 18

Getting Results from ANOVA

In This Chapter

➤ Getting into the idea of analysis of variance

➤ Understanding the characteristics of the *F* distribution

➤ Organizing data into a one-way and a two-way ANOVA table

➤ Understanding treatments and blocking variables

➤ Conducting hypothesis testing among two, three, or more treatment means

In the previous chapters you learned how to compare the means of two samples using either the *t*-test (for small samples) or the *z* statistic (for large samples). The problem is you still don't know how to compare the means of more than two samples—and in business there are many times when more than two samples need to be compared.

In this chapter I'll focus on another technique for testing the equality of different population means. The technique is *ANOVA*, which stands for *analysis of variance*. The technique uses variance-like measures to make inferences about population means. ANOVA can simultaneously compare several populations' means (meaning two or more).

Introducing the *F* distribution

The ANOVA technique you're about to learn uses a new distribution, called the *F* distribution. It was named to honor Sir Ronald Fisher, one of the founders of modern statistics. This probability is used to test whether two samples are from populations having equal variances; it also is applied when several populations' means need to be compared simultaneously.

The *F* distribution has some specific characteristics that you could have probably guessed by now:

➤ It is continuous.

➤ Its values cannot be negative.

➤ It is positively skewed.

➤ There is a family of *F* distributions. When the degrees of freedom change in either the denominator of the numerator of the formula for the *F* statistic, a different distribution results.

Statistical Wisdom

Testing variances among populations, while not as exciting as a nudist computer dating service, does have its own rewards. It is particularly useful to people who are interested in manufacturing products and marketing them more efficiently.

—*Jefferson Hane Weaver,*
Conquering Statistics, 1997

Comparing Training Results

To understand how ANOVA and the *F* statistic works, let's start with a simple example. Suppose you have observed the training scores for your new staff for 3 different groups of 10 people. Each group had a different trainer; you want to know whether the training results are the same for all three groups. Here's the data you have to work with:

Group 1	69	79	67	64	65	69	64	72	66	69
Group 2	87	94	91	89	89	84	92	89	89	86
Group 3	74	82	76	84	79	77	84	81	69	74

Is seems generally apparent that these three groups are not really too much different. But is this really true? ANOVA and the *F* statistic can answer that question. The null hypothesis used for testing the three means is that all three means are the same. The alternate hypothesis is simply that the means are not all the same.

The first obvious thing to do is calculate the sample average for each group. After doing that, you can calculate the average for all the numbers by adding the means for the three groups and dividing by three. You also can calculate the sample variance for these three averages, which we'll refer to as S^{2*}. (Notice the asterisk after the two.)

With what you already know, you also can calculate the sample variances for each of the three individual groups. For purposes of this analysis, it also is useful to calculate the average of the three sample variances, which we'll call S^2.

The F statistic is calculated with the following formula:

Statistical Wisdom

By the expressiveness of numbers, we can express what is inexpressible, describe what is indescribable, predict what is reasonable to expect, or infer a logical conclusion to a series of events.

—*Paul D. Leedy,* Practical Research, *1997*

$$F = \frac{nS^{2*}}{S^2}$$

where S^2 is the sample variance of the three sample variances. If you think about it you'll realize that the larger the value of S^2, the *more* likely it will be necessary to accept the null hypothesis. If the means are truly equal, F should be close to 1. If it is much larger than 1 (it can't get much smaller), you should reject the null hypothesis.

The F statistic will have $K - 1$ degrees of freedom in the numerator because the sample variance is calculated from k treatments for the statistic. (The k stands for the number of treatments we are testing.) It will have $n - k$ degrees of freedom in the denominator because we calculate a sample variance of n cases in each of the k groups. In the example, $k = 3$ and $n = 10$. Therefore, the F statistic will have 2 and 27 degrees of freedom.

There is an F distribution table in Appendix C, "Sample Statistical Tables." If you examine the table you'll see that an F statistic with 2 and 27 degrees of freedom has about a 95 percent chance of being less than a value about 3.3. Thus, if the calculated F statistic is greater than 3.3, you can reject the null hypothesis.

You were smart; you used a computer to make the actual calculation. The F statistic for the 3 groups has a value of 1061/16.996 = 62.426. This means you should reject the hypothesis. The test scores indeed are statistically different among the three groups.

When using ANOVA, the term *treatment* is used to identify the populations being examined; in this example each of the instructors would be considered a treatment. This term comes from agriculture, where ANOVA had its beginnings. In agriculture you apply treatments to different crops to determine what works best to improve yield. Here we're determining whether the different instructors yield different results from their students (the cases) on the training tests.

Statistical Wisdom

Here are the general steps for calculating the F statistic in simple language when you have k groups and each has n (the same number of cases):

1. Calculate the sample average for each group.

2. Calculate the average of all averages.

3. Calculate the sample variance of the averages.

4. Calculate the sample variance for each group.

5. Calculate the average of all the sample variances.

6. Calculate the value of the F statistic.

7. Look up the value in an F statistic table, like the one in Appendix C.

8. If the observed value of F is greater than the critical value, reject the null hypothesis.

9. Better yet: Use a computer program to make the calculations for you!

The problem with the example I've just provided is that not very many problems are so simple when comparing variances. When you really want to compare the means of three or more samples to determine whether they come from equal populations, you need to understand the sum of squares (actually the sum of squared deviations). There are three types of variations in completing an ANOVA test (which you just learned without realizing it):

➤ **Total variation** This is the sum of the squared differences between each observation and the overall mean.

➤ **Treatment variation** This is the sum of the squared differences between each treatment mean and the overall mean. This variation quantifies the source of variation due to treatments. (Treatments is a statistical term for changes, experiments, or processes that have been applied.)

➤ **Random variation**   This is the sum of the squared differences between each observation and its treatment mean. This variation also is called the *error component* or *random component.*

Conceptually then, the *F* statistic is the ratio between the two estimates of the population variance, based on this equation:

$$F = \frac{\text{Estimate of the population mean based on the differences between sample means}}{\text{Estimate of the population variance based on variation within samples}}$$

Although conceptually simple, the actual sum of squares calculations necessary to accurately calculate *F* are quite tedious; especially when numbers other than whole ones are involved. For this reason, the ANOVA table and other statistical shortcuts have been developed to help make it easier to summarize the calculations necessary for an *F* statistic. (Of course, it's still easier to let Excel or a statistics program do the calculations for you.)

Watch Out!

Computer programs and authors use the term *factor* instead of *treatment* for ANOVA calculations; the meaning is the same.

Do Customers Who Like Our Advertising Buy More?

Here is an example, based on an advertising campaign that was evaluated as excellent, good, fair, or poor. The rating (the treatment) was matched to the customer's purchase totals (in thousands). The sample information looks like the following table. This table provides the information necessary for calculating the value of *F*.

Excellent		Good		Fair		Poor		Total
X	X^2	X	X^2	X	X^2	X	X^2	
80	6400	75	5625	70	4900	68	4624	
85	7225	68	4624	73	5329	70	4900	
90	8100	77	5929	76	5776	72	5184	
94	8836	84	6889	78	6084	65	4225	
		88	7744	80	6400	74	5476	
				68	4624	65	4225	
				65	4225			

continues

	Excellent		Good		Fair		Poor		Total
	X	X^2	X	X^2	X	X^2	X	X^2	
T_c	349		391		510		414		1664
n_c	4		5		7		6		22
X^2	30,561			30,811		37,338		28,634	127,344

The format for the actual ANOVA table looks like this:

Source of Variation	Sum of Squares	Degrees of Freedom	Mean Square	F
Treatments	SST	k - 1	SST/(k-1) = MST	MST/MSE
Error	SSE	n - k	SSE/(n-k) = MSE	
Total		n - 1		

Work your way across the table to find the value of *F*. The term *mean square* is another term for an estimate of the variance. *SST* stands for the sum of squares of the treatment. *SSE* stands for sum of squares of the error (random variation). To get SSE you subtract the SST from the total sum of squares (SS). (You'll see these terms used in reports; so I mention them here.)

Based on the values given in the first table, the ANOVA table would look like the following, with the *F* value calculated as shown in the following table.

Source of Variation	Sum of Squares	Degrees of Freedom	Mean Square	F
Treatments	890.68	3	296.89	8.99
Error	594.41	18	33.02	
Total	1,485.09	21		

The *F* value in the preceding table is much greater than the critical value of 5.09 calculated for the .01 significance level. Therefore, we conclude that the populations' means are not at all equal. We know that the purchases vary by rating but at this point we know only that there is a difference in the treatment means. We can't determine which groups differ or how many treatment groups differ. To determine this, you must do further analysis of each of the treatment groups or ask further questions of the customers.

The main thing you probably noticed is the complexity of the required calculations to complete the ANOVA table. It's a good thing that most computer programs used for statistical analysis produce ANOVA tables that look a lot like the example here.

The program will even calculate the significance level and sometimes chart the range of scores on useful graphs.

Inferences About Treatments

As in the example I've just completed, you can see that it isn't always satisfying to know that the treatment means differ. You really want to know between which groups the means differ. You can calculate the *confidence interval* for the difference between two population means with this calculation based on the t distribution you already know; the complete formula looks like this:

$$\left(\overline{X}_1 - \overline{X}_2\right) \pm t \sqrt{MSE\left(\frac{1}{n_1} + \frac{1}{n_2}\right)}$$

If this value contains a zero when calculated, you can conclude that there is no difference between the two means. Thus, if the confidence interval was calculated to range from –3.0 to 12.5, you could conclude that there is no significant difference in the selected treatment means because the range includes zero. On the other hand, if the range includes the same sign, you can conclude that the two means differ.

Based on the example of customer purchases and advertising opinions comparing the excellent and poor treatments, you'd calculate the end points of the range to be 10.46 to 26.04. This tells you that these two treatments (ratings of excellent and ratings of poor) differ significantly.

You can observe that the customers who thought the ads were excellent purchased more than the customers who rated the ads poor; however, be careful when looking at this conclusion. Without running a correlation and regression analysis, you can't really tell how strongly the advertising opinions and purchases are correlated. (By the way, if you run the confidence interval test to compare other means, you'll find that the difference between the means of excellent and fair also are significantly different, but the difference between excellent and good are not.)

Considering Two-Way Analysis of Variance

At this point you've been looking at between treatment variance and within treatment variance using the ANOVA tables. However, you haven't considered factors other than an initial type of treatment. Analysis of variance doesn't get any easier than what you've seen. There is considerably more to know if you want to do the calculations on your own; personally, I leave it up to the computer. ANOVA can also help you consider more factors that might be affecting the differences in treatment means.

Statistical Wisdom

We cannot feel strongly toward the totally unlike because it is unimaginable, unrealizable; nor yet toward the wholly like because it is stale—identity must always be dull company. The power of other natures over us lies in a stimulating difference which causes excitement and opens communication, in ideas similar to our own but not identical, in states of mind attainable but not actual.

—*Charles Horton*, Human Nature and the Social Order, 1902

The benefit of considering other factors is that you can reduce the error variance, which means you can reduce the denominator of the F statistic and the value of F will be larger. As such, you'll more easily reject the hypothesis of equal treatment means.

To see whether there is another factor affecting the treatment means, you'd establish something called a *blocking variable*. This is the other factor that might be affecting your decision to reject or not reject that the treatment means are the same. When the blocking variable is included in the ANOVA analysis it will have the effect of reducing the SSE (error) term in the ANOVA table.

ANOVA analysis that includes a blocking variable is called two-way analysis of variance. The two-way ANOVA table uses the same format as the one-way table, except there is an additional row for the blocking variable. SS total and SST are calculated as before. SSB, the sum of squares for the block variable, is found by a specific formula; we won't go into detail about that here. If you're interested, refer to a more advanced book on statistics.

Here is an example of a two-way ANOVA table that uses a blocking variable:

Source of Variation	Sum of Squares	Degrees of Freedom	Mean Square	F
Treatments	32.4	3	10.8 (MST)	4.531
Blocks	78.2 (SSB)	4	19.55 (MSB)	8.202
Error	28.6	12	2.3833 (MSE)	
Total	139.2	19		

The preceding example is based on truck drivers and their average travel time from Pittsburgh to your battery factory (the drivers are the treatment). The blocking variable (denoted by the letter B in the table) is the different routes taken by the drivers at different times. At the .05 significance level, the critical value of F for 12 degrees of freedom for the treatments is 3.49, which means you can reject the null hypothesis for treatments. Further, the critical value for the block is 3.26. Thus, the null hypothesis for the blocking variable (that there is no difference among the treatments) is rejected as well.

You'll be happy to learn that Excel has a two-factor ANOVA procedure. It even calculates the p-value and critical values for your analysis. The p-values calculated by Excel for the preceding example are .0019 for the treatment and .024 for the blocking variable. These p-values confirm that the null hypotheses for treatment and blocks both should be rejected at the .05 significance level. In this case, both the route taken and the drivers make a difference.

Other examples of problems that might require a two-way ANOVA analysis include these:

➤ Do different products sell differently during different seasons of the year? (Treatment: sales of different products. Blocking variable: seasons of the year.)

➤ Do workers produce more volume on different shifts? (Treatment: the workers' output. Blocking variable: shifts of day, evening, and night.)

➤ Do different machines produce different amounts of pollution at the different factory locations? (Treatment: the different machines. Blocking variable: the locations.)

➤ Do people in different locations take more days off at certain times of the month? (Treatment: the people. Blocking variable: the locations.)

You get the idea. You need to have two factors: the treatment and the potentially mediating factor.

This was a tough chapter. If you made it through the mathematical concepts, bravo! If not, I hope at least understand you the basic concepts behind the ANOVA procedure. The F statistic is used in many reports in business, so it's a good thing to understand (even at the basic level).

At this point I've concluded the foray into hypothesis testing and inferential statistics. The next section covers some general topics, including ways to use and interpret statistics wisely. I'll also look at the computer programs available to help you with statistics (mentioned many times already). Finally, now that you know how to use and interpret the fundamental statistical analyses used in business, you'll learn some ways to expand your statistical skills in the future. It's all downhill from here—enjoy the ride!

The Least You Need to Know

➤ ANOVA is a technique used to test simultaneously whether the means of several populations are equal.

➤ The *F* distribution is used as the test statistic for ANOVA analysis.

➤ The value of *F* is never negative.

➤ The critical areas for the *F* calculations are determined from an *F* table. An *F* statistic table is available in Appendix C.

➤ The various means being tested in a one-way ANOVA are called *treatments*, the specific source of variation in the data.

➤ A two-way ANOVA analysis includes a second treatment variable, called a *blocking variable*.

➤ The calculations for ANOVA, using sum of squares, are so cumbersome they're best handled with a computer program.

Part 5
Going On from Here

You've made it through all the hard stuff. With the understanding of statistics you've gained thus far, you'll be able to truly appreciate the programs available on computers that make using statistics fast and easy. (I'll tell you all about them in this section.) You'll also appreciate the insights in this section on ways to avoid common pitfalls in using and interpreting statistics. This will keep you from making the mistakes that have hindered others.

Finally, I provide some guidelines for learning even more about statistics in the future. You'll be glad to discover that there's great information available to keep your statistics skills up-to-date for free—on the Internet, of course. When you're done with the book, you can impress all your colleagues with your newfound statistics power!

Chapter 19

Interpreting Business Data Correctly

In This Chapter

➤ Knowing which mistakes to avoid

➤ Recognizing ways statistics can lie

➤ Knowing how to recognize hyperbole

We all are familiar with disparaging words about statistics. The most famous quote probably is "There are three kinds of lies: lies, damned lies, and statistics," attributed to either Mark Twain or Disraeli, depending on whom you ask. It's no secret that many people, including many businesspeople, harbor misgivings about statistics.

Statistics can be a powerful force for making decisions in business, as I hope you've concluded by now. However, statistics can create misconceptions, lead to poor decisions, or even disrupt the normal operation of business if used inappropriately. As Darrell Huff points out in *How to Lie with Statistics*, a best-selling tome of statistical gaffes, "Averages and relationships and trends and graphs are not always what they seem. There may be more to them than meets the eye, and there may be a good deal less."

It might be helpful to consider some aspects of statistics that can lead people to distrust statistical claims. First, statistics requires the capability to consider things from a probabilistic perspective. You must use quantitative concepts such as confidence, reliability, and significance, which seem complex and obscure. This is in contrast to the way nonstatisticians define problems, preferring concrete, habitually dichotomous viewpoints over mathematical ones. Those not trained in statistics might see things as right or wrong, large or small, this or that.

Additionally, the untrained might dread quantitative data, believing that numbers should be unquestionably correct. In grade school we learn that there is a clearly defined process for finding the answer, and that answer is the only satisfactory one. It often astounds people that different research studies can produce different, often contradictory, results. If the statistical techniques used are really supposed to represent reality, how can it be that different studies produce dissimilar results?

To resolve this contradiction, many naive readers conclude that statistics must not really provide reliable (in the nontechnical sense) indicators of truth after all. Further, if statistics aren't right, they must be wrong. It is easy to see how even well-educated people can become suspicious if they don't understand the basics of statistical reasoning and analysis. By now I hope you've mastered some of those subtleties and diminished your doubt of statistical reasoning.

Statistical Wisdom

The core value of statistical methodology is its ability to assist one in making inferences about a large group (a population) based on observations of a smaller subset of that group (a sample). In order for this to work correctly, a couple of things have to be true: The sample must be similar to the target population in all relevant aspects; and certain aspects of the measured variables must conform to assumptions which underlie the statistical procedures to be applied.

—*Clay Helberg, an employee of SPSS (a statistics software company)*

Even with your recently developed reasoning skills and knowledge of statistics, there are problems in statistical analysis that could ensnare you into inappropriate conclusions. This chapter provides examples in which you could go wrong by incorrectly applying statistical concepts and tests. The information in this chapter also will help you expose those charlatans who use statistics to manipulate or mislead people. These aren't in any particular order: each example covers a commonly found error and discusses ways to recognize or avoid it in your own analyses. The guidelines provided after the problem is exposed will help you avoid the most common statistical errors in business research.

Beware of Nonrandom Nonsamples

If you wanted to investigate the age ranges of your employees, you might do something like this poor human resources manager. He collected information from the files of all 106 employees and found the average age to be 42 with a standard deviation of 10. He then proceeded to use a hypothesis testing procedure to see whether the age is significantly different from 40 using the following (inappropriate) z statistic calculation, because he figures he doesn't have to use the t distribution because the *n* is over 30:

$$z = \frac{\overline{X} - \mu}{s\sqrt{n}} = \frac{42 - 40}{10\sqrt{92}} = \frac{2}{95.91} = .02$$

As a result, he concluded that the average age is not significantly different from 40. So why did the CEO call this poor HR manager a fool when the information was presented at the staff meeting?

The problem is that the whole analysis is inappropriate—not to mention silly. First, all of your employees is not a sample; it's the entire population. Even if you were doing research on businesspeople in general, the sample of all your employees isn't a random sample from that population.

Further, there's no point doing any hypothesis testing when you already know the true value of the parameter—the mean—really is 42. You can't substitute a hypothetical mean for the population mean in the z calculation either, as he did; so the analysis is even more ludicrous, even though the numbers are calculated correctly.

Statistical Wisdom

I have a great subject [statistics] to write upon, but feel keenly my literary incapacity to make it easily intelligible without sacrificing accuracy and thoroughness.

—*Sir Francis Galton (1822–1911), English scientist and anthropologist*

Beware the Ploys of Advertisers

Advertising—which is popularly described as "the science of arresting human intelligence long enough to get money from you"—often is a source of both humorous and manipulative uses of statistics. The founder of Revlon says, "In the factory we make cosmetics; in the store we sell hope." Advertising most frequently deceives by omission of important statistical facts. Here are some classic examples:

➤ **The classic claim of taste preference** "In recent side-by-side blind taste tests, nationwide, more people preferred Pepsi over Coca-Cola." Some details remain unmentioned: In which tests, the sample size, and why doesn't it say, "In all recent tests ..." Obviously some people preferred Coke.

➤ **Amazing claim of the Paperboard Packaging Council** "University studies show paper milk cartons give you more vitamins to the gallon." Amazing! I never knew paperboard contained vitamins. Bet those cartons taste good too.

➤ **Safer than most?** "Last year 35 people drowned in boating accidents. Only five were wearing life jackets. The rest were not. Always wear a life jacket when boating." What percentage of boaters wear life jackets? This is a misuse of conditional probability—and a common type of mistake that leads people to believe that things are worse or better than they are.

➤ **Toyota expands space and time** "How can it be that an automobile that's a mere nine inches longer on the outside gives you over two feet more room on the inside? Maybe it's the new math!" A Toyota Camry ad in which Toyota confused volume with length. Maybe they didn't take math in school.

Use the Correct Scale

It's easy to misrepresent data with charts and graphs, even when you don't intend to. One of the most common innocent mistakes is to start a graph's Y scale just below the lowest data point and stop it just above the highest data value. Almost any line graph of histogram constructed this way can misrepresent the magnitude of data changes. It's okay to do this if you're showing details for emphasis, but you should always couple the detail chart with a nondistorted view with a vertical scale that starts at zero. For representing any data that involves a change with time you should always start the vertical axis at zero.

The following figure shows an example of a company that wants to emphasize its consistent cut prices. The cuts look dramatic over the more than six months shown—but look at the total range of prices. It's only a total change of less than five dollars on a price of more than $200.

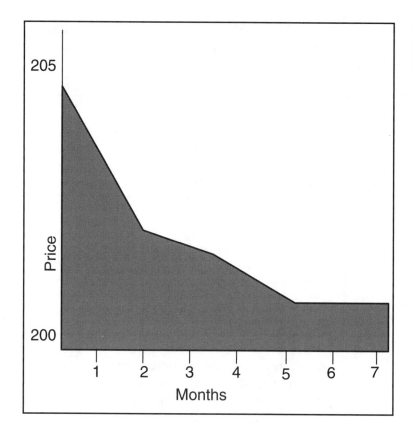

The wrong scale can misrepresent change over time.

Correlation Needs Matched Pairs

Correlation analysis is easy to use incorrectly. Those new to statistics often make errors in how they compare variables and groups, when the variables being compared aren't really meaningful. The following table represents a sample of research that a zealous political researcher came up with.

Democrats	Beer Consumption (in gallons per year)	Republicans	Beer Consumption (in gallons per year)
Sally	5	Tony	2
Fred	15	Michael	10
John	13	Harry	8
Kim	8	Helen	4

The researcher wants to determine whether there is a relationship between political party and beer consumption. She creates the following scatter plot to prove the correlation.

Political party and beer consumption—an inappropriate correlation.

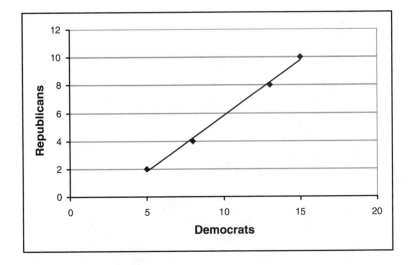

Why was this researcher fired when the results came across the candidate's desk? The answer is pretty clear. First, there are no matched observations for the scatter plot. Each point in a scatter plot needs to come from one person, one time period, or one something. How do you label the point $x = 15$ and $y = 10$ on this plot? Well you can't, because x equals Fred and y equals Michael. The entire analysis is irrational.

Beware of Significant but Unimportant Findings

There are many tests that show that men favor certain products, jobs, or pastimes over those of women—and vice versa. Some of these findings are significant.

Watch Out!

Sometimes things just go wrong, no matter how well you plan your statistical analysis. Luckily, usually there are things you can do to avoid common mistakes before you make the wrong decision.

When some researchers discover these results, they proudly proclaim that one sex or the other is significantly different on this skill or capability; however, often the differences are not very large.

For example, you might find a significant difference in mean scores on a national math test based on a mean of 96 for women and 94 for men. However, this difference really doesn't seem very important. The difference really is too small to make any proclamations. There probably is more variability within the scores of each sex than between the sexes in general.

Statistical Wisdom

Round numbers are always false.

—*Samuel Johnson (1709–1784), British writer*

The terminology in statistics (namely the word "significant") often obscures results behind the normal curve. First of all, "significant" results sometimes are proclaimed based on a questionable level of significance, such as .2 or .4; thus making conclusions suspect even if the results literally are significant at this level. Further, most people who are unfamiliar with statistical significance would know, based on common sense, that the differences in the scores cited above don't really make any difference.

The warning here is to be cautious when you claim or read about differences based on statistical difference alone. Make sure the differences are important as well as significant.

Beware of Data Mining Without Hypotheses

Imagine administering a test with 500 questions on it to a randomly selected sample of 1000 potential customers. You're trying to find out the primary interests of potential customers. To find out exactly which questions show significant interest in your product, you run regressions on every question to show which questions show a significant correlation with interest in your product.

What's the problem with doing this?

Well, if you remember the steps of hypothesis testing, first introduced in Chapter 13, "Testing Your Hypothesis," you should know that you should state your hypotheses before you start testing for results in the data. It would have been better to state hypotheses about the relationships between questions in advance of running the regressions. It's often hard to resist stating conclusions that emerge for hypotheses you can construct after you have the results in hand. Beware of the value of this type of research. Such data mining can lead to conclusions based on coincidence rather than meaningful results.

Avoid Extrapolation That Goes Beyond Observed Ranges

Making bold forecasts and gutsy extrapolations based on a limited range of data often seems warranted because you need to forecast future results, costs, or performance in business. These weak extrapolations often are made when regression calculations are performed on two variables. Unsophisticated researchers often predict values that are outside the range of previously observed data using the current regression formula to fill in the values. This is always a tempting mistake, because you want to be able to predict the future in business, as in life. The regression line makes it seem as if we're being reasonable, even when you're totally off base in making the prediction.

If your regression is based on a small sample, extrapolation beyond observed data ranges is especially dangerous. Often if you take a larger sample in another experiment, the shape of the regression line could change markedly. If you make extrapolations before you have evidence that the regression is valid for all value ranges, you could make decisions based on costs, performance, or sales potential that don't really hold up on more complete analysis. This could have disastrous effects on the decisions you make based on these questionable extrapolations.

Avoid Basic Mistakes That Affect Business Results

In addition to the types of statistical falsehoods I've gone over already, there are other general traps you should always avoid. Some of these have been mentioned elsewhere in the book, but they deserve mentioning again. Remember that you're making important business decisions based on your research and statistics. For this reason, it's prudent to pay attention to the details.

Here's a list of things you should keep at your desk when you're reading research reports or computing statistics on your own:

➤ Use the correct version of the standard deviation, variance, and mean in your formulas. There is a population version and a sample version for each of these: Some formulas use one; some use the other. Know the difference. For easy reference here are the correct symbols:

μ Population mean

$\overline{X}$ Sample mean

σ Population standard deviation (the positive square root of the variance)

s Sample standard deviation

σ^2 Population variance (the square of the standard deviation)

s^2 The sample variance

➤ Always know that the addition rule applies to mutually exclusive outcomes. If outcomes can occur simultaneously or together, the probability of their occurrence must be subtracted from the total *addition rule* of probability you learned about in Chapter 7, "Playing the Probability Game."

➤ Be cautious to not confuse a confidence level with a confidence interval. Remember that a confidence level (also referred to as the level of significance or significance level of the statistical test) is the likelihood of obtaining a result by chance. The confidence interval is a range of values, the values between the lowest and the highest that an estimated parameter could take at a given confidence level.

Reduce the Risk

You'll never remember how all the formulas in statistics work (unless you plan to get a Ph.D. in the subject). Keep a statistics book with tables for the basic tests on your desk at all time. Even if you use a computer program for calculating your statistical tests, it's good to have a reference to refer to.

➤ Don't confuse the addition rule with the multiplication rule when determining probabilities. The multiplication rule applies if all favorable outcomes must occur in a series of trials. The addition rule applies when at least one success must occur in a series of trials. If you don't remember what these rules are, reread Chapter 7.

➤ Be aware of the difference between a statistic and a parameter. Parameters are characteristics of the population, and are not usually easy to discern. Statistics are characteristics of samples that you can compute. Statistics are computed so you can estimate (infer) the parameters of a population. Know the difference— the two are not interchangeable.

➤ Know that interval width and margin of error are not the same thing. A confidence interval is always a point estimate plus or minus a margin of error. For example, if a population parameter is estimated to be 54 percent plus or minus 3 percent, the interval width is 6 percent (not 3 percent).

➤ Never fail to include information on the sample size, confidence intervals, and appropriately worded margin of error information for your research. For example, news reports on polls often leave this information out, making the polling information only marginally valuable.

➤ Put the points in the right place on a frequency diagram. The points of a frequency polygon or plot are always at the center of each of the class intervals—and at the end.

➤ Remember to average the two middle values of an even-numbered data set when you're calculating the median and (often) quartiles. If an ordered series of values contains an even number of measures, the median is the mean of the two middle measures.

Watch Out!

Beware of others' claims that violate the rules and guidelines you've learned in this book. If the statistics aren't properly used, don't believe the claims or use the research as a basis for your own decisions.

➤ Remember to split the alpha level for two-tailed tests. If overall significance level is .05, you must look up the critical value (in a table) for a probability of .025. The alpha level is always divided in two when computing confidence intervals for two-tailed tests.

➤ Keep in mind that you must use $n - 1$ degrees of freedom in a one-sample t-test. (Sometimes people mistakenly use n.) You must subtract 1 from n to get the correct df (degrees of freedom) that you will look up in the t-test table.

➤ Use one-tailed or two-tailed tests appropriately. If your hypothesis predicts only one value will be higher than another, the one-tailed test is required. If it predicts that two values will be higher, of that they are equal, you need to use a two-tailed test. Further, if you simply state that there will be a difference between two values and no direction to that difference (positive or negative), you are specifying a two-tailed test. And make sure your null and alternative hypotheses cover all the possibilities you're interested in researching—less than, equal to, and greater than—as relevant to your research questions.

From Inferences to Your Future

I've provided some examples and guidelines in this chapter that will help you avoid common errors when developing your own business research and statistical analyses. You've learned all the things you need to start doing your own statistical computations at this point. However, if you really don't want to do all the math and calculations by hand, there's advice in the following chapter to help you choose the right computer program for your analyses. A computer makes statistics a lot more fun, because all you really need to know is how to interpret the numbers—and hopefully you have a pretty good idea about that by now.

The Least You Need to Know

➤ Pay attention to the details. It's in the details that most statistical analyses go wrong.

➤ When making a report on statistics, make sure you include all the information necessary for others to interpret your results appropriately.

➤ Know when a population is being discussed and when a sample is being used.

➤ If the sample isn't random, don't make inferences about the population that are unfounded.

➤ Never use statistics to manipulate or coerce people into an erroneous conclusion.

➤ Always double check your calculations before you base your business decisions on the data.

Chapter 20

Using Statistics Programs for Your Company

In This Chapter

➤ Using software to help your statistical analyses

➤ Understanding what software can't do for you

➤ Looking at the types of statistical software

➤ Choosing the right software for your analysis

Creating a complex research design on important business questions and then computing the statistics to report your results can be a very time-consuming process if completed manually. It isn't that the statistical calculations are in themselves difficult. You've learned already that the most difficult math involved is calculating a square root (which you can do without effort using most handheld calculators). The difficult part is the number of steps in the calculations.

The number of steps and calculations can be overwhelming to someone inexperienced in statistics techniques or short on pencils. And, as you've hopefully concluded by now, statistics entails more than just the calculations. Producing the reports, updating the charts, and incorporating changes to a research project along the way add complexity and more paperwork. Of course, if you need to manage research analyses at the same time, the calculations, graphs, and reports can seem impossible.

In this chapter, you'll learn about software that can help you keep it all straight. And because most modern statistical programs are easy to use, you won't have any excuses for not using statistics to help you make better decisions and conclusions for your business.

Using Software That Simplifies the Details

All the calculations can drive you crazy if you're completing a research project with large samples. Even projects with small samples can require considerable calculation, especially if you're using ANOVA analysis or regressions. Some naive managers simply reject statistical methods because of the data entry and calculations involved. Instead, they choose to manage their business with intuition and guesswork (and much of the time they guess wrong). The benefits of statistical methods are too important to ignore just because the charts and graphs take time to produce.

Today, thanks to the rise of the personal computer and the World Wide Web, there are solutions that enable everyone to benefit from using statistics. There are easy-to-use electronic spreadsheet programs such as Microsoft Excel that anyone can master in a few hours. There are also highly sophisticated systems that can handle the huge databases of data required for large corporate analyses (called "data mining" in current lingo).

With the right statistics program, you can concentrate on answering questions and making decisions for your business. You can let the computer provide tactical support for your statistical analyses in the form of charts, graphs, and detailed data analysis. This chapter covers the basics of selecting and using computerized statistics programs so you won't give up on statistics before you get started.

What Can Statistics Programs Do?

Statistics programs range in capabilities from simple programs that produce basic descriptive statistics and simple charts, to prodigious mainframe applications that are integrated with the corporation's budgeting, marketing, manufacturing, personnel, and other management information systems.

The underlying methods supported by most statistics programs, whether designed as general-purpose spreadsheets (like Microsoft Excel) or stand-alone statistics-specific applications, are similar to those presented in this book. Depending on the capabilities of the program, you enter data or import it from another database, and then tell the program to calculate the tests you want to examine. Most programs even draw the charts, graphs, and distributions for you, if you want them.

Most of the time, you'll enter your research data into a form that looks like a spreadsheet with columns and rows. You can usually import the data from database programs and other standard sources as well.

Reduce the Risk

As always, a major benefit of using the computer is the speed with which it accomplishes tasks. It can take several hours to manually complete a single analysis of variance with a reasonable set of groups and total data points. With a handheld calculator, such problems might be completed in less than an hour. Now, however, with a computer, a whole series of these problems can be completed in a matter of minutes or even seconds.

—*Paul D. Leedy,* Practical Research, *1997*

Not even the most sophisticated software package is a substitute for competent statistical judgment and skilled decision making, and by itself, it can't correct any poor choices in the research design or the statistical tests you use. Statistics software can, however, be a terrific boon to the speed and accuracy of your statistical analyses. Although not all programs do everything, most of them can help you do some or all of the following:

➤ Sort your data in a variety of ways to make data easier to review. Data is usually recorded very randomly, just as it is received. You might want to list the data by scores or locations or names associated with the cases. All this can be done in a few seconds with a computer, but could take months by hand.

➤ Produce a wide range of descriptive graphs, plots, and diagrams to visually describe your data. Generally, the type of graph produced is selected from a number of options (scatter graphs, line charts, pie charts, histograms, and others). You can select the colors you'll use, how the axes are labeled, how the legend is created, and how the data points are listed.

➤ Calculate a wide range of formulas, from simple descriptive statistics to the most complex formulas imaginable.

➤ Create free-format reports with an integrated word processor or other report generator for incorporating personalized research annotations.

➤ Display relevant information on the Web or corporate intranet so that other people in the company can view results and conclusions based on your statistical analyses.

➤ Communicate and collaborate with other businesspeople who want to know about the analysis across locations. (This is called virtual communication.)

So What's in It for Me?

One of the most powerful benefits of using software to assist in statistical analysis is the what-if analysis capabilities facilitated by interactive software products. Even the products that aren't Web-enabled allow you to do this. Changes to the tests requested can be made in a few minutes—and the results will be available almost immediately. Imagine trying to do that with a pencil and eraser; it would take hours. With a computer, it takes seconds!

To facilitate what-if analyses, many programs establish a separate, duplicate research database before changes are entered. The software then performs a comparative analysis and displays the new against the old analysis in tabular or graphical form. This makes it fast and easy for managers to review the impact of changes and come to better, more informed conclusions from their statistical analyses.

Simple vs. Complex Software Tools

For a statistics software program to be considered for general business use today, it must facilitate interactive changes and support high-quality graphics. And, by modern standards, it probably should have the ability to use collaborative capabilities provided by networks and the World Wide Web.

Traditionally, statistics-driven organizations preferred mainframe software, like the still-popular SAS and SPSS systems. Today, the companies that offer large-scale statistics programs also offer desktop versions that can be integrated into a corporate-level analysis systems. SPSS is one such company that offers a full range of statistical programs for almost every type of data analysis.

In the past, organizations that were less statistics-driven looked for less expensive, personal-computer software that was either networked or not, depending on the size and consistency desired in statistical procedures. Today, companies don't have to compromise between one or the other—they can have power and large data handling capability on personal computers that can work in conjunction with the corporate, server-based systems.

The Types of Statistical Programs

For purposes of easy classification, statistical software products can be divided into three categories based on the functions and features they provide. These include basic spreadsheets, robust data analysis programs, and corporate-level data analysis programs. Let's take a closer look at each of these.

Basic Spreadsheet Programs

Basic spreadsheets programs typically are designed for people who only need to calculate or present descriptive-level statistics. These programs usually produce simple graphs and charts and work in a fashion similar to more robust spreadsheet programs like Microsoft Excel. A large number of these programs are available for most common personal computers. Some of them are available on the Internet for downloading and typically cost less than $50 or $100 to license for permanent use. These programs are usually limited to producing a small number of charts and reports.

Choose a spreadsheet program like this if you only have very simple analyses to do on your own. If your reporting requirements are simple and your research projects are small, one of these programs can be very useful. The good ones are easy to learn and provide color display capabilities.

Robust Data Analysis Programs

Full-featured spreadsheet programs like Microsoft Excel are designed for handling fairly robust data sets. With the add-on statistical analysis programs (which come packaged with Excel, but need to be specifically loaded into the program), you can handle all but the largest or most specialized statistical analyses. Excel, like other full-featured spreadsheet programs, is still relatively easy to learn, and the output is easy to understand. There are also hearty stand-alone statistics programs, like StatPac (www.statpac.com) and other similar software designed specifically for statistical analysis on a personal computer.

Watch Out!

Excel is certainly not the most capable statistical package available today—it is inferior in that respect to Minitab, not to mention real research tools like SAS or Stat. A student who really plans to concentrate in statistics will certainly need to become exposed to more capable statistical software.

—*John L. Neufeld*, Learning Business Statistics with Excel 2000, 2001

243

Most of the programs in this category provide the ability to produce charts, graphs, and plots in a variety of formats. Microsoft Excel also has a variety of programs available to further extend the power of the standard package that are produced by third-party vendors, like Analyse-It (www.analyse-it.com/default.htm). These programs can add advanced statistical analysis functions that go beyond the functions discussed in this book, including complex multiple regression or linear programming functions.

Excel Functions You Might Want to Know

Many of you will already own Microsoft Excel. For many reasons it is a good tool to use when first learning statistics: It is visual and accessible. It comes as part of the popular Microsoft Office package that includes Microsoft Word (a robust word-processing package) and other general-purpose programs of great utility in business. When you load Excel on your computer, it comes standard with functions for basic descriptive statistics, including the following commands with the data to be entered shown in parentheses:

➤ AVERAGE (range) calculates the mean or mathematical average.

➤ STDEVP (range) calculates the standard deviation of a population.

➤ STDEV (range) calculates the standard deviation of a sample.

➤ MEDIAN (range) calculates the median.

➤ PERCENTRANK (range, value) calculates the percentile rank of a value within the list *range*.

Statistical Wisdom

Man is still the most extraordinary computer of all.

—John F. Kennedy (1917–1963), 35th U.S. President

If you do use Microsoft Excel (and you should be using a current version), you should be aware of the special functions that are a part of the standard package. Some of these require you to load a set of programs from the installation disk called Analysis Tools.

In the newer versions of Excel, these tools are pre-loaded on installation. If you don't have the Analysis Tools available from the pull-down menus, go to the help menu to request information on loading the Analysis Tools. When everything is loaded, here are a few of the hundreds of functions you'll have available in Microsoft Excel:

➤ BINOMDIST(k, n, p, FALSE) calculates the probability that $X = k$, where X has a binomial distribution with parameters n and p.

➤ BINOMDIST(k, n, p, TRUE) calculates the cumulative probability that X is less than or equal to k; in other words, it sums the probabilities from $X = 0$ up to $X = k$.

➤ CHIDIST(a, df) gives the probability that a chi square random variable with df degrees of freedom will be greater than a.

➤ CHIINV(p, df) gives the value of a such that $Pr(\chi_{df}^2 > a) = p$, where χ_{df}^2 is a chi square random variable with df degrees of freedom. This function is the inverse of the previous one.

➤ COMBIN(n, j) gives the number of combinations when j objects are selected from n objects.

➤ FACT(n) gives $n!$ (n factorial).

➤ FDIST(a, df_{num}, df_{den}) gives the probability that an F random variable with df_{num} and df_{den} degrees of freedom will be greater than a.

➤ FINV(p, df_{num}, df_{den}) gives the value of a such that $Pr(F > a)$ p, where F is an F random variable with df_{num} and df_{den} degrees of freedom. This function is the inverse of the previous one.

➤ HYPGEOMDIST(k, ns, M, N) gives $Pr(X = k)$, where X has a hypergeometric distribution with population size N, sample size ns, and M objects in the population of type M, and k objects in the sample of type M.

➤ NORMDIST(x, mu, sigma, TRUE) gives the probability that a normal random variable (with mean mu and standard deviation sigma) will be less than x.

➤ NORMINV(p, mu, sigma) gives the value of a such that $Pr(X < a) = p$ where X has a normal distribution. This function is the inverse of the previous one.

➤ NORMSDIST(a) gives $Pr(Z < a)$, where Z has a standard normal distribution.

➤ NORMSINV(p) gives the value a such that $Pr(Z < a) = p$, where Z has a standard normal distribution. This function is the inverse of the previous one.

➤ TDIST(a, df, 1) gives the one-tail probability for a t distribution: $Pr(T > a)$, where T is a random variable with the t distribution with df degrees of freedom.

➤ TDIST(a, df, 2) gives the two-tail probability for a t distribution: $Pr(T > a) + Pr(T < -a)$, or $2Pr(T > a)$.

➤ TINV(p, df) give the value a such that $Pr(T > a) = p$, where T is a random variable with the T distribution with df degrees of freedom.

The following functions can be used in Excel for simple regression and correlation analyses:

➤ SLOPE(*vrange, xrange*): slope of simple regression line

➤ INTERCEPT(*yrange, xrange*): y intercept of simple regression

➤ RSQ(*yrange, xrange*): r squared value of simple regression

➤ CORREL(vrange, *xrange*): correlation coefficient between two ranges

The help feature of Microsoft Excel provides examples on using the functions. Further, there are some good books available on using Excel for statistical analysis. One that I like is *Learning Business Statistics with Microsoft Excel* by John L. Neufeld (published by Prentice Hall). At this writing, the book covers the 2000 version of Excel; hopefully Mr. Neufeld will do another version for the new 2002 version of Excel and other versions as they are released.

Corporate-Level Statistics Programs

As I've mentioned earlier, it used to be that you needed a mainframe computer (now known as a server) to complete complex data analyses. Now you can do it on your personal computer. But there are still some companies that produce statistics programs that handle larger data sets and more complex mathematical procedures than are feasible on spreadsheet programs—even those as robust as Excel.

These corporate-level programs extend the features already discussed for the other two categories of software, and most run versions for personal computers that can interact with the large database-handling capabilities of the server-based programs. Some of the companies known for corporate-level analysis programs include SPSS, SAS, and Minitab. I've provided links to these companies below so you can see the wide range of data analysis tools they offer for corporate use.

Choices and More Choices

As features and functions continue to be added to the less sophisticated programs over time, the division between the types of programs is not as clear-cut as presented here. With more than 100 different software packages available for statistics that I found in searching the Internet, the evaluation and selection of software can become a tedious process.

Other sources of information about statistics programs include computer magazines and the Internet. The computer magazines in bookstores and on the Web frequently run reviews of popular statistics programs. You can do an Internet search using one of the major search engines (Yahoo!, for example) to discover Web sites that focus on statistics software.

Here are some Internet sites to get your started on your quest for the perfect statistics software for your business:

➤ **www.microsoft.com/office/excel/default.htm**

Microsoft's site for Excel. As of this writing, the current version is 2002 with even more advanced analysis functions than ever. Many of the functions that were add-ons in Excel 2000 are now standard fare.

➤ **www.spss.com**

The SPSS software site that provides links to all the company's various data analysis and statistics software. SPSS now owns and markets the popular StatView as an alternative to its very robust SPSS statistics software family.

➤ **www.sas.com**

The SAS site which provides complete information on all its data analysis and business intelligence software.

➤ **www.minitab.com**

The Minitab site with information on its capable statistics software products.

How Do You Choose?

After you determine the category of software you need for your statistics and data analysis needs, you should consider several critical factors for evaluating software before you make a purchase decision. These are detailed in the sections that follow.

Cost/Feature Analysis

Prices for statistics software vary greatly. Depending on the kinds of projects you intend to manage, study the features of products under consideration to match your requirements. The most expensive products are not always the most capable. On the other hand, unless your budget is heavily constrained, rule out programs that skimp on features just to save a few dollars. A product that lacks basic functionality results in frustration because it won't do what you need it to.

As you evaluate different products, add features to your requirements list that you hadn't considered before studying the software options. Don't make the mistake of selecting a package simply because it has more features at its price than any other package. Consider the other factors discussed later in this section, but make sure there are enough features for your current needs and those in the foreseeable future.

If you have the opportunity to evaluate products before purchase (either at a dealer's showroom, through a demo disk, or at the company's Web site), try using the package to assemble a simple research or data analysis problem. That way, you can test the package's reliability and see how it performs. Also check the program's speed when saving to disk and its printing efficiency. A program with strong features that takes all day to print an analysis is probably not the one for you.

Once you select what appears to be the right product, try to purchase it from a source that gives you a 30-day money-back guarantee. That way, if the product performs poorly or ultimately doesn't fill the bill, you can return it and try something else. If you purchase software through mail order, use a credit card. You'll have more leverage returning the product because your credit card company may take your side.

When considering the cost of the software, don't forget the other system configuration requirements. Will the program work on your existing system or do you need to buy new hardware?

Ease of Use and Consistency of the Interface

One of the most important aspects of choosing software for data analysis and statistics is to select a package that's easy to use and that responds consistently throughout its interface. The easier the product is to use, the more likely it is you'll keep using it.

For example, if you choose the most feature-laden package, you may get a product with a number of menus, commands, dialog boxes, and cryptic functions that not only get in your way but actively interfere with analyzing your data. Although these may be important functions for a professional statistician, unless you have four months to learn the package, it may get shelved and never used. Such a package forces you into overmanaging even comparatively simple research projects, thereby negating its usefulness.

Flexibility to Adapt to Various Analyses

Because research in business varies from small to large and from simple to complex, you want a package that's flexible in how it adapts to various research analysis requirements.

Compatibility with Other Programs

In many cases, you will want to use statistics-oriented charts and combine them with documents such as reports and presentation materials. If this is important to you, look for a package that can save or export images in a format compatible with the word-processing, page-layout, or presentation software you own or plan to acquire. Excel is especially good at doing this, and SPSS has great import and export capabilities as well.

Documentation and Support for the Program

When learning how to use a product, your first point of reference when looking for a solution to a problem is the manual (whether it's online or printed in a book). Check the documentation and help menus carefully before purchase.

Statistical Wisdom

Computer science only indicates the *retrospective* omnipotence of our technologies. In other words, an infinite capacity to process data (but only data, i.e., the *already given*) and in no sense a new vision. With that science, we are entering an era of exhaustivity, which is also an era of exhaustion.

—*Jean Baudrillard, French sociologist*

Study the documentation carefully. The information should be well organized, have a detailed index, and offer plenty of screen shots showing how the product works. A lengthy troubleshooting section doesn't hurt, either. Keyboard templates, quick-reference cards, and disk-based sample projects are also useful. Complex products with skimpy manuals should be avoided at all costs. Also, make sure the company offers training options for the program that are commensurate with the complexity of the software.

Also, see if there is online training available. Many well-supported products even have free guidebooks and training materials available on the Internet that have been developed by universities, business schools, and consultants for the programs. These extra materials can be a great help in getting your research projects up and running quickly.

Reputation of the Product Manufacturer

If you are purchasing an expensive product that will get considerable day-to-day use, check up on the company that designed the product. If the company discontinues the product or closes its doors, you'll be on your own with the software. Look for a stable company with a strong track record of designing useful software and providing regular updates and bug fixes. Once a product becomes incompatible with the current version of your computer's operating system, statistical analyses that could have been revamped for future use become unavailable if the software is not updated.

Word-of-Mouth Experiences

Talk to other users of a particular package to get feedback on how well the product performs with real-world projects. The users you query should use the package for projects similar in scope to the ones you plan to carry out. If calling references provided by the manufacturer, take anything less than a glowing tribute to mean that the product performs less adequately than expected.

Technical Support

When considering any software product, evaluate the technical support provided by the manufacturer. Find out if it's free or if you must pay an annual fee after 90 days or a per-use fee after a certain number of calls. Do they provide a toll-free number? Must you listen to an automatic telephone system recite a long list of options before connecting you to a technician at your expense? Dial the number and see what happens. Check out the technical support information on the company's Web site. If you're fortunate enough to have other users to ask for recommendations, query them on the quality of technical support.

So which computerized statistics tool is best for you? The one that meets your feature requirements with the most flexibility, with an acceptable learning curve, from a reliable and supportive vendor, and at a price you can afford. (This is pretty much the standard formula for choosing any software or computer product, not just statistics software.)

Things Statistics Software Can't Do

As powerful and efficient as statistics programs are, many aspects of the statistics process are not within the computer's realm. Using computer-assisted statistics streamlines administration, reporting, analysis, and even communication, but the following are things the computer can't and shouldn't be allowed to do:

➤ **Statistics software can't gather data.** You'll have to decide how much and what type of information you need to answer your business questions. You or members of your team will still need to gather data. The computer only helps compute and display the information after it is gathered and entered.

➤ **Statistics software can't make decisions.** The computer can make it easier and faster to look at alternatives, but it is ultimately you and your staff who will have to make the choice between the alternatives and take responsibility for the decisions.

➤ **Statistics software can't solve problems that require subjective judgments.** Sometimes human intuition is the most important ingredient in statistics, especially when dealing with people. People require understanding. Software is programmed and is not intuitive. It only reports back what you put into it. If you selected a biased sample or asked for the wrong statistical tests, the computer won't question your judgment or your research design.

➤ **Statistics software can't find the errors in your input.** If you put biased, incomplete, or erroneous data into the statistics program, it will output biased, incomplete, and erroneous data analysis. Don't blame the computer for human error. The best way to eliminate this problem is to check the reports and entries a couple of times before they are distributed.

Statistical Wisdom

Computers are good at swift, accurate computation and at storing great masses of information. The brain, on the other hand, is not as efficient a number cruncher and its memory is often highly fallible; a basic inexactness is built into its design. The brain's strong point is its flexibility. It is unsurpassed at making shrewd guesses and at grasping the total meaning of information presented to it.

—*Jeremy Campbell, British journalist*

➤ **Statistics software can't communicate for you.** Software is great at producing reports that look good and contain a wealth of detailed information, but there is more to reporting on research than sending out the report.

➤ **Statistics software won't save money by reducing the need for personnel to design the research and analyze the result of the data analysis.** Automation almost never really reduces the personnel costs on any type of work. The software can make you more efficient and make decision making more effective because the information is better, but statistics software will not significantly reduce the need for people with training in the use of statistics.

Go Get Yourself Some!

Now you have been introduced to the features for selecting statistics software for your needs. Now, if you don't already own something like Microsoft Excel, go out, select a program, and get started in analyzing your data. Follow the step-by-step guidelines for hypothesis testing and data analysis you've read in the book. With each successful research project, you will contribute to the business, the economy, and your own career—no mean feat for having just learned some terms and procedures in business statistics. You've done a good job so far—so keep on reading to learn how you can continue to gain knowledge about the power of statistics in business. The next and final chapter in this book provides information on resources that can help you do just that.

The Least You Need to Know

➤ There are statistics programs for projects of all sizes and complexities that run on most common personal computers.

➤ Statistics programs help simplify data analysis and reporting.

➤ To get the most benefit from its features, practice using the software regularly.

➤ No software program can replace the basic knowledge of statistics you need to use the program effectively and make good decisions based on the data.

Chapter 21

Advancing Your Business with Statistics

In This Chapter

➤ Continuing to build on your new statistical skills

➤ Learning where to find more information on statistics

➤ Using the World Wide Web as a resource for your statistical analyses

---

You have arrived at the end of your venture into business statistics. You've learned how to organize and display your data. You've gained knowledge of modeling and re-search. You know how to analyze frequencies, understand associations between vari-ables, and find significant differences among groups. You know the difference between a mean and a mode and a critical value and a confidence interval. You can even spot the errors in others' data analyses when they fail to report on the selection of the sam-ple or the level of significance for their tests.

Although this seems like a lot to know about statistics and their value in business, this book is only a first step. To make your new knowledge work for you, you need to practice the skills you've learned. Invest in statistical software, if you don't already have a program, and practice some basic analyses. Try creating a database of key meas-urements in your job and update them regularly. Begin tracking your results and ana-lyze them with statistics; start with descriptive statistics and then move into testing a hypothesis and gathering the data to prove your hypothesis. If you use statistics regu-larly, you'll find your skills improve—and you may quickly find that you want to know even more than you mastered in this book.

In the rest of this chapter you'll learn about some additional statistical tests you might want to make use of in the future. You'll also be introduced to resources on the World Wide Web that will expand your knowledge of statistics and help you further enhance your statistical research and reasoning skills.

Statistical Wisdom

More than 100 years ago H. G. Wells, an English author and historian, noted that "statistical thinking will one day be as necessary for efficient citizenship as the ability to read." He made no mention of business because the Industrial Revolution was just beginning. Were he to comment on statistical thinking today, he would probably say that "statistical thinking is necessary not only for effective citizenship but also for effective decision making in various facets of business."

—*Robert D. Mason, Douglas A. Lind, and William G. Marchal,* Statistical Techniques in Business and Economics, *10th Edition, 1999*

More Statistical Functions to Learn

The diagram below summarizes the broad categories of statistics you've learned about in this book already. You may recall the introduction to these various realms of statistical analysis in the first chapters of the book: parametric statistics and nonparametric statistics.

Statistical Wisdom

With a little practice, and the success and failures that accompany it, you will understand complicated problems more easily. You will tease useful information from muddled situations. Most important of all, you will act when others are only confused.

—*Terry Dickey,* Using Business Statistics, *1994*

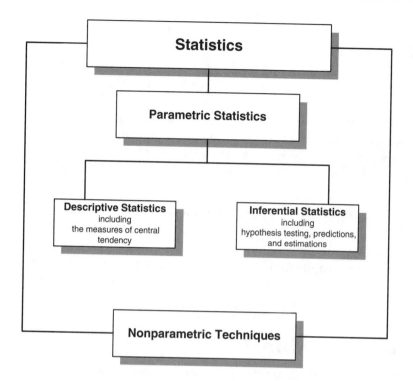

The branches of statistics you now know.

In each of the major areas there are more tests which can be conducted than would be appropriate for an introduction to business statistics. Even so, the basic principles, methods, concepts, and formulas covered in this book can be extended to solve more complex business problems than were covered here. Thus, you've learned the necessary terms and tests to prosper in your business career, but if you were to go into a full-time research position, you'd probably want to learn even more.

Some more advanced statistical concepts you might want to pursue that build on your current knowledge include

➤ **Multivariate data analysis,** including cluster analysis, discriminant analysis, and factor analysis.

Statistical Wisdom

Statistics is a tool that helps us to learn about the world around us. It can be used in as creative a manner as we desire to solve complex problems faced by business and industry.

—Jefferson Hane Weaver, Conquering Statistics, *1997*

➤ **Advanced probability analysis,** including random walk models, image analysis, and resampling.

➤ **Additional parametric tests,** including the Kruskal-Wallis test, the Kendall coefficient of concordance, and the Wilcoxon rank sum test, among others.

And there are many more advanced correlation tests to extend your ability to measure and predict relationships, with multiple correlation being one I mentioned in Chapter 15, "Recognizing the Relationships of Business Variables." Other correlation tests include Kendall's coefficient of concordance and the Spearman rank-order correlation.

The point in mentioning all these new cryptic functions is not to make you feel unskilled, but to let you know that there is still more to know. But more importantly, even without knowing these more advanced techniques, you should feel secure that you know enough to conduct meaningful research for your business without further study. In fact, almost everything else you might learn in statistics is based on the core concepts you've already learned in this book.

Where Can You Learn More?

You can always expand your knowledge with a higher-level textbook and courses in statistics. Since you have already studied the fundamental concepts, additional statistical techniques will be much easier to learn. However, some of the ongoing training you desire is available for free and without the effort of leaving your office—from sources on the World Wide Web.

The following Web sites are some of my favorite statistical resources on the Internet. Many of these are simply good references to know about, and some offer extended training and detailed research designs. Mark the ones you like as "favorites" in your browser so they're always at your fingertips when you have an important statistical analysis to complete for making a major business decision:

➤ davidmlane.com/hyperstat/

A fantastic site by David Lane that includes his online statistics textbook and links to many other useful statistical sites. Thank you, David, for a great resource!

➤ www.statsoftinc.com/textbook/stathome.html

Another online resource that includes a (free) textbook on all the basic and most of the advanced techniques in statistics. Statsoft also sells statistics software.

Statistical Wisdom

A point estimate is a single statistic that is taken as the best indication of the corresponding population parameter. We have discussed the variability within samples—the error of the means of random samples from the true mean of the total population. We must recognize and take into account this variability when making any kind of estimate, particularly with point estimates, where we are shooting for a statistical bull's eye.

—Paul D. Leedy, Practical Research, *1997*

➤ www.spss.org/wwwroot/

V.J. Inc.'s private consultant site that offers a great free paper on interpreting linear regression, among other useful links.

➤ www.indiana.edu/~statmath/stat/spss/win/index.html

The stat/math site at Indiana University that provides a free tutorial for using basic SPSS software.

➤ www.ats.ucla.edu/stat/Qtr_Schedule.htm

The UCLA (University of California at Los Angeles, in case you didn't know) site for statistical education and consulting.

➤ trochim.human.cornell.edu/kb/

The research methods knowledge base developed by William Trochim of Cornell University.

➤ www.psychstat.smsu.edu/sbk00.htm

David Stockburger's online textbook. It's for psychology majors, but it has lots of useful statistics information that can be used by businesspeople.

➤ ubmail.ubalt.edu/~harsham/Business-stat/opre504.htm

Professor Hossein Arsham's site dedicated to training people on the use of business statistics.

There is also a wide range of web sites that specialize in supplying business statistics for general analysis. Many of these are sponsored by the U.S. government.

By the way, the Web is constantly changing. If some of the sites I've suggested have changed or cease to exist, there are likely many new sites out there in the same vein. Simply type in "business statistics" as the key words in a major search engine and you'll get links to hundreds of sites with valuable information you can use to expand your command of statistical analysis.

Statistical Wisdom

The researcher should consider very early while developing a research problem which statistical tools are to be used. This should be done when the hypotheses and/or question are being formulated. One should certainly *not* collect the data first and then ponder what to do with them.

—*Gerhard D. Land and George D. Hess,* A Practical Guide to Research Methods, *Fifth edition, 1994*

You're Ready to Compute!

At this juncture, after what has been a somewhat long and, at times, meticulous discussion, it's important to remember what you set out to learn when you picked up this book in the first place. As a businessperson you wanted to learn how to analyze data statistically so that you could discern the dynamic and potentially forceful impacts on your business. You wanted to find the clues in your business data that would allow you to investigate those areas that truly warrant further research. And at a quite basic level, you wanted to understand the language of statistics so you could read research reports with a critical eye and write reports on your business with statistical flair.

I hope this book has helped you meet those goals—even if only in part. After all, your own effort in taking time to understand the concepts and get to this final section in the book took focus and intent.

I know you're ready to put your knowledge of statistics to good use. And in your continuing pursuit of better ways to analyze and manage your business, may statistics help guide you to the successes you seek.

The Least You Need to Know

➤ Statistics can help you guide your business to bigger and better things.

➤ Keeping your statistics skills honed requires ongoing effort in using what you've already learned.

➤ There are myriad resources on the Web to help you expand your statistical skills.

➤ Nothing worth working for is wasted time.

Answer Key

In many of the chapters you are asked to try out calculations and procedures based on the types of examples that were discussed. This chapter provides answers to the questions and exercises in those chapters. If you want to try more practice exercises, you might want to pick up a textbook on statistics that provides exercises and answers in the back of the book.

Chapter 2

Here are the answers to the exercise in the "Try It on Your Own" section:

1. ratio
2. nominal
3. ratio
4. interval or ratio (assumed)
5. ordinal
6. ordinal
7. ratio
8. interval
9. nominal
10. interval

Chapter 5

The exercise was adapted from *Using Business Statistics* by Terry Dickey. Here are the answers to the Simple Practice exercise:

Range	Variance	Standard Deviation
4	3.2	1.79
100	1250	35.36
50	500	22.36
20	50	7.07
8	8	2.83

Chapter 6

Here are the answers to the "Providing Your Own Answers" exercise:

1. 99.9%
2. The value minus the mean divided by the standard deviation which is equal to the number of standard deviations the value is from the mean
3. The mean and the standard deviation
4. Approximately 34%
5. The median
6. Interval or ratio data

Chapter 7

Here are the answers to the "Try Some of Your Own" questions:

1. If you don't get a result close to .5 for heads and .5 for tails, extend the experiment to 100 tosses. You might have just been "lucky" in the domain of the largest occurrence (heads or tails).

2. Start with all the probabilities for dice throws, in a table like the one below:

(1,1)	(1,2)	(1,3)	(1,4)	(1,5)	(1,6)
(2,1)	(2,2)	(2,3)	(2,4)	(2,5)	(2,6)
(3,1)	(3,2)	(3,3)	(3,4)	(3,5)	(3,6)
(4,1)	(4,2)	(4,3)	(4,4)	(4,5)	(4,6)
(5,1)	(5,2)	(5,3)	(5,4)	(5,5)	(5,6)
(6,1)	(6,2)	(6,3)	(6,4)	(6,5)	(6,6)

   a. (2,6) (3,5) (4,4) (5,3) (6,2)

   $4/36 = 1/9 = .1111$

   b. (1,1) $= 1/36 = .0278$

   c. (1,6) (2,5) (3,4) (4,3) (5,2) (6,1) $= 6$

   (5,6) (6,5) $= 2$

   $8/36 = 2/9 = .2222$

Chapter 9

The answer to the "Try It on Your Own" exercise is simple: go to the city. The odds are always better. The decision tree is shown in the following figure:

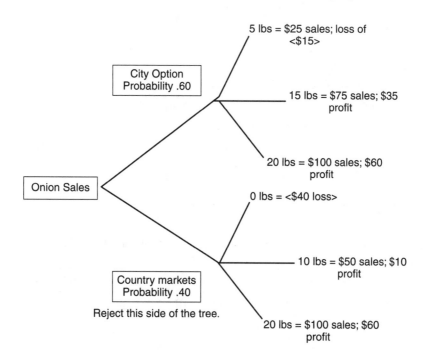

Chapter 12

Here are the answers to the "Try It on Your Own" table:

Mean ($\bar{x}$)	Standard Deviation (s)	Number of Cases (n) the Mean	Standard Error of Confidence Interval of 95%
100	10	30.........1.83	96.4 to 103.6
500	50	65.........6.2	487.8 to 512.2
85	3	35.........0.51	84 to 86
20	2	40.........0.32	19.2 to 20.8

Note: Critical points (z-scores) for a two-tailed test are plus and minus 1.96 for 95 percent confidence interval above.

Chapter 13

Based on the data given in the "Try It on Your Own" exercise, a random sample of cases of the 12-volt batteries showed a mean turnover of 5.84 for this year.

Here are the answers to the questions:

1. $H_0 : \mu = 6.0$; $H_1 : \mu \neq 6.0$
2. .05
3. $$z = \frac{\overline{X} - \mu}{\sigma / \sqrt{n}}$$
4. The null hypothesis will not be rejected if the computed z-value falls between −1.96 and 1.96, the values for .05 significance level.
5. Yes. The z-value would equal −2.56.

   Reject the null hypothesis at the .05 level and accept the alternate hypothesis. The mean turnover rate is *not* 6.0.

Chapter 14

Here are the answers for the "Try Using a Contingency Table on Your Own" exercise in Chapter 14:

The null hypothesis could be stated formally like this:
H_0 : *Current* = .60; *Late* = .30; *Uncollectable* = .10.

You would reject the null hypothesis if $\chi 2 > 5.991$.

Given that $\chi 2 = 9.33$, you would reject the null hypothesis and conclude that the data does not reflect the industry standards.

Chapter 15

Here is the table of the "Try Some Regression Calculations on Your Own" exercise completely filled in. Does yours match mine?

m	x	b	y = (m × x) + b	Relationship? Positive or Negative
−2	3	10	4	Positive
4	2	8	16	Positive
−1	1	5	4	Positive
−4	6	3	−21	Negative
5	3	7	22	Positive
−5	2	4	−6	Negative

Chapter 16

Here is the answer to the "Try Using a t-Test on Your Own" exercise:

You would reject the null hypothesis that the two factories have equal production if $t > 2.624$ for 14 degrees of freedom $(9 + 7 - 2 = 14)$.

The t value equals 0.234. Therefore, you conclude that there is no significant difference in the average production and Factory Two is not producing more than Factory One.

Chapter 17

Here are the answers to the "Try Solving a Problem on Your Own" exercise:

1. You'd use the formula for calculating a z-score for two independent means.
2. Two-tailed test.
3. Reject the null hypothesis if $z < -2.05$ and $z > 2.05$. The null hypothesis states that there is no difference between the two customer groups.

4. 2.59, calculated as:

$$z = \frac{102 - 99}{\sqrt{\dfrac{5^2}{40} + \dfrac{6^2}{50}}} = 2.59$$

5. Reject the null hypothesis and accept the alternative hypothesis. This means that there is a significant difference in opinion between the old and the new customers.

6. p = .0096.

Statistics Formulas

This chapter provides definitions of the symbols used in statistics. It's a handy reference when you can't remember what a symbol stands for. This appendix also provides a list of the most commonly used formulas in business statistics. Don't worry about memorizing these; your computer program can do the calculations for you. Just make sure you know what the formula is used for. To do that, you need to read the book!

The Greek Characters and Other Symbols

This section lists the symbols you need to know to read business statistics books and reports that use statistics.

Greek Characters

μ	Lowercase mu, pronounced *mew;* stands for the mean of a random variable.
σ	Lowercase sigma; stands for the standard deviation of a random variable.
χ	Lowercase chi, pronounced *kye.*
χ^2	Chi squared; represents an important random variable distribution.
π	Lowercase pi, pronounced *pie;* represents a special number about equal to 3.1416 that is used extensively in mathematics.
ϕ	Capital phi, pronounced *fie;* ϕ is used to represent the cumulative distribution function for a standard normal random variable.

Σ   Capital sigma; this symbol represents summation.

For an explanation, refer to the section "Notation and Convention" in this appendix.

Other Symbols

λ Lowercase lambda; λ is used for the parameter in the Poisson and exponential distributions.

Δ Capital delta; represents "change in."

φ Lowercase psi, pronounced *sigh;* represents a moment-generating function.

ϵ Lowercase epsilon; represents a small positive number.

Γ Capital gamma; represents the gamma function.

Notation and Convention

Statisticians use symbols and formulas to make working with statistics easier. Formulas written the usual way would be very long; for this reason, statisticians use certain conventions to write statistical formulas. Here are some of them.

Σ   The summation symbol, the uppercase Greek letter sigma, means calculate the value of the formula to the right after substituting the first values (of a given variable in the data set) for x. Repeat the process, using the second value, third, fourth, and so on, until you reach the last case. Then, total the results of all the calculations and use the total for the answer.

x The value of the variable for a single case or occurrence of the variable.

n The number of cases in a data set. Specifically, a lowercase n stands for the number of cases in the sample. An uppercase N stands for the number of cases in the complete population.

z The standard normal value corresponding to the desired level of confidence.

Y' Y-Prime, the symbol for linear regression.

The Formulas

The following formulas are discussed in the book. Again, don't worry about memorizing them; instead, try to remember why they are important in statistical analyses.

$$\mu = \frac{\Sigma(x)}{N}$$

Mean of a population.

$$\overline{X} = \frac{\Sigma(x)}{n}$$

Mean of a sample.

$$\sigma = \sqrt{\frac{\Sigma(X-\mu)^2}{N}}$$

The standard deviation of a population.

$$s = \sqrt{\frac{\Sigma(X-\overline{X})^2}{(n-1)}}$$

The standard deviation of a sample. Notice that the number of cases is reduced by 1, to make the value a more accurate estimator.

$$s = \sqrt{\frac{\Sigma x^2 - \frac{(\Sigma x)^2}{n}}{(n-1)}}$$

Standard deviation of a sample, raw data.

$$\sigma^2 = \frac{\Sigma(X-\mu)^2}{N}$$

Variance of a population, the square of the standard deviation.

$$s^2 = \frac{\Sigma(X-\overline{X})^2}{(n-1)}$$

Variance of a sample.

$$s_{\overline{X}} = \frac{s}{\sqrt{n}}$$

Standard error of the mean.

$$\overline{X} \pm z\frac{s}{\sqrt{n}}$$

Confidence interval for mean.

$$n = \left(\frac{zs}{E}\right)^2$$

Sample size for mean where E is the maximum allowable error.

$$x^2 = \Sigma \left(\frac{\left(\text{actual - expected}^2\right)}{\text{expected}} \right)$$

Chi-squared calculation (for contingency tables).

$$x^2 = \Sigma \left(\frac{(f_0 - f_e)}{f_e} \right)$$

Chi-square test statistic (all tables), where f_0 is observed occurrences and f_e is expected frequency or occurrences.

$$z = \frac{\overline{X}_c - \mu_1}{\sigma \sqrt{n}}$$

Type II error probability, where $\overline{X}_c$ equals the critical value.

$$z = \frac{\overline{X} - \mu}{s \sqrt{n}}$$

Z statistic, σ unknown; test for single sample mean.

$$z = \frac{\overline{X}_1 - \overline{X}_2}{\sqrt{\frac{s_1^2}{n_1} + \frac{s_2^2}{n_2}}}$$

Test of means, two samples.

$$z = \frac{\left(\overline{X}_1 - \overline{X}_2\right) - difference}{\sqrt{\frac{s_1^2}{n_1} + \frac{s_2^2}{n_2}}}$$

Test of means, two samples (alternate calculation).

$$z = \frac{p_1 - p_2}{\sqrt{\frac{p_c(1 - p_c)}{n_1} + \frac{p_c(1 - p_c)}{n_2}}}$$

Two-sample test of proportions.

$$p_c = \frac{x_1 + x_2}{n_1 + n_2}$$

Pooled proportions.

$$t = \frac{\overline{X} - \mu}{s \sqrt{n}}$$

One sample test of a mean, small samples.

$$t = \frac{\overline{X}_1 - \overline{X}_2}{\sqrt{s_p^2 \left(\frac{1}{n_1} + \frac{1}{n_2}\right)}}$$

Two sample test of means, small samples, where S_p^2 is the pooled estimate of the population variance.

$$s_p^2 = \frac{(n_1 - 1)(s_1^2) + (n_2 - 1)(s_2^2)}{n_1 + n_2 - 2}$$

Pooled estimate of the variance.

$$t = \frac{\bar{d}}{s_d \sqrt{n}}$$

Paired test, where d is the mean of the difference between paired or related observations, s_d is the standard deviation of the differences between the paired or related observations, and n is the number of paired observations. The standard deviation of the differences is calculated with the sample standard deviation formula for raw data, except that d is substituted for x.

$$r = \frac{n(\sum XY) - (\sum X)(\sum Y)}{\sqrt{\left[n(\sum X^2) - (\sum X)^2\right]\left[n(\sum y^2) - (\sum y)^2\right]}}$$

Coefficient of correlation (Pearson's r).

$$t = \frac{r\sqrt{n-2}}{\sqrt{1-r^2}}$$

Correlation test of hypothesis.

$$Y' = a + bX$$

Linear regression equation, general form.

$$y = (m \times x) + b$$

Model for a straight line, alternate for linear regression above, where y is the value of the dependent variable, x is the value of the independent variable, m is the slope of the line, and b is a constant (the place on the y-axis where the line crosses).

$$r_s = 1 - \frac{6\sum d^2}{n(n^2 - 1)}$$

Spearman's coefficient of rank-order correlation, where d is the difference between the ranks for each pair and n is the number of paired observations.

$$F = \frac{nS^{2*}}{S^2}$$

F statistic, where S^{2*} is the sample variance of the averages (means) for all samples and S^2 is the average of the sample variances for each of the individual samples.

Sample Statistical Tables

Table 1: Two-Tailed Standard Normal (Z) Table

$p = \Pr(-a < Z < a)$

The following table lists the probability p that a standard normal random variable Z (mean 0, standard deviation 1) will be between $-a$ and a. The values in *boldface* are those commonly used for confidence intervals and hypothesis testing in most business research, with .9500 and .9900 being the most common of these.

a	p	A	p
0.100	0.0796	1.400	0.8384
0.200	0.1586	**1.439**	**0.8500**
0.300	0.2358	1.500	0.8664
0.400	0.3108	1.600	0.8904
0.500	0.3830	**1.645**	**0.9000**
0.600	0.4514	1.700	0.9108
0.700	0.5160	1.800	0.9282
0.800	0.5762	1.900	0.9426
0.900	0.6318	**1.960**	**0.9500**
1.000	0.6826	2.000	*0.9544*
1.100	0.7286	2.500	0.9876
1.200	0.7698	**2.576**	**0.9900**
1.282	**0.8000**	3.000	0.9974
1.300	0.8064	3.100	0.9980

Table 2: One-Tailed Standard Normal (Z) Random Variable Table

The two-part table on the next pages gives the probability p that a standard normal random variable Z will be less than the specified value $a : p = \Pr(Z < a)$. It also gives the area under the standard normal density function to the left of the specified value a.

The connection between Table 1 and Table 2 (parts 1 and 2) is the following: If $p_2 = \Pr(-a < Z < a)$ (the value from the two-tailed table), and $p_1 = \Pr(Z < a)$ (the value from the one-tailed table), then $p_2 = 2p_1 - 1$.

Part 1 of One-Tailed Standard Normal (Z) Random Variable Table

a	P	a	p	a	p	a	p	a	p	a	p
-2.99	.0014	-2.30	.0107	-1.99	.0233	-1.49	.0681	-0.99	.1611	-0.49	.3121
-2.98	.0014	-2.29	.0110	-1.98	.0239	-1.48	.0694	-0.98	.1635	-0.48	.3156
-2.97	.0015	-2.28	.0113	-1.97	.0244	-1.47	.0708	-0.97	.1660	-0.47	.3 192
-2.96	.0015	-2.27	.0116	-1.96	.0250	-1.46	.0721	-0.96	.1685	-0.46	.3228
-2.95	.0016	-2.26	.0119	-1.95	.0256	-1.45	.0735	-0.95	.1711	-0.45	.3264
-2.94	.0016	-2.25	.0122	-1.94	.0262	-1.44	.0749	-0.94	.1736	-0.44	.3300
-2.93	.0017	-2.24	.0125	-1.93	.0268	-1.43	.0764	-0.93	.1762	-0.43	.3336
-2.92	.0018	-2.23	.0129	-1.92	.0274	-1.42	.0778	-0.92	.1788	-0.42	.3372
-2.91	.0018	-2.22	.0132	-1.91	.0281	-1.41	.0793	-0.91	.1814	-0.41	.3409
-2.90	.0019	-2.21	.0136	-1.90	.0287	-1.40	.0808	-0.90	.1841	-0.40	.3446
-2.89	.0019	-2.20	.0139	-1.89	.0294	-1.39	.0823	-0.89	.1867	-0.39	.3483
-2.88	.0020	-2.19	.0143	-1.88	.0301	-1.38	.0838	-0.88	.1894	-0.38	.3520
-2.87	.0021	-2.18	.0146	-1.87	.0307	-1.37	.0853	-0.87	.1922	-0.37	.3557
-2.86	.0021	-2.17	.0150	-1.86	.0314	-1.36	.0869	-0.86	.1949	-0.36	.3594
-2.85	.0022	-2.16	.0154	-1.85	.0322	-1.35	.0885	-0.85	.1977	-0.35	.3632
-2.84	.0023	-2.15	.0158	-1.84	.0329	-1.34	.0901	-0.84	.2005	-0.34	.3669
-2.83	.0023	-2.14	.0162	-1.83	.0336	-1.33	.0918	-0.83	.2033	-0.33	.3707
-2.82	.0024	-2.13	.0166	-1.82	.0344	-1.32	.0934	-0.82	.2061	-0.32	.3745
-2.81	.0025	-2.12	.0170	-1.81	.0351	-1.31	.0951	-0.81	.2090	-0.31	.3783
-2.80	.0026	-2.11	.0174	-1.80	.0359	-1.30	.0968	-0.80	.2119	-0.30	.3821

a	P	a	p	a	p	a	p	a	p	a	p
-2.79	.0026	-2.10	.0179	-1.79	.0367	-1.29	.0985	-0.79	.2148	-0.29	.3859
-2.78	.0027	-2.09	.0183	-1.78	.0375	-1.28	.1003	-0.78	.2177	-0.28	.3897
-2.77	.0028	-2.08	.0188	-1.77	.0384	-1.27	.1020	-0.77	.2206	-0.27	.3936
-2.76	.0029	-2.07	.0192	-1.76	.0392	-1.26	.1038	-0.76	.2236	-0.26	.3974
-2.75	.0030	-2.06	.0197	-1.75	.0401	-1.25	.1056	-0.75	.2266	-0.25	.4013
-2.74	.003 1	-2.05	.0202	-1.74	.0409	-1.24	.1075	-0.74	.2296	-0.24	.4052
-2.73	.0032	-2.04	.0207	-1.73	.0418	-1.23	.1093	-0.73	.2327	-0.23	.4090
-2.72	.0033	-2.03	.0212	-1.72	.0427	-1.22	.1112	-0.72	.2358	-0.22	.4129
-2.71	.0034	-2.02	.0217	-1.71	.0436	-1.21	.1131	-0.71	.2389	-0.21	.4168
-2.70	.0035	-2.01	.0222	-1.70	.0446	-1.20	.1151	-0.70	.2420	-0.20	.4207
-2.69	.0036	-2.00	.0228	-1.69	.0455	-1.19	.1170	-0.69	.2451	-0.19	.4247
-2.68	.0037	-2.30	.0107	-1.68	.0465	-1.18	.1190	-0.68	.2483	-0.18	.4286
-2.67	.0038	-2.29	.0110	-1.67	.0475	-1.17	.1210	-0.67	.2514	-0.17	.4325
-2.66	.0039	-2.28	.0113	-1.66	.0485	-1.16	.1230	-0.66	.2546	-0.16	.4364
-2.65	.0040	-2.27	.0116	-1.65	.0495	-1.15	.1251	-0.65	.2578	-0.15	.4404
-2.64	.0041	-2.26	.0119	-1.64	.0505	-1.14	.1271	-0.64	.2611	-0.14	.4443
-2.63	.0043	-2.25	.0122	-1.63	.0516	-1.13	.1292	-0.63	.2643	-0.13	.4483
-2.62	.0044	-2.24	.0125	-1.62	.0526	-1.12	.1314	-0.62	.2676	-0.12	.4522
-2.61	.0045	-2.23	.0129	-1.61	.0537	-1.11	.1335	-0.61	.2709	-0.11	.4562
-2.60	.0047	-2.22	.0132	-1.60	.0548	-1.10	.1357	-0.60	.2743	-0.10	.4602
-2.59	.0048	-2.21	.0136	-1.59	.0559	-1.09	.1379	-0.59	.2776	-0.09	.4641
-2.58	.0049	-2.20	.0139	-1.58	.0570	-1.08	.1401	-0.58	.2810	-0.08	.4681
-2.57	.005 1	-2.19	.0143	-1.57	.0582	-1.07	.1423	-0.57	.2843	-0.07	.4721
-2.56	.0052	-2.18	.0146	-1.56	.0594	-1.06	.1446	-0.56	.2877	-0.06	.4761
-2.55	.0054	-2.17	.0150	-1.55	.0605	-1.05	.1469	-0.55	.2912	-0.05	.4801
-2.54	.0055	-2.16	.0154	-1.54	.0618	-1.04	.1492	-0.54	.2946	-0.04	.4840
-2.53	.0057	-2.15	.0158	-1.53	.0630	-1.03	.1515	-0.53	.298 1	-0.03	.4880
-2.52	.0059	-2.14	.0162	-1.52	.0642	-1.02	.1539	-0.52	.3015	-0.02	.4920
-2.51	.0060	-2.13	.0166	-1.51	.0655	-1.01	.1562	-0.51	.3050	-0.01	.4960
-2.50	.0062	-2.12	.0170	-1.50	.0668	-1.00	.1587	-0.50	.3085	0.00	.5000

Part 2 of One-Tailed Standard Normal (Z) Random Variable Table

a	p	a	p	a	p	a	p	a	p	a	p
0.01	.5040	0.51	.6950	1.01	.8438	1.51	.9345	2.01	.9778	2.51	.9940
0.02	.5080	0.52	.6985	1.02	.8461	1.52	.9357	2.02	.9783	2.52	.9941
0.03	.5120	0.53	.7019	1.03	.8485	1.53	.9370	2.03	.9788	2.53	.9943
0.04	.5160	0.54	.7054	1.04	.8508	1.54	.9382	2.04	.9793	2.54	.9945
0.05	.5199	0.55	.7088	1.05	.8531	1.55	.9394	2.05	.9798	2.55	.9946
0.06	.5239	0.56	.7123	1.06	.8554	1.56	.9406	2.06	.9803	2.56	.9948
0.07	.5279	0.57	.7157	1.07	.8577	1.57	.9418	2.07	.9808	2.57	.9949
0.08	.5319	0.58	.7190	1.08	.8599	1.58	.9429	2.08	.9812	2.58	.9951
0.09	.5359	0.59	.7224	1.09	.8621	1.59	.9441	2.09	.9817	2.59	.9952
0.10	.5398	0.60	.7257	1.10	.8643	1.60	.9452	2.10	.9821	2.60	.9953
0.11	.5438	0.61	.7291	1.11	.8665	1.61	.9463	2.11	.9826	2.61	.9955
0.12	.5478	0.62	.7324	1.12	.8686	1.62	.9474	2.12	.9830	2.62	.9956
0.13	.5517	0.63	.7357	1.13	.8708	1.63	.9484	2.13	.9834	2.63	.9957
0.14	.5557	0.64	.7389	1.14	.8729	1.64	.9495	2.14	.9838	2.64	.9959
0.15	.5596	0.65	.7422	1.15	.8749	1.65	.9505	2.15	.9842	2.65	.9960
0.16	.5636	0.66	.7454	1.16	.8770	1.66	.9515	2.16	.9846	2.66	.9961
0.17	.5675	0.67	.7486	1.17	.8790	1.67	.9525	2.17	.9850	2.67	.9962
0.18	.5714	0.68	.7517	1.18	.8810	1.68	.9535	2.18	.9854	2.68	.9963
0.19	.5753	0.69	.7549	1.19	.8830	1.69	.9545	2.19	.9857	2.69	.9964
0.20	.5793	0.70	.7580	1.20	.8849	1.70	.9554	2.20	.9861	2.70	.9965
0.21	.5832	0.71	.7611	1.21	.8869	1.71	.9564	2.21	.9864	2.71	.9966
0.22	.5871	0.72	.7642	1.22	.8888	1.72	.9573	2.22	.9868	2.72	.9967
0.23	.5910	0.73	.7673	1.23	.8907	1.73	.9582	2.23	.9871	2.73	.9968
0.24	.5948	0.74	.7704	1.24	.8925	1.74	.9591	2.24	.9875	2.74	.9969
0.25	.5987	0.75	.7734	1.25	.8944	1.75	.9599	2.25	.9878	2.75	.9970
0.26	.6026	0.76	.7764	1.26	.8962	1.76	.9608	2.26	.9881	2.76	.9971
0.27	.6064	0.77	.7794	1.27	.8980	1.77	.9616	2.27	.9884	2.77	.9972
0.28	.6103	0.78	.7823	1.28	.8997	1.78	.9625	2.28	.9887	2.78	.9973
0.29	.6141	0.79	.7852	1.29	.9015	1.79	.9633	2.29	.9890	2.79	.9974

a	p	a	p	a	p	a	p	a	p	a	p
0.30	.6179	0.80	.7881	1.30	.9032	1.80	.9641	2.30	.9893	2.80	.9974
0.31	.6217	0.81	.7910	1.31	.9049	1.81	.9649	2.31	.9896	2.81	.9975
0.32	.6255	0.82	.7939	1.32	.9066	1.82	.9656	2.32	.9898	2.82	.9976
0.33	.6293	0.83	.7967	1.33	.9082	1.83	.9664	2.33	.9901	2.83	.9977
0.34	.6331	0.84	.7995	1.34	.9099	1.84	.9671	2.34	.9904	2.84	.9977
0.35	.6368	0.85	.8023	1.35	.9115	1.85	.9678	2.35	.9906	2.85	.9978
0.36	.6406	0.86	.8051	1.36	.9131	1.86	.9686	2.36	.9909	2.86	.9979
0.37	.6443	0.87	.8078	1.37	.9147	1.87	.9693	2.37	.9911	2.87	.9979
0.38	.6480	0.88	.8106	1.38	.9162	1.88	.9699	2.38	.9913	2.88	.9980
0.39	.6517	0.89	.8133	1.39	.9177	1.89	.9706	2.39	.9916	2.89	.9981
0.40	.6554	0.90	.8159	1.40	.9192	1.90	.9713	2.40	.9918	2.90	.9981
0.41	.6591	0.91	.8186	1.41	.9207	1.91	.9719	2.41	.9920	2.91	.9982
0.42	.6628	0.92	.8212	1.42	.9222	1.92	.9726	2.42	.9922	2.92	.9982
0.43	.6664	0.93	.8238	1.43	.9236	1.93	.9732	2.43	.9925	2.93	.9983
0.44	.6700	0.94	.8264	1.44	.9251	1.94	.9738	2.44	.9927	2.94	.9984
0.45	.6736	0.95	.8289	1.45	.9265	1.95	.9744	2.45	.9929	2.95	.9984
0.46	.6772	0.96	.8315	1.46	.9279	1.96	.9750	2.46	.9931	2.96	.9985
0.47	.6808	0.97	.8340	1.47	.9292	1.97	.9756	2.47	.9932	2.97	.9985
0.48	.6844	0.98	.8365	1.48	.9306	1.98	.9761	2.48	.9934	2.98	.9986
0.49	.6879	0.99	.8389	1.49	.9319	1.99	.9767	2.49	.9936	2.99	.9986
0.50	.6915	1.00	.8413	1.50	.9332	2.00	.9772	2.50	.9938	3.00	.9987

Table 3: Chi-Square Table

The following table gives the value of a such that $\Pr(\chi^2_{DF} < a) = p$, where χ^2 is a chi-square random variable with DF degrees of freedom. For example, there is a probability of .95 that a chi-square random variable with 6 degrees of freedom will be less than 12.6.

DF	p =.005	.01	.025	.05	.25	.5	.75	.90	.95	.975	.99
1	.000	.000	.001	.004	.10	.45	1.32	2.71	3.84	5.02	6.64
2	.010	.020	.051	.10	.58	1.39	2.77	4.61	5.99	7.38	9.21
3	.072	.11	.22	.35	1.21	2.37	4.11	6.25	7.81	9.35	11.3
4	.21	.30	.48	.71	1.92	3.36	5.39	7.78	9.49	11.1	13.3
5	.41	.55	.83	1.15	2.67	4.35	6.63	9.24	11.1	12.8	15.1
6	.68	.87	1.24	1.64	3.45	5.35	7.84	10.6	12.6	14.4	16.8
7	.99	1.24	1.69	2.17	4.25	6.35	9.04	12.0	14.1	16.0	18.5
8	1.34	1.65	2.18	2.73	5.07	7.34	10.2	13.4	15.5	17.5	20.1
9	1.73	2.09	2.70	3.33	5.90	8.34	11.4	14.7	16.9	19.0	21.7
10	2.16	2.56	3.25	3.94	6.74	9.34	12.5	16.0	18.3	20.5	23.2
11	2.60	3.05	3.82	4.57	7.58	10.3	13.7	17.3	19.7	21.9	24.7
12	3.07	3.57	4.40	5.23	8.44	11.3	14.8	18.5	21.0	23.3	26.2
13	3.56	4.11	5.01	5.89	9.30	12.3	16.0	19.8	22.4	24.7	27.7
14	4.07	4.66	5.63	6.57	10.2	13.3	17.1	21.1	23.7	26.1	29.1
15	4.60	5.23	6.26	7.26	11.0	14.3	18.2	22.3	25.0	27.5	30.6
16	5.14	5.81	6.91	7.96	11.9	15.3	19.4	23.5	26.3	28.8	32.0
17	5.70	6.41	7.56	8.67	12.8	16.3	20.5	24.8	27.6	30.2	33.4
18	6.26	7.01	8.23	9.39	13.7	17.3	21.6	26.0	28.9	31.5	34.8
19	6.84	7.63	8.91	10.1	14.6	18.3	22.7	27.2	30.1	32.9	36.2
20	7.43	8.26	9.59	10.9	15.5	19.3	23.8	28.4	31.4	34.2	37.6
21	8.03	8.90	10.3	11.6	16.3	20.3	24.9	29.6	32.7	35.5	38.9
22	8.64	9.54	11.0	12.3	17.2	21.3	26.0	30.8	33.9	36.8	40.3
23	9.26	10.2	11.7	13.1	18.1	22.3	27.1	32.0	35.2	38.1	41.6
24	9.89	10.9	12.4	13.8	19.0	23.3	28.2	33.2	36.4	39.4	43.0
25	10.5	11.5	13.1	14.6	19.9	24.3	29.3	34.4	37.7	40.6	44.3
26	11.2	12.2	13.8	15.4	20.8	25.3	30.4	35.6	38.9	41.9	45.6
27	11.8	12.9	14.6	16.1	21.7	26.3	31.5	36.7	40.1	43.2	47.0

DF	p =.005	.01	.025	.05	.25	.5	.75	.90	.95	.975	.99
28	12.5	13.6	15.3	16.9	22.7	27.3	32.6	37.9	41.3	44.5	48.3
29	13.1	14.3	16.0	17.7	23.6	28.3	33.7	39.1	42.6	45.7	49.6
30	13.8	14.9	16.8	18.5	24.5	29.3	34.8	40.3	43.8	47.0	50.9
35	17.2	18.5	20.6	22.5	29.0	34.3	40.2	46.1	49.8	53.2	57.3
40	20.7	22.2	24.4	26.5	33.7	39.3	45.6	51.8	55.8	59.3	63.7
50	28.0	29.7	32.4	34.8	42.9	49.3	56.3	63.2	67.5	71.4	76.2
60	35.5	37.5	40.5	43.2	52.3	59.3	67.0	74.4	79.1	83.3	88.4
70	4.3.3	4.5.4	48.8	51.7	61.7	69.3	77.6	85.5	90.5	95.0	100.4
80	51.2	53.5	57.2	60.4	71.1	79.3	88.1	96.6	101.9	106.6	112.3
90	59.2	61.8	65.6	69.1	80.6	89.8	98.6	10./6	113.1	118.1	124.1
100	67.3	70.1	74.2	77.9	90.1	99.3	109.1	118.5	124.3	129.6	135.8

Table 4: Students Distribution

Level of Significance for One-Tailed Test						
	0.100	0.050	0.025	0.010	0.005	0.0005

Level of Significance for Two-Tailed Test

DF	0.20	0.10	0.05	0.02	0.01	0.001
1	3.078	6.314	12.706	31.821	63.657	636.619
2	1.886	2.920	4.303	6.965	9.925	31.599
3	1.638	2.353	3.182	4.541	5.841	12.924
4	1.533	2.132	2.776	3.747	4.604	8.610
5	1.476	2.015	2.571	3.365	4.032	6.869
6	1.440	1.943	2.447	3.143	3.707	5.959
7	1.415	1.895	2.365	2.998	3.499	5.408
8	1.397	1.860	2.306	2.896	3.355	5.041
9	1.383	1.833	2.262	2.821	3.250	4.781
10	1.372	1.812	2.228	2.764	3.169	4.587
11	1.363	1.796	2.201	2.718	3.106	4.437
12	1.356	1.782	2.179	2.681	3.055	4.318
13	1.350	1.771	2.160	2.650	3.012	4.221
14	1.345	1.761	2.145	2.624	2.977	4.140
15	1.341	1.753	2.131	2.602	2.947	4.073
16	1.337	1.746	2.120	2.583	2.921	4.015
17	1.333	1.740	2.110	2.567	2.898	3.965
18	1.330	1.734	2.101	2.552	2.878	3.922
19	1.328	1.729	2.093	2.539	2.861	3.883
20	1.325	1.725	2.086	2.528	2.845	3.850
21	1.323	1.721	2.080	2.518	2.831	3.819
22	1.321	1.717	2.074	2.508	2.819	3.792
23	1.319	1.714	2.069	2.500	2.807	3.768
24	1.318	1.711	2.064	2.492	2.797	3.745
25	1.316	1.708	2.060	2.485	2.787	3.725
26	1.315	1.706	2.056	2.479	2.779	3.707
27	1.314	1.703	2.052	2.473	2.771	3.690
28	1.313	1.701	2.048	2.467	2.763	3.674

Level of Significance for One-Tailed Test

	0.100	0.050	0.025	0.010	0.005	0.0005

Level of Significance for Two-Tailed Test

DF	0.20	0.10	0.05	0.02	0.01	0.001
29	1.311	1.699	2.045	2.462	2.756	3.659
30	1.310	1.697	2.042	2.457	2.750	3.646
40	1.303	1.684	2.021	2.423	2.704	3.551
60	1.296	1.671	2.000	2.390	2.060	3.460
120	1.289	1.658	1.980	2.358	2.617	3.373
	1.282	1.645	1.960	2.326	2.576	3.291

Table 5: Sample *F* Distribution Table

In the two tables below, the numerator degrees of freedom are read along the top, and the denominator degrees of freedom are read along the left side. The table gives the value of a such that $\Pr(F < a) = p$ where F is a random variable with an F distribution with DF_{num} numerator degrees of freedom and DF_{den} denominator degrees of freedom.

Each table has a different value of p; first .99, then .95. These are the two of the most commonly used levels of significance for hypothesis testing. Another way to describe the table is to give the value of $1 - p$, which is the right tail area (that is, the area to the right of the given value of a). For example, there is a .99 probability that an F random variable with 10 numerator degrees of freedom and 9 denominator degrees of freedom will be less than 5.26.

$\Pr(F < a) = .99$; right tail area = .01

DF_{den}	$DF_{num}=2$	3	4	5	10	15	20	30	60	120
2	99.00	99.16	99.25	99.30	99.40	99.43	99.45	99.47	99.48	99.49
3	30.82	29.46	28.71	28.24	27.23	26.87	26.69	26.50	26.32	26.22
4	18.00	16.69	15.98	15.52	14.55	14.20	14.02	13.84	13.65	13.56
5	13.27	12.06	11.39	10.97	10.05	9.72	9.55	9.38	9.20	9.11
6	10.92	9.78	9.15	8.75	7.87	7.56	7.40	7.23	7.06	6.97
7	9.55	8.45	7.85	7.46	6.62	6.31	6.16	5.99	5.82	5.74
8	8.65	7.59	7.01	6.63	5.81	5.52	5.36	5.20	5.03	4.95
9	8.02	6.99	6.42	6.06	5.26	4.96	4.81	4.65	4.48	4.40
10	7.56	6.55	5.99	5.64	4.85	4.56	4.41	4.25	4.08	4.00
15	6.36	5.42	4.89	4.56	3.80	3.52	3.37	3.21	3.05	2.96
20	5.85	4.94	4.43	4.10	3.37	3.09	2.94	2.78	2.61	2.52
30	5.39	4.51	4.02	3.70	2.98	2.70	2.55	2.39	2.21	2.11
60	4.98	4.13	3.65	3.34	2.63	2.35	2.20	2.03	1.84	1.73
120	4.79	3.95	3.48	3.17	2.47	2.19	2.03	1.86	1.66	1.53

$Pr(F < a) = .95$; right tail area $= .05$

DF_{den}	$DF_{num}=2$	3	4	5	10	15	20	30	60	120
2	19.00	19.16	19.25	19.30	19.40	19.43	19.45	19.46	19.48	19.49
3	9.55	9.28	9.12	9.01	8.79	8.70	8.66	8.62	8.57	8.55
4	6.94	6.59	6.39	6.26	5.96	5.86	5.80	5.75	5.69	5.66
5	5.79	5.41	5.19	5.05	4.74	4.62	4.56	4.50	4.43	4.40
6	5.14	4.76	4.53	4.39	4.06	3.94	3.87	3.81	3.74	3.70
7	4.74	4.35	4.12	3.97	3.64	3.51	3.44	3.38	3.30	3.27
8	4.46	4.07	3.84	3.69	3.35	3.22	3.15	3.08	3.01	2.97
9	4.26	3.86	3.63	3.48	3.14	3.01	2.94	2.86	2.79	2.75
10	4.10	3.71	3.48	3.33	2.98	2.85	2.77	2.70	2.62	2.58
15	3.68	3.29	3.06	2.90	2.54	2.40	2.33	2.25	2.16	2.11
20	3.49	3.10	2.87	2.71	2.35	2.20	2.12	2.04	1.95	1.90
30	3.32	2.92	2.69	2.53	2.16	2.01	1.93	1.84	1.74	1.68
60	3.15	2.76	2.53	2.37	1.99	1.84	1.75	1.65	1.53	1.47
120	3.07	2.68	2.45	2.29	1.91	1.75	1.66	1.55	1.43	1.35

A Glossary of Statistical Terms

alternative hypothesis   The hypothesis that states that the null hypothesis is false. Symbolized by H_1.

analysis of variance   Known generally as ANOVA, a method for testing the hypothesis that several different groups all have the same mean.

analysis of covariance   Known as ANCOVA, a test of significance which statistically adjusts the two groups to make them equivalent. It does not replace random assignment. Used when compared groups are initially unequal.

ANOVA table   A table that summarizes the results of an analysis of variance calculation.

applied research   Applying research techniques to practical problems of some general concern. Goes beyond action research in scope and rigor. Can involve sophisticated procedures and aims to apply the research results to the larger population of study.

autocorrelation   See *serial correlation*.

average   Equivalent to the term mean.

base year   An arbitrary year relative to which a price index measures the average level of prices or which serves as the base for other statistical analysis to establish trends or changes.

basic research   Applying research techniques to conceptual or theoretical problems in business, social science, or science. There need be no practical application in mind; the aim is to discover new knowledge and build new theory as an end in themselves.

Bayesian approach   An approach to statistics where the researcher starts with a prior distribution and then uses results from observations to calculate an updated distribution.

Bayes's rule   A rule that tells how to calculate the conditional probability $\Pr(B|A)$ provided that $\Pr(A|B)$ and $\Pr(A|B^C)$ are known.

Bernoulli trial   An experiment that has only two possible results: one referred to as "success" and one called "failure."

bimodal   Having two modes. Applies to distributions of values. See *mode.*

binomial distribution   The discrete probability distribution that applies when an experiment is conducted a number of times, with each trial having a probability p of success and each trial being independent of every other trial.

bivariate   The study of two variables at the same time.

case   A case is generally one instance of a variable or combination of variables being observed. There are many definitions of case, depending on the research problem. For example, a case could be a customer, a production lot, or a sales figure.

cell   One of the locations in a contingency table or an Excel spreadsheet.

central limit theorem   A theorem that states that the average of a large number of independent, identically distributed random variables will have a normal distribution.

central tendency   A measure that indicates the typical medium value of a distribution of a continuous discrete variable; the mean, median, and mode are examples of measures of central tendency.

Chebyshev's theorem   A theorem that states that for any group of numbers, the fraction that will be within k standard deviations of the mean will be at least $1-1/k^2$; also spelled Tchebysheff's theorem.

chi-square distribution   A continuous probability distribution related to the normal distribution; used in the chi-square test.

chi-square test   A statistical method to test the hypothesis that two or more factors are independent. Related to the goodness of fit test.

class limits   The two boundaries of a class used to group a data class which establish the midpoint of a class.

classical approach to probability   An approach to probability based on defining a probability space consisting of all possible outcomes of an experiment where it is assumed that each outcome is equally likely.

cluster sampling   A sampling method where the population is divided into clusters; clusters are selected at random, and then members of the chosen clusters are selected at random to make up the sample.

coefficient of determination   A value between 0 and 1 that indicates how well variations in the independent variable in a regression explain variations in the dependent variable (symbolized by r^2).

coefficient of variation   The standard deviation divided by the mean; this value indicates how big the dispersion is compared to the mean.

combinations   The number of different ways of selecting objects from a group of objects when the order in which the objects are selected does not matter.

common logarithm   A logarithm to the base 10.

complement for an event   All outcomes that are not part of that event or trial.

conditional probability   The probability that a particular event will occur when it is given that another event has occurred.

confidence interval   An interval based on observations of a sample and constructed such that there is a specified probability that the interval contains the unknown actual (true) value of a parameter. For example, it is common to calculate confidence intervals that have a 95 percent chance of containing the true value.

confidence level   The degree of confidence associated with a confidence interval; the probability that the interval contains the true value of the parameter.

consistent estimator   An estimator that tends to converge toward the true value as the sample size becomes larger.

consumer price index (CPI)   A measure of the average price level at a particular time based on the cost of purchasing a fixed market basket of consumer goods.

critical ratio   A ratio that measures an important characteristic. This ratio is often plotted or tracked in some way to determine priorities among items or events.

contingency table   A table that shows how many observations fall within each cell, where the cells represent all of the possible combinations of two (or more) factors; a contingency table is used in the chi-square test to determine whether two factors are independent.

continuous random variable   A random variable that can take on any real-number value within a certain range; it is characterized by a density function curve such that the area under the curve between two numbers represents the probability that the random variable will be between those two numbers. For contrast, see *discrete random variable*.

convenience sampling   A method of sampling where the items that are most conveniently available are selected as part of the sample; it is not appropriate to apply statistical analysis to samples selected in this manner.

correction factor   See *finite population correction factor.*

correlation   An indication of the degree of association between two quantities; the correlation value is always between –1 and 1.

covariance   An indication of the degree of association between two quantities; it is related to the correlation but is not constrained to be between –1 and 1.

critical region   If the calculated value of the test statistic falls within the critical region, the null hypothesis is rejected (same as *rejection region*).

critical value   The value (or values) at the boundary of the critical region.

cumulative distribution function   The function that gives the probability that a random variable will be less than or equal to a specific value.

Current Population Survey   A monthly survey of over 100,000 people conducted by the Census Bureau.

cyclical component   The component of a time series that moves up or down with the overall level of business activity in the economy.

decision theory   The study of making decisions designed to achieve some goal, typically under conditions of uncertainty.

decision tree   A diagram that illustrates all possible consequences of different decisions in different states of nature.

degrees of freedom   The nature of a chi-square or a *t*-distribution is characterized by its degrees of freedom, which is equal to the number of cases minus 1; the *F* distribution is characterized by the degrees of freedom in the numerator and the degrees of freedom in the denominator.

demographic data   Identification and background information obtained on research subjects, such as age, gender, income, social class, and so on.

density function   See *probability density function.*

dependent variable   The variable in a research study or regression analysis that is assumed to be caused by or changed by the independent variable(s). Also, the variable that is changed by or "depends" on the experimental treatment for its value. Sometimes referred to as the outcome or criterion variable.

depreciation   The loss in value of capital goods as they wear down.

descriptive research   Research studies that seek to explain and predict. Existing conditions and variables are used with no manipulation; therefore, no direct cause-and-effect relationships can be obtained.

descriptive statistics   The study of summarizing data, specifically procedures and formulas for collecting, organizing, analyzing, interpreting, and presenting numerical data that has been obtained from a sample or population. Specifically calculating measures of central tendency, variability, relative position, and relationship.

discrete random variable   A random variable for which it is possible to make a list of all possible values. For contrast, see *continuous random variable*.

disjoint events   Two events that cannot both happen.

dispersion   The degree to which a distribution is spread out (same as *spread*).

dummy variable   An independent variable used in regression analysis that has the value 1 when a specified condition is met and otherwise has the value 0 (same as *indicator variable*).

Durbin-Watson statistic   A statistic used in regression analysis to test for the presence of serial correlation.

econometrics   The branch of economics that uses statistical analysis to analyze and forecast the economy.

empirical data   Verifiable information derived from careful observation and measurement.

error   A random term included in regression and analysis of variance that represents the effects of all factors other than those that have been specifically included in the analysis.

error sum of squares   A quantity that indicates the degree of random error in analysis of variance or regression.

estimate   The value of an estimator in a particular circumstance.

estimator   A quantity based on observations of a sample whose value is taken as an indicator of the value of an unknown population parameter. For example, the sample average is commonly used as an estimator of the unknown population mean.

expectation   The average value that would appear if a random variable was observed many times; also called the *expected value* or *mean* and symbolized by μ.

expected payoff   The expected value of the payoff resulting from a decision.

expected value   See *expectation*.

exponential smoothing   A method for analyzing the trend in a time series.

extrapolation   A forecast that attempts to predict what will happen in a situation that is outside the range of previously observed data.

F-distribution   A continuous random variable distribution related to the chi-square distribution; it is used in the analysis of variance procedure and in regression analysis.

F-statistic   In analysis of variance, a statistic to test the null hypothesis that all the groups come from populations with the same mean; in regression analysis, a statistic to test the null hypothesis that there is no connection between the independent variables and the dependent variable.

factorial   For a particular whole number, the product of all the whole numbers from 1 up to that number.

finite population correction factor   When sampling without replacement, the formulas for the standard deviation of the sample mean and sample proportion need to be multiplied by $\sqrt{(N-n)/(N-1)}$, where N is the population size and n is the sample size; this is not necessary if the population is much larger than the sample.

fitted value   For a given set of values of independent variables, the value of the dependent variable that is predicted by the regression equation.

frequency diagram   A bar diagram that illustrates how many observations fall within each category.

frequency polygon   A diagram that illustrates a frequency distribution with the use of line segments instead of bars.

frequency table   A table showing how many observations fall within each category of observations or data.

Friedman Fr test   A procedure to test the hypothesis that there is no difference between preferences when there are more than two possibilities.

GDP deflator   A measure of the average price level.

goodness-of-fit test   A statistical procedure to test the hypothesis that a particular probability distribution fits an observed set of data.

grand mean   The mean of all elements in an analysis of variance test.

gross domestic product (GDP)   A measure of the total value of all goods and services produced in the United States.

gross national product   Measure of national output related to gross domestic product; it includes production by inputs owned by U.S. citizens but not production from domestic inputs that are foreign-owned.

grouped data   A way of arranging data where, instead of listing each individual value, a table is made that shows how many values fall within certain categories.

heteroscedasticity   A situation in regression analysis where the error terms do not all have the same variance.

histogram   A bar diagram that illustrates a frequency distribution; each bar is drawn so that its area is proportional to the number of items in the interval it represents.

hypergeometric distribution   The discrete probability distribution that applies when a group of items is sampled without replacement.

hypothesis testing   A statistical procedure that involves collecting evidence and then making a decision as to whether a particular hypothesis should be accepted or rejected.

independent events   Two or more events that do not affect the value or outcome of each other.

independent random variables   Two random variables that do not affect each other; knowing the value of one of the random variables does not provide any information about the value of the other variable.

independent variable   The variable that is manipulated in experimental research to cause change in the dependence variable. Also called the experimental and treatment variable. Also, a variable in a regression study that affects the dependent variable, but is assumed not to be affected by the other variables in the regression.

index of leading indicators   An index consisting of 12 different economic time series that tend to turn up or down before the whole economy shows a similar trend.

indicator variable   See *dummy variable*.

inference   See *statistical inference*.

inferior good   A good that people buy less of as their income increases.

inflation rate   The rate of change in the average price level.

interquartile range   The value of the third quartile minus the value of the first quartile. Half of the items in a list fall within the interquartile range.

intersection for two sets   The set that consists of all elements that are in both of the two sets.

interval data   A level of measurement in which there are equal intervals between units on a scale. The numerical data at this level are continuous, thus allowing a full range of mathematical operations.

interval estimate   An estimate for a parameter that gives a range of likely estimates for the parameter, instead of just a single value. See also *confidence interval.*

irregular component   The component of a time series that moves up or down with no apparent pattern.

Kruskal-Wallis H test   A generalization of the Wilcoxon rank sum test to the condition where there are more than two populations.

law of large numbers   A law stating that, if a random variable is observed many times, the average of those observations will tend toward the mean of that random variable.

least-squares estimators   The estimates for the coefficients found from regression analysis; these estimates are calculated because they minimize the square of the error between the actual values of the dependent variable and the values predicted by the regression equation.

levels of measurement   A hierarchy of four levels of measurement scales arranged from simple to complex according to the properties of each level. The quantitative value and thus the statistical power of the data increase at each level: nominal, ordinal, interval, and ratio.

level of significance   For a hypothesis-testing procedure, the probability of committing a type 1 error—the probability of rejecting the null hypothesis when it is true. Also known as the alpha level.

logarithm   If $a^2 = y$ then x is the logarithm to the base a of y.

marginal probability function   The probability function for a specific random variable that is calculated from a joint probability function.

maximum likelihood estimator   An estimator with the following property: If the true value of the unknown parameter has the value of this estimator, then the probability of obtaining the sample that was actually observed is maximized.

mean   The value that is equal to the sum of a list of numbers divided by the number of numbers. Same as *average* or *arithmetic average*. It is a measure of central tendency or typicality. The mean of a random variable is the average value that would appear if you observed the random variable many times (same as *expectation*). It is symbolized by the Greek letter μ (mu) for a population and by $\overline{X}$ (X-bar) for a sample.

mean absolute deviation   The average value of the absolute values of the distances from all numbers in a list to their mean.

mean square   A quantity, used in analysis of variance, that is equal to a sum of squares divided by its degrees of freedom.

mean square error (MSE)   A quantity used in regression to estimate the unknown value of the variance of the error term.

mean square variance   See *mean square.*

median   The value such that half of the numbers in a list are above it and half are below it.

mode   A measure of central tendency that is the value or score that occurs most frequently in a list of numbers or distribution.

moving average   The average value of the observations in a time series that are closest to one particular value.

multicollinearity   A problem that arises in regression analysis when two or more of the independent variables are closely correlated.

multiple regression   A statistical method for analyzing the relation between several independent variables and one dependent variable.

multiplication principle   A principle that states that if there are *m* possible outcomes of the first experiment and *n* possible outcomes of the second experiment, then there are *mn* possible combined outcomes of both experiments (if the two experiments are independent).

national income   The sum of all income earned in a country; equal to the gross national product minus depreciation and indirect taxes.

negatively correlated   Two quantities related so that one tends to be large when the other tends to be small.

net national product (NNP)   A measure of the national economy equal to gross national product minus depreciation.

nominal data   The lowest level of measurement, where data can only be assigned to categories; numerals function only to identify and classify.

nominal gross domestic product   The gross domestic product measured in current dollars, not corrected for inflation. For contrast, see *real gross domestic product.*

nonparametric method   A statistical method that does not make assumptions about the specific forms of distributions and therefore does not focus on estimating unknown parameter values. Used to measure categorical data or higher level data treated as categorical that are not normally distributed.

normal curve   See *normal distribution.*

normal distribution   The most important continuous random variable distribution; its density function is bell-shaped with the mean, median, and mode at the same point on the curve. It is a symmetrical frequency distribution where most of the scores fall near the mean but fewer and fewer scores fall near the extremes of the distribution. Many real populations are distributed according to the normal distribution. All called the *normal curve*.

null hypothesis   The hypothesis that is being tested in a hypothesis-testing situation; often the null hypothesis is of the form, "There is no relation between two quantities." Symbolized by H_0.

objective variable   A variable that the researcher is trying to maximize or minimize in decision theory.

ogive   A graph showing cumulative distribution.

one-tailed test   A hypothesis test where the critical region consists of only one tail of a distribution; the null hypothesis is rejected only if the test statistic has an extreme value in one direction. In other words, the area of rejection in only one end of the sampling distribution is used.

open-ended class   A class for grouping data with no upper-class limit or no lower-class limit.

open-ended question   An item on a questionnaire or interview that does not suggest any choice of answers and the respondent is free to give his/her own answer.

operational definition   A definition of a variable that assigns meaning to it by specifying the observable behaviors or measures that will represent the variable. This is a crucial step in making research objective and verifiable.

ordinal data   A level of measurement which permits data to be classified and ranked, but which does not allow numbers to represent exact scores; there is not a fixed value between ranks.

outcome   One of the possible results of a probability or other type of experiment.

outlier   An observation that is significantly different from the other observations.

parameter   A quantity (usually unknown) that characterizes a population. For example, the population mean and population standard deviation are parameters.

payoff table   A table showing payoffs in different states of nature in decision theory.

percentile   The th percentile of a list is the number such that P percent of the elements in the list are less than that number.

perfectly correlated   Two quantities X and Y are perfectly correlated if there is a relation between them of the form *Y=aX+b*, where *a* and *b* are two constants; their correlation will be 1 if *a* is positive and –1 if *a* is negative.

permutations   The number of different ways of selecting objects from a group of *n* objects when each distinct way of ordering the chosen objects counts separately.

pie chart   A graph where a circle represents the whole amount and wedge-shaped sectors indicate the fraction in each category.

point estimate   A single value used as an estimator for an unknown parameter. For contrast, see *interval estimate.*

Poisson distribution   The discrete probability distribution that gives the frequency of occurrence of certain types of random events; it can be used as an approximation for the binomial distribution.

population   The set of all items (cases) of interest in a research study. The research sample is drawn from the population.

population standard deviation   The standard deviation calculated when the values of all items in the population are known. For contrast, see *sample standard deviation.*

population variance   The variance calculated when the values of all items in the population are known. For contrast, see *sample variance.*

positively correlated   Two quantities are positively correlated if they are related so that, if one quantity is large, the other tends to be large; their correlation is greater than zero.

practical significance   The degree to which research results are suitable or can be adapted to real-world conditions and problems. Data may be statistically but not practically significant.

predicted value   A value of a dependent variable that is calculated from a regression equation and values of the independent variables.

prediction interval   An interval so constructed that there is a specified probability that a explicit random variable will be within that interval.

predictive validity   The degree to which an assessment or experimental technique predicts the performance of the case (person, machine, element) in question on some future task or measurement.

price index   A measure of the price level.

price level   The average level of all prices in the country; it can be measured by the GNP deflator, consumer price index, or producer price index.

probability   The study of chance phenomena or the likelihood of something happening by chance.

probability density function   For a discrete random variable, the probability that the random variable will have a specific value; for a continuous random variable, the probability density function is represented by a curve such that the area under the curve between two numbers is the probability that the random variable will be between those two numbers.

probability function   For a discrete random variable, the probability function at a specific value is the probability that the random variable will have that value.

probability of an event   The number of outcomes that corresponds to that event divided by the total number of possible outcomes.

probability space   The set of all possible outcomes from a random experiment (same as *sample space)*.

producer price index (PPI)   A measure of the price level based on a fixed market basket of goods used by producers.

qualitative research   A study that relies heavily upon data collected using open-ending narrative and observation. It is based on detailed descriptions of events, people, and excerpts from documents and other records. Both the data and the analysis are basically verbal (as opposed to quantitative).

quantitative research   A study that relies upon variables that can be measured. The data can be collected, organized, and interpreted with statistical techniques.

quartile   The first quartile of a list is the number such that one quarter of the numbers in the list are below it; the third quartile is the number such that three quarters of the numbers are below it; the second quartile is the same as the *median.*

quasi-experiment   An experiment characterized by lack of control over subjects.

r^2 A measure of how well the independent variable in a simple linear regression can explain changes in the dependent variable; its value is between zero (meaning poor fit) and one (meaning perfect fit).

R^2 A measure of how well a multiple regression equation is able to explain changes in the dependent variable.

random sample   A sample selected by a method such that each possible sample had an equal chance of being selected; also, a collection of independent random variables all selected from the same distribution.

random variable   A variable whose value depends on the outcome of a random experiment.

range   The simplest measure of variability, expressed as largest value in a list minus the smallest value.

rating scale   An assessment or research device that contains a series of number points, descriptive statements, or behavioral categories that an observer or research subject uses to indicate the degree of a characteristic a person or other research object possesses.

ratio data   The most refined level of measurement, as it has all the properties of nominal, ordinal, and interval levels plus a true zero point. Thus, a full range of statistical operations can be used with ratio data.

ratio to moving average method   A method for seasonally adjusting the values in a time series.

raw data   The initial data a researcher starts with before beginning analysis. Data that has not been manipulated using statistical tests or other formulas.

real gross domestic product   A measure of the GDP that corrects for inflation; it increases when there is an increase in the goods and services produced in a nation.

recession   A period of time when there is a slowdown in business activity in a country or the world.

regression line   A line calculated in regression analysis that is used to estimate the relation between two quantities (the independent variable and the dependent variable.)

regression sum of squares   A quantity that indicates the degree to which a regression equation can explain the variations in the dependent variable.

rejection region   The set of values of the test statistic for which the hypothesis will be rejected.

relative frequency view of probability   A view that regards the probability of an event as being the fraction of times the event would occur if an experiment was repeated many times.

reliability   The degree to which a research device or instrument is consistent or dependable.

reliability coefficient   A numerical indicator of the degree of consistency shown by a measuring instrument.

research problem   A succinct description of the research topic so that a clear-cut purpose of the research project is evident. "Problem" may be used interchangeably with "purpose of the study."

residual   The difference between the actual value of the dependent variable and the value predicted by the regression equation.

sample   A group of items or cases selected from the population and used to estimate the properties of the population.

sample space   See *probability space.*

sample standard deviation   The standard deviation calculated from the values in a sample. Used to estimate the value of the population standard deviation.

sample variance   The variance calculated from the values in a sample which is used to estimate the value of the population variance.

sampling bias   The degree to which the sample does not reflect the characteristics of the population.

sampling distribution   The frequency distribution that consists of the means obtained from drawing repeated random samples of a fixed size from the same population; also a probability distribution of a statistic, such as the sample average $\overline{X}$ (x-bar).

sampling error   The difference between a statistic and the corresponding parameter (the true value).

sampling with replacement   A method for choosing a sample where an item that has been selected is put back in the population and therefore has a chance of being selected again.

sampling without replacement   A method for choosing a sample where an item that has been selected is not put back in the population and therefore cannot be selected again.

scatter diagram   A diagram showing the relation between two quantities; one quantity is measured on the vertical axis, the other quantity is measured on the horizontal axis, and each observation is represented by a dot.

scientific method   A procedure or steps for generating empirical data, generally characterized by tentativeness, openness, rigorous reasoning, and verifiability of data and results.

seasonal adjustment   A procedure for adjusting time-series data to compensate for seasonal variation in order to make nonseasonal changes in the data more apparent.

serial correlation   A problem that arises in regression analysis involving time-series data when successive values of the random error term are not independent (same as *autocorrelation*).

set   A well-defined collection of objects, observations, or cases.

sign test   A procedure to test the hypothesis that there is no difference between two quantities for which there are rankings instead of numerical values.

simple linear regression   A method for analyzing the relation between one independent variable and one dependent variable.

skewed   Not symmetrical.

slope   A number that describes the orientation of a line; a horizontal line has zero slope and a vertical line has infinite slope; the slope can be found by calculating the vertical distance between any two points on the line and dividing by the horizontal distance between those two points.

spread   See *dispersion*.

stability   The degree to which a research instrument produces similar results with repeated administrations. Can be estimated statistically by a test-retest reliability coefficient.

standard deviation   The square root of the variance. A measure of the dispersion or heterogeneity of a set of scores around the mean of the set or sample.

standard error of the mean   The estimated standard deviation for a sample statistic which is also the standard deviation of a sampling distribution of means. The statistical bridge that connects the sample and the population and forms one of the bases of inferential statistics.

standard error for coefficient   In regression analysis, the estimated standard deviation of the estimated coefficient; a small value of the standard error means that the estimated coefficient is a more precise estimate of the true coefficient.

standard normal distribution   The normal distribution with mean 0 and variance 1.

state of nature   In decision theory, an unpredictable outcome.

statistic   A value calculated from the items (cases) in a sample, such as the sample average $\overline{X}$; a statistic is often used as an estimator of an unknown population parameter.

statistical inference   The process of using observations of a sample to estimate the properties of the population.

statistics   The study of ways to analyze data; it consists of *descriptive statistics* and *statistical inference* (also known as inferential statistics).

stratified sampling   A sampling method where the population is divided into strata that are as much alike as possible.

subjective view of probability   A view that regards the probability of an event as being an individual's estimate of the likelihood of occurrence of that event.

subscript   A small number or letter written next to and slightly below another character.

subset   A portion of a set, such that set *A* is a subset of set *B* if all elements in *A* are also in *B*.

sum of squares   The sum of the squared deviations of the elements in a list about a specified quantity; several sum of squares statistics are used in analysis of variance and regression.

summation notation   A notation that uses the Greek capital letter sigma, Σ, to mean "add up the values"; for example, Σ*X* means "add up all values of *X*."

symmetrical distribution   A distribution is symmetrical about a particular line if the halves of the distribution on either side of that line are mirror images of each other; for example, a normal distribution is symmetrical about its mean.

table of random numbers   A table used to select subjects or cases randomly and made up of a list of numbers compiled by a random process, often using a computer.

true score   The score a person or research object would obtain on a perfectly reliable test; the score obtained on a test with an infinite number of items or equivalent forms; a theoretical score never obtainable in the real world.

***t* distribution**   A continuous random variable distribution related to the normal and chi-square distributions; it is used for confidence interval calculations and hypothesis testing for small samples.

***t* statistic**   A statistic used to test the null hypothesis that the true value of a coefficient in regression analysis is zero and to test significant differences between sample means.

***t*-test**   A statistical procedure to determine significant differences between sample means and the significance of correlation coefficients. See also *t distribution* and *t statistic.*

tail   The extreme upper or lower end of a distribution.

test statistic   A quantity calculated from observed quantities used to test a null hypothesis; the test statistic is constructed so that it will come from a known distribution if the null hypothesis is true; therefore the null hypothesis is rejected if it seems implausible that the observed value of the test statistic could have come from that distribution.

time-series data   Data that consist of several observations of a variable, such as sales, income, or other quantity, at different points in time.

total sum of squares   The sum of the squares of the deviations of all numbers in a list from the mean; used in analysis of variance and regression.

treatment sum of squares   In analysis of variance, a quantity that indicates the degree to which differences in the observations can be explained by the fact that the observations come from different groups.

trend component   The component in a time series that increases or decreases smoothly with time.

two-tailed test   A hypothesis test where the critical region consists of both tails of the distribution, so that the null hypothesis is rejected if the test statistic value is either too large or too small.

two-way analysis of variance   A test procedure that can be applied to a table of numbers in order to test two hypotheses: (1) there is no significant difference between the rows; and (2) there is no significant difference between the columns.

type 1 error   An error that occurs in hypothesis testing when the null hypothesis is rejected when it is actually true.

type 2 error   An error that occurs in hypothesis testing when the null hypothesis is accepted when it is really false.

unbiased estimator   An estimator whose expected value is equal to the true value of the parameter that it is trying to estimate.

union   In set theory, for set A and set B, the set consisting of all elements that are in A or B or both.

validity   The degree to which a procedure or device does what it claims to do. Content, concurrent, predictive, and construct validity all deal with how well a statistical instrument or device (such as a questionnaire or test) does what it is supposed to do. The two types of experimental validity (internal and external) ask the question, Did the experimental treatment really produce the results attained?

variance   A measure of dispersion for a random variable or a list of numbers. It takes into account every score and its size and distance from the mean of its set. Symbolized for a population by σ^2, where σ is the Greek lowercase letter sigma; the standard deviation is the square root of the variance, or $\sqrt{\sigma^2}$ which is symbolized by σ.

vertical intercept   The point where a line crosses the vertical axis.

Wilcoxon rank sum test   A procedure to test the hypothesis that there is no difference between the means of populations.

Wilcoxon signed rank test   A procedure to test the hypothesis that there is no difference between the means of populations.

within-groups variance   The variation of scores from all groups or cases in a study around the mean of the scores. It is assumed that the variance reflects the variations of the larger population from which the subjects or cases where drawn. This variation is due to sampling error and also called chance variation.

zone of acceptance   If the calculated value of the test statistic falls within the zone of acceptance, the null hypothesis is accepted. For contrast, see *critical region*.

Index

A

absolute values, 50
accidental sampling, 132
action research, 120
addition rule, 82-83
additive model
    gross domestic product
    (GDP), 95
advertisers' ploys (recognition and avoidance tips),
    229-230
alternative hypotheses,
    153-154
analysis of variance
    (ANOVA), 215-219
    confidence interval calculations, 221
    example, 219-221
    two-way analysis of variance, 221-223
    variation types
        random variation,
        219
        total variation, 218
        treatment variation,
        218
ANOVA (analysis of variance), 215-219
    confidence interval calculations, 221
    example, 219-221
    two-way analysis of variance, 221-223

variation types
    random variation,
    219
    total variation, 218
    treatment variation,
    218
answers
    example exercises,
    261-265
    questions and answers
        business research
        data, 36-37
        standard normal
        distribution and
        z-scores, 68
applied research, 121
arrays (stem and leaf
    plots), 33-34
averages
    moving, 94-95
    ratio to moving, 97
    standardized, 99

B

bar graphs, 31
basic research, 121
bell-shaped curves, 58-59
Bernoulli trials, 138
    confidence intervals,
    139-140
    samples, 139-141

binomial
    distribution, 86-87
    experiments, 86
    formulas, 86
    tables, 86
    variables, 85-86
bivariate analysis, 177
branches (statistics), 7
    descriptive statistics, 7
    inferential statistics, 8-9
business applications
    common questions
        regarding research
        data, 36-37
    statistical method utilizations, 6
        determining advertising effectiveness, 6
        quality control, 7
        understanding product demand, 6

C

cases, 18
catchment, 6
categorical variables, 19,
    34-36
    nominal, 34-35
    ordinal, 34-35
central limit theory, 87-88,
    142-143
central tendency measures
    applications, 44
    calculating, 44

mean value, 39-41
median, 42-43
mode, 41-42
characters, Greek, 267-268
chi square test, 171. *See also* goodness of fit test
  equal expected frequencies, 171-173
  example, 174
  unequal expected frequencies, 173-174
Chi-Square table, 278-279
classical probability, 75
  formula, 76-77
  theory, 75-76
classification trees. *See* decision trees
cluster sampling, 133-134
coefficients
  correlation, 181-182
  determination, 183
  variation, 52-53
common errors
  preventing business mistakes, 234-237
  recognition and avoidance tips
    advertisers' ploys, 229-230
    correlation analysis pairings, 231-232
    data mining without hypotheses, 233
    extrapolation beyond observed ranges, 234
    incorrect scale, 230
    nonrandom nonsamples, 229
    significant but unimportant findings, 232-233
conditional probability, 85

confidence intervals, 139-146, 189
content validity, 124
contingency tables, 164
  creating, 164
  examples, 169-171, 174
  negative values, 165-166
  no relationship outcomes, 166
  positive relationships, 165
  testing significance, 167-169
continuous variables (versus discrete variables), 85-86
convenience sampling, 132
conventions, 268
  formula conventions and notations, 268
  Greek characters, 267-268
corporate-level software programs, 246
correlations, 178-179
  calculating the significance of "r," 184
  coefficient of determination, 183
  common errors, 231-232
  correlation coefficient statistic, 181-182
  negative, 179-180
  positive, 179
  spurious correlation, 183
  uncorrelated variables, 180
  variables
    scatterplots, 31-34
cumulative frequency distributions, 29-30

curves
  bell-shaped, 58-59
  probability, 87-88
  skewed
    standard distributions, 67-68
cyclical variation, 95-96

D

data, 15
  common questions regarding business research data, 36-37
  files
    components, 18
    converting observations to data files, 13, 17-20
  presentation forms, 22
    bar graphs, 31
    histograms, 26-31
    line graphs, 25-26
    pie charts, 24
    tables, 22-24
  time series
    components, 92-93
    cyclical variation, 95-96
    seasonal variation, 96-100
    trends, 93-95
  types, 14
    determination exercise, 17
    interval, 15-16
    limitations of type choices, 16-17
    nominal, 14
    ordinal, 14-15
    parametric, 15-16
    ratio, 15-16
    raw, 7-8

decisions
 based on data files,
  17-20
 decision theory, 104
 strategies for decision
  making, 113-114
  equal likelihood deci-
   sion criterion, 113
  minimum regret crite-
   rion, 114
  optimistic decision
   criterion (maximax),
   113
  pessimistic decision
   criterion (maximin),
   113
 trees, 105-106
  calculating benefits,
   108-109
  evaluating options,
   108
  exercise, 114
  incorporating costs,
   109-110
  listing options,
   106-107
  objective variables,
   110-111
  payoff tables, 111-113
 types, 104
  decisions under con-
   ditions of certainty,
   104
  decisions under con-
   flict, 105
  decisions under
   uncertainty, 105
dependent
 events (probability),
  83-85
 samples (*t*-tests),
  201-202
 variables, 19

descriptive
 research, 122
 statistics, 7, 10
deseasonalized values, 99
Dewey's theory of cogni-
 tion, 119-120
discrete variables (versus
 continuous variables),
 85-86
dispersion measures. *See
 also* spread and variability
 absolute values, 50
 exercises, 54
 interquartile range
  (IRQ), 48-49
 range, 48
 selecting, 53
 standard deviation,
  51-53
 variance, 51-52
distribution
 binomial, 86-87
 normal, 59
 Poisson distribution, 87
distributions, frequency, 19

E

equal likelihood decision
 criterion strategy, 113
errors
 preventing business mis-
  takes, 234-237
 recognition and avoid-
  ance tips
  advertisers' ploys,
   229-230
  correlation analysis
   pairings, 231-232
  data mining without
   hypotheses, 233

extrapolation beyond
 observed ranges, 234
 incorrect scale, 230
 nonrandom nonsam-
  ples, 229
 significant but unim-
  portant findings,
  232-233
evaluation (versus
 research), 122-123
events
 dependent, 83-85
 independent, 76
 probability, 74
Excel (Microsoft) software
 program, 244-246
exercises
 answers, 261-265
 data types, 17
 decision trees, 114
 dispersion measures, 54
 linear regression, 186
 probability, 89
 t-tests, 202
 z-tests and proportions,
  213
experimental research, 122
experiments, binomial
 (successes and failures),
 86
exponential smoothing, 96

F

F distribution, 216-221
 calculation steps, 218
 example, 219-221
 two-way analysis of variance, 221-223
face validity, 124
factorials, 74, 79-81

factors, 19
failures, 86
forecasting, 100
  price indices
    inflation, 101-102
  time series data
    components, 92-93
    cyclical variation,
      95-96
    seasonal variation,
      96-100
    trends, 93-95
formulas, 269-272
  binomial, 86
  classical probability,
    76-77
  conventions and nota-
    tions, 268
Fourier analysis, 96
frequency
  distribution, 19
  polygons, 30
  tables, 23
    histograms, 26-31

G

GDP (gross domestic prod-
  uct), 95, 101
  additive model, 95
  multiplicative model, 96
goodness of fit test, 164.
  See also chi square test
graphs, 24
Graunt, John, 5
Greek characters, 267-268
gross domestic product
  (GDP), 95, 101
  additive model, 95
  multiplicative model, 96

H

hierarchy of research levels, 120-122
  action research, 120
  applied research, 121
  pure research, 121
histograms, 26-31
historical-documentary
  research, 122
history (origins of statistics), 5
hypotheses testing, 74, 152
  example, 158-161
  five-step process,
    152-158
  z-scores, 149-152

I-J

independent
  events, 76
  samples
    t-tests, 201-202
  variables, 19
inductive-deductive
  process, 119
inferential statistics, 8-10
infinite populations, 130
inflation, 101-102
interpretations (scatter-
  plots), 32
interquartile range (IRQ),
  48-49
intervals
  confidence, 139-146,
    189
  interval data, 15-16
  prediction, 189
  samples, 141-43

IRQ (interquartile range),
  48-49

joint occurences (probability and dependent
  events), 84

K-L

kurtosis, 68

large number theory, 88
least squares principle,
  185-187
leptokurtic distributions,
  68
levels
  research (hierarchy),
    120-122
  significance (hypotheses
    testing), 154-155
line graphs, 25-26
linear regression, 184-185
  exercise, 186
  general form equation,
    187
  goals, 185-186
  predicting business val-
    ues, 187-189
    standard error of esti-
      mate, 189
literacy research, 123-124

M

mean, 39-41
mean absolute deviation,
  50

measures
  central tendency
    applications, 44
    calculating, 44
    mean, 39-41
    median, 42-43
    mode, 41-42
  dispersion, 48
    absolute values, 50
    exercises, 54
    interquartile range
      (IRQ), 48-49
    range, 48
    selecting, 53
    standard deviation,
      51-53
    variance, 51-52
  nominal, 19
median, 42-43
mesokurtic distributions,
  68
Microsoft Excel software
  program, 244-246
minimum regret criterion
  strategy, 114
mode, 41-42
models, research, 125-126
multiple regression and
  correlation analysis, 190
monthly trend ratio, 98-99
moving averages, 93-95
multiplicative model
  gross domestic product
    (GDP), 96

N

national income account-
  ing, 95
negative
  correlation, 179-180
  skews, 25

nominal
  data, 14
  scales, 19
  variables, 34-35
nonrandom nonsamples
  (recognition and avoid-
  ance tips), 229
normal
  convergence theorem,
    88
  curves, 58-59
  distribution, 59
notations, 268
  formula conventions
    and notations, 268
  Greek characters,
    267-268
null hypotheses, 153-154

O

objective variables (decision trees), 110-111
observations (organizing
  into data files), 12-13
one-tailed analysis, 62
One-Tailed Standard
  Normal (Z) Random
  Variable table, 274-277
optimistic decision criterion (maximax) strategy,
  113
ordinal
  data, 14-15
  variables, 34-35

P

paired *t*-tests, 200-201
parametric data, 15-16
payoff tables, 111-113

Pearson's "r," 181-182
percentage
  predicting
    z-scores, 63-67
  versus percentile, 49
percentile (versus percentage), 49
personal probability, 75
pessimistic decision criterion (maximin) strategy,
  113
pie charts, 24
platykurtic distributions,
  68
plots, scatter, 178-179
Poisson distribution, 87
polygons, 30
pooled estimates, 212
populations, 8-9, 131
  cluster sampling,
    133-134
  determining sample size,
    134-135
  infinite, 130
  random sampling,
    131-133
  stratified sampling, 134
  systematic sampling,
    133
positive
  correlation, 179
  skews, 25
predictions, 184
  intervals, 189
  linear regression,
    184-185
    exercise, 186
    general form equa-
      tion, 187
    goals, 185-186
    predicting business
      values, 187-189

multiple regression and correlation analysis, 190
percentages
  z-scores, 63-67
price indices, 101-102
probabilistic modeling, 5
probability, 10, 74
  binomial experiments, 86
  calculating factorials, 79-81
  central limit theorem, 87-88
  classical, 75
    formula, 76-77
    theory, 75-76
  dependent events, 83-84
    conditional probability, 85
    joint occurences, 84
  exercises, 89
  history, 5
  odds and outcomes of tossing 46 heads in a row, 77-79
  personal, 75
  Poisson distribution, 87
  relationship with statistics, 9-10
  relative frequency, 75, 77
  sampling with replacement, 81-82
    addition rule, 82-83
  variables, 76
    discrete versus continuous, 85-86
programs, software, 240-243
  basic spreadsheets, 243
  benefits, 242
  capabilities, 240-242

corporate-level, 246
full-featured spreadsheets, 243-244
limitations, 250-252
Microsoft Excel, 244-246
recommendations, 252
selection criteria, 247-250
simple versus complex, 242
Web site resources, 246-247
proportions, 76, 86, 208-209. *See also* ratios
  election prediction calculations, 209-211
  exercise, 213
  testing two population proportions, 211-213
pure research, 121

Q

qualitative variables, 19, 31
quantitative variables, 19, 34-36
questions and answers
  business research data, 36-37
  standard normal distribution and *z*-scores, 68

R

random
  sampling, 131-133
  variables, 19
    normal distributions, 59
range, interquartile (IRQ), 48-49

ratios, 76. *See also* proportions
  data, 15-16
  monthly trend ratios, 98-99
  samples, 141, 143
  standardized average adjusted ratio, 99
raw data presentations, 7-8, 22
  bar graphs, 31
  histograms, 26-31
  line graphs, 25-26
  pie charts, 24
  tables, 22-24
realization, 19
records. *See* cases
regression
  analysis, 6
  linear, 184-185
    exercise, 186
    general form equation, 187
    goals, 185-186
    predicting business values, 187-189
relationships. *See* correlations
relative frequency, 75-77
reliability, 124-125
replacement (sampling with replacement), 81-83
research
  categories
    descriptive research, 122
    experimental research, 122
    historical-documentary research, 122
  deciding when to use research, 118-119

hierarchy of research
  levels, 120-122
    action research, 120
    applied research, 121
    pure research, 121
  indentifying appropriate
    research projects, 120
  literacy, 123-124
  methods, 119-120
  models
    developing, 125-126
  populations, 131
    cluster sampling,
      133-134
    determining sample
      size, 134-135
    infinite, 130
    random sampling,
      131-133
    stratified sampling,
      134
    systematic sampling,
      133
  preparing for statistical
    analysis, 126-127
  reliability, 124-125
  sampling methods, 131
    cluster, 133-134
    determining sample
      size, 134-135
    random, 131-133
    stratified, 134
    systematic, 133
  validity, 124-125
    content validity, 124
    face validity, 124
  versus evaluation,
    122-123
resources
  references and expanded
    study sources, 256-258

Web sites
  references and
    expanded study
    sources, 256-257
  software programs,
    246-247

S

Sample Distribution Table,
  282-283
sampling, 8-9, 131
  accidental, 132
  Bernoulli trials, 139-141
  cluster, 133-134
  convenience, 132
  determining sample size,
    134-135
  interval, 141, 143
  random, 131-133
  ratio, 141, 143
  sample mean, 41
  stratified, 134
  systematic, 133
  with replacement, 81-82
    addition rule, 82-83
scales, nominal, 19
scattergraphs, 180
scatterplots, 31-32,
  178-179
  interpreting, 32
  stem and leaf plots,
    33-34
scientific method, 119
seasonal variation, 96-100
skews, 25-26
  curves
    standard distribu-
      tions, 67-68
  negative, 25
  positive, 25
  symmetric distribution
    (no skew), 26

software programs,
  240-243
  basic spreadsheets, 243
  benefits, 242
  capabilities, 240-242
  corporate-level, 246
  full-featured spread-
    sheets, 243-244
  limitations, 250-252
  Microsoft Excel, 244-246
  recommendations, 252
  selection criteria, 247
    analyses flexibility,
      248
    compatibility with
      other programs, 249
    cost/feature analysis,
      247-248
    documentation and
      support, 249
    ease of use and con-
      sistency of the inter-
      face, 248
    manufacturer reputa-
      tion, 250
    technical support,
      250
    word-of-mouth expe-
      riences, 250
  simple versus complex,
    242
  Web site resources,
    246-247
spread, 47. *See also* dispersion measures
spreadsheet programs
  basic, 243
  full-featured, 243-244
spurious correlation, 183
standard deviation, 51-53
  coefficient of variation,
    52-53
  interpretations, 52

translating into values, 63, 68

two-tailed and one-tailed analysis, 62

standard

distributions

normal, 58-62

skewed curves, 67-68

error of estimate, 189

standardized average adjusted ratio, 99

statistics

branches, 7

descriptive statistics, 7

inferential statistics, 8-9

business utilizations, 6

determining advertising effectiveness, 6

quality control, 7

understanding product demand, 6

history, 5

programs, 240-243

basic spreadsheets, 243

benefits, 242

capabilities, 240-242

corporate-level, 246

full-featured spreadsheets, 243-244

limitations, 250-252

Microsoft Excel, 244-246

recommendations, 252

selection criteria, 247-250

simple versus complex, 242

Web site resources, 246-247

recommended concepts for further study, 254-258

relationship with probability, 9-10

resources for further study, 256-258

stem and leaf plots, 33-34

strategies (decision making), 113-114

equal likelihood decision criterion, 113

minimum regret criterion, 114

optimistic decision criterion (maximax), 113

pessimistic decision criterion (maximin), 113

stratified sampling, 134

successes, 86

symbols, 267-268

formula conventions and notations, 268

Greek characters, 267-268

symmetric distribution (no skew), 26

systematic sampling, 133

T

t distribution tests, 194

comparing two population means, 196-198

calculations, 198-199

dependent and independent samples, 201-202

exercise, 202

paired *t*-test example, 200-201

student's distribution (one- and two-tailed) table, 280-281

testing a mean, 195-196

tables, 18, 22-24

binomial, 86

Chi-Square, 278-279

contingency, 164

creating, 164

example, 169-171, 174

negative value example, 165-166

no relationship example, 166

positive relationship example, 165

testing significance, 167-169

frequency, 23

one-tailed standard normal (Z) random variable, 274-277

sample distribution, 282-283

student's distribution (one- and two-tailed), 280-281

two-tailed standard normal (Z), 273

testing, hypotheses, 74, 152-156

example, 158-161

five-step process, 152-158

z-scores, 149-152

theories

central limit theory, 142-143

classical probability, 75-76

formula, 76-77

decision, 104
  types of decisions,
    104-105
  Dewey's theory of cogni-
    tion, 119-120
  large number theory, 88
  probability of relative
    frequency, 75, 77
time series data
  components, 92-93
  cyclical variation, 95-96
  seasonal variation,
    96-100
  trends, 93-95
treatments, 217-218, 221
trees, decision, 105-106
  calculating benefits,
    108-109
  evaluating options, 108
  exercise, 114
  incorporating costs,
    109-110
  listing options, 106-107
  objective variables,
    110-111
  payoff tables, 111-113
trends
  time series data, 93-95
two-tailed
  analysis, 62
  standard normal (Z)
    table, 273

variability, 47. *See also* dispersion measures
variables, 18-19
  categorical, 19
  continuous versus
    discrete, 85-86
  dependent, 19
  discrete versus continu-
    ous, 85-86
  independent, 19
  objective decision trees,
    110-111
  probability variables, 76
  qualitative, 19, 31
  quantitative, 19
  random, 19
  relationships, scatter-
    plots, 31-34
variance, 51-52
variation
  cyclical, 95-96
  seasonal, 96-100
variables
  categorical, 34-36
  quantitative, 34-36

z-tests
  investment turnover
    example, 207-208
  proportions, 208-209
    election prediction
      calculations,
        209-211
    exercise, 213
    testing two popula-
      tion proportions,
      211-213
  testing the mean, stan-
    dard deviation known,
    206
  testing the mean, stan-
    dard deviation
    unknown, 206-207

W–X–Y

Web sites
  references and expanded
    study sources, 256-257
  software programs,
    246-247

U–V

uncorrelated variables, 180

validity, 124-125
  content, 124
  face, 124
values, 18

Z

z-scores, 63-65
  answering questions,
    66-67
  calculating, 65-66
  hypotheses testing,
    149-152

 THE COMPLETE **IDIOT'S** GUIDE TO

 Arts & Sciences

Business & Personal Finance

 Computers & the Internet

Family & Home

Hobbies & Crafts

Language Reference

 Health & Fitness

 Personal Enrichment

 Sports & Recreation

 Teens

IDIOTSGUIDES.COM

Introducing a new and different Web site

Millions of people love to learn through *The Complete Idiot's Guide*® books. Discover the same pleasure online in **idiotsguides.com**–part of The Learning Network.

Idiotsguides.com is a new and different Web site, where you can:

※ Explore and download more than 150 fascinating and useful mini-guides—FREE! Print out or send to a friend.

⊕ Share your own knowledge and experience as a mini-guide contributor.

● Join discussions with authors and exchange ideas with other lifelong learners.

🏛 Read sample chapters from a vast library of *Complete Idiot's Guide*® books.

✗ Find out how to become an author.

✂ Check out upcoming book promotions and author signings.

🏠 Purchase books through your favorite online retailer.

Learning for Fun. Learning for Life.

...SGUIDES.COM • LEARNINGNETWORK.COM